THE ACCIDENTAL BOND

THE
ACCIDENTAL BOND

How Sibling Connections Influence Adult Relationships

Susan Scarf Merrell

FAWCETT COLUMBINE • NEW YORK

The names and identifying details of all siblings described in this book have been changed to protect their privacy.

A Fawcett Columbine Book
Published by Ballantine Books
Copyright © 1995 by Susan Scarf Merrell

Grateful acknowledgment is made to the following for permission to reprint previously published material:
Doubleday, a division of Bantam Doubleday Dell Publishing Group, Inc.: Excerpt from *Shot in the Heart* by Mikal Gilmore. Reprinted by permission of Doubleday, a division of Bantam Doubleday Dell Publishing Group, Inc.
HarperCollinsPublishers and Faber and Faber Limited: "The Rivals" from *Ariel* by Sylvia Plath. Copyright © 1962 by Ted Hughes. Copyright renewed. Rights throughout Canada and the Open Market are administered by Faber and Faber Limited. Reprinted by permission of HarperCollins*Publishers* and Faber and Faber Limited.
Alfred A. Knopf, Inc.: "The Couple" from *The Dead and the Living* by Sharon Olds. Copyright © 1983 by Sharon Olds. Reprinted by permission of Alfred A. Knopf, Inc.

http://www.randomhouse.com

Cover design by David Stevenson
Cover photos (from top to bottom):
    © Uniphoto
    © Sharon J. Wohlmuth
    © 1996 Picture Perfect
    © Image Bank

Library of Congress Catalog Card Number: 96-97065

ISBN: 0-449-91119-5

Manufactured in the United States of America

This edition published by arrangement with Times Books, a division of Random House, Inc.

LSI 001

To my sisters, with love and admiration

"Bessie and I have been together since time began, or so it seems. Bessie is my little sister, only she's not so little. She is 101 years old, and I am 103. . . .

"Neither one of us ever married and we've lived together most of our lives, and probably know each other better than any two human beings on this Earth. After so long, we are in some ways like one person. She is my right arm. If she were to die first, I'm not sure if I would want to go on living because the reason I am living is to keep *her* living."

—Having Our Say: The Delaney Sisters' First 100 Years

THE COUPLE

On the way to the country, they fall asleep
in the back seat, those enemies,
rulers of separate countries, sister and
brother. Her big hard head
lolls near his narrow oval skull
until they are crown to crown, brown
hair mingling like velvet. Mouths
open, the rosebud and her cupid's bow,
they dream against each other, her calm
almond eyes and his round blue eyes
closed, quivering like trout. Their toes
touching opposite doors, their hands in
loose fists, their heads together in
unconsciousness, they look like a small
royal bride and groom, the bride still a
head taller, married as children
in the Middle Ages, for purposes of state,
fighting all day, and finding their only
union in sleep, in the dark solitary
power of the dream—the dream of ruling the world.

—Sharon Olds

ACKNOWLEDGMENTS

I must begin by thanking those people who encouraged me from the very moment I mentioned my interest in writing a book on sibling relationships: my parents, Herb and Maggie Scarf; my agent, Suzanne Gluck; and, in particular, my husband, Jim, who has already packed a lifetime's worth of support and encouragement into the years we have been together.

Among the many sibling experts who gave so generously of their time, I want to single out Judy Dunn, Judith Lasky, and Brian Sutton-Smith. Each of them provided expert guidance at critical moments. Victor Cicirelli, Robert Plomin, David Reiss, and Thomas Weisner all kindly enlightened me about their own work, as did Eliot Rosen and Donald Meyer.

I am also indebted to a number of psychologists, social workers, and psychiatrists who so patiently guided me through the muddy waters of interpreting the siblings' stories. The exercise itself was problematic: speculations about people whom they'd never met. Time and again, the experts I consulted reminded me that we were only talking about possible interpretations of a particular sibling's behavior. My goal, of course, was never definitively to analyze the siblings I interviewed; rather, I was merely trying to place their stories in the context of the most fundamental aspects of brother-sister relationships. In particular, I want to thank Hannah Fox, who was an invaluable resource; she made herself available to me on dozens of occasions and the acuity of her insights was frequently startling. I also want to thank David Ertel for providing me with crucial direction on several sets of siblings. My dear friends Bettina Volz and Wendy

Grolnick, and my sister, Betsy Stone, were always available when I called upon their expertise, and often would drop whatever they were doing to go over case histories with me: for their wisdom and good friendship alike, I am exceedingly grateful.

Thanks also to Betsy Rapoport of Times Books for her insightful editing (and for support when it was most needed!), to Felicia Dickinson for so ably and cheerfully transcribing many of my interview tapes, to my saintly friend Bobbie Cohen for reading and re-reading the manuscript in its earliest stages, and to the Southampton College Library for the use of the John Steinbeck Room. Above all, I must express my deep gratitude to the many siblings who so generously gave of their time and of themselves. Although their identities are disguised, their intelligence and eagerness to participate in this project will, I hope, be apparent. I owe each sister and brother a tremendous debt.

CONTENTS

———

———

THE ACCIDENTAL BOND

CHAPTER ONE

The Accidental Bond

We do not select our beginnings. We are cast from Eden when one of a million sperm connects, in a random instant, with an egg; our creation occurs because two previously unacquainted genomes—without benefit of clergy or even a moment for mutual assessment—select one another and marry for life. Such a wonderful intricacy of circumstance joins gene to gene, supplies the nascent human with the parameters of its adult personality and physical form. At that moment of primary connection, the person-to-be is endowed with propensities toward engineering or music, toward conversation or silence, toward athletic prowess or a fondness for animals or alcohol.

No one receives a gene to be a social worker or a murderer in the lottery of genetic chance; one's endowment is a tendency toward a range of outcomes, not a blueprint for a single way of being. Such predispositions are further molded by life's early lessons. At birth, a child's world is given to him; the lessons of acting, reacting, and interacting will be learned with a certain set of parents, siblings, and others. The influence is mutual, for these others—each as inadvertently a particular self as any of the rest—react and change in response to the newcomer as well. And as each person evolves and grows, her relationships will influence the development of myriad aspects of her personality, from sense of self to ambition, talent, and energy. The basic self is a genetic inheritance, an accident of birth. In relation to others, then, each person becomes a more specific, durable individual.

A young mother gazes affectionately at her sleeping infant, and says, "She's so peaceful; her brother was wild, he never slept." The actual hours each child slept at six weeks of age may not be all that different, but the perception that the little girl is quieter than her brother—the family's need to differentiate them in this particular way—will be one tiny factor that affects what sorts of people both children will eventually become. Nature's bequest and nurturing's behest work in concert: Our roots are immutable, but each tree grows in a unique way, depending on its response to the light, the care, and the room it receives.

That peaceful little girl, only a few weeks old, is already being affected and having her own effect on the world around her. Up until his sister's birth, her two-year-old brother's nickname, "Wild Man," had always seemed a term of affection. At this moment, the accident of her birth has combined with his parents' perceptions of critical characteristics to remake the world. Wild and peaceful are traits this family recognizes, while another family might focus on other descriptive terms—alert, curious, accepting, passive—that subtly alter the child's sense of what is important. That big brother will never again know a universe in which aspects of his self and others will not be measured, at least in part, in relation to who his sister is or is not.

Shared and Unshared Environment

The urge to measure one's accomplishments against those of a sibling is an ongoing feature of life, natural and normative. Even in adulthood, and despite the fact that so many of us no longer have a day-to-day intimacy with our siblings, we continue to regard them as yardsticks against whom our own achievements can be estimated. (Oddly enough, those "yardsticks" often fail to reflect who our siblings have actually become during their lives; rather, we tend to view them as grown-up versions of their childhood family labels.) Nevertheless, brothers and sisters tend to be so completely different from each other that comparing oneself to a sibling is a little like Albert Einstein assessing his accomplishments in terms of Florence Nightingale's. Of course, one can draw such a comparison, but what purpose does it serve?

How can a set of siblings be so different from one another, since they all come from the same family? In order to understand our differences, we need first to look in the other direction, and examine to what extent children in the same family actually are similar. Conception, that first random bonding of sperm to egg, results in the creation of twenty-three pairs of chromosomes: One of each duo of chromosomes comes from the mother and one from the father. On each chromosome are thousands of different genetic components that determine different physical and psychological traits. For each minuscule genetic component, two siblings have, on average, a fifty-fifty chance of inheriting the same propensity. The range, researchers believe, is between 35 percent and 65 percent; thus, some sets of siblings are much more alike than others. (Note: Interestingly enough, siblings who are more alike genetically can actually tell that this is so at a glance; physical resemblance is a marker of genetic resemblance. And somehow those who have more in common know it: In one study, sets of twins were asked if they were fraternal or identical. Those fraternal twins whose blood analysis showed that they actually *were* more similar genetically than other fraternals were the ones who believed, albeit incorrectly, that they were identical.)

If siblings are 50 percent alike genetically, they are also 50 percent different. And yet, in fact, on most measures of personality, siblings are more dissimilar than that; in study after study, they have been shown to be far more unalike than alike. For more than a century, a series of devoted researchers has compared siblings on a huge variety of traits and characteristics. Since Sir Francis Galton's first comparison of brothers and their relative heights in the 1880s, scientists have studied everything from height and weight to the incidence of cancer, from mental illness and alcoholism to personality characteristics such as liveliness, sociability, and moodiness. What they continually find is that siblings only rarely share more of a particular propensity or trait than random members of the population. For example, about 80 percent of brothers and sisters have different eye colors; hair color, hair curliness, and skin complexion are visibly different for a full 90 percent of siblings. One brother's asthma, ulcer, or colon cancer has little bearing on whether his sibling will be vulnerable to the same illnesses. The story is the same for intelligence and reasoning abilities, although school success is also related to environmental factors, which tend to place siblings on a more even footing scholastically. Perhaps the sole measure upon which siblings have actually been found to be more alike than different is the question of whether or not they believe in the existence of God.

By looking more closely at a particular example, we can better understand the nature of the dissimilarities among blood-related siblings. Studies of schizophrenics, for example, have shown that the likelihood of a sibling also having the illness is about 10 percent. In the general population, the risk of schizophrenia is only 1 percent, so the risk is obviously higher for a sibling. But at the same time the most important thing to note is that *90 percent of siblings of schizophrenics do not themselves become mentally ill.* That 90 percent figure holds true also for a range of illnesses, from breast cancer to Alzheimer's disease to diabetes. Alcoholism, a tendency thought to be highly influenced by genetics, has a slightly higher rate; if one sibling is alcoholic, it appears that another will share the trait approximately 20 percent of the time.

One of the world's leaders in sibling research, behavioral geneticist Robert Plomin, of the Institute of Psychiatry at the University of London, was among the first to grasp that siblings' similarities are best explained by the genes they have inherited in common, while their differences are equally a matter of genetics and the environment in which they grow up. Thus, on average, 50 percent of the differences between any two siblings' personalities is genetic in origin. The other 50 percent is a result of the environment in which the siblings are raised. As Plomin argues, two siblings only *seem* to have the exact same environment. Even if their worlds were identical—an unlikely event—each child would experience the world in an extremely individual manner. Furthermore, parents actually *do* treat each child differently, because they perceive each child to have different advantages and needs. And siblings, friends, and outside social and academic experiences continue to contribute to what is called "unshared environment," that factor that makes each sibling develop so uniquely.

In this past century, during which geneticists have evaluated a great deal of evidence and become convinced of the vast differences among any set of siblings, much of psychological theory has tended to lump children into one rearing environment. Conventional thinking has always been that a mother has a single rearing style and treats each of her children in a similar manner; the father is assumed to be consistent as well. But parents act differently toward each child, a truth of which children are well aware. Consider that familiar battle cry: "It's not fair!" Every child experiences a different set of parents, unique relationships with one another and with caretakers, teachers, and friends. Each child grows up in a world that only he or she perceives.

Even identical twins—who have precisely the same genes and enter the family at almost exactly the same moment in time—end up becoming unique, separate people with at least some different ideas about themselves and the world. Identical twins who select identical careers and marry identical twins will nevertheless have diverging self-definitions: One will be the "creative one," one the "scientific"; one will be the cook, the other the seamstress.

In an often-quoted passage, psychologist and sibling expert Sandra Scarr of the University of Virginia makes this point:

> Lest the reader slip over these results, let us make clear the implication of these findings: Upper-middle-class brothers who attend the same school and whose parents take them to the same plays, sporting events, music lessons and therapists, and use the same child-rearing practices on them, are little more similar in personality measures than they are to working class or farm boys, whose lives are totally different.

Siblings, to put it bluntly, are not at all alike.

Multiple Realities

Our differences from one another can be a wonderful source of mutual appreciation. As Bessie Delany said about her 103-year-old sister, Sadie, in the best-selling book *Having Our Say: The Delany Sisters' First 100 Years*: "If Sadie is molasses, then I am vinegar! Sadie is sugar and I'm the spice. . . . We were best friends from Day One."

As the standard-bearers of our first families, our siblings are the only people who can truly share our happy and unhappy memories with us, who can help reconstruct that early sense that the world was manageable and we would always be cared for. They can also be discomforting reminders that each person grows up in a family that is his and his alone. Thus, one adult sibling's memory of an overwhelming and unsympathetic mother can be difficult to reconcile with another's recollection of a loving caretaker. Each person's truth is valid, a function of the unique individuals doing the perceiving, and of the particular life phases and experiences of each. This is one reason that, so frequently, grown brothers and sisters go through uncomfortable phases in their relationships; the discovery that there are unshared—even misunderstood—memories of the original intent and structure of our first childhood universe may make it easier to part ways, rather than to acknowledge that every family exists at multiple points of reality.

This book is called *The Accidental Bond* in acknowledgment of the phenomenon of chance that forces two vastly different children into relationship with each other and has an amazing, long-reaching impact on both their lives. We are placed in the world with a gorgeous randomness, cheek by jowl with these look-somewhat-alike/talk-somewhat-alike/think-somewhat-alike others, our siblings. They resemble us just enough to make all their differences confusing, and no matter what we choose to make of this, we are cast in relation to them our whole lives long.

The stories told here are primarily those of siblings from two- and three-child families. By looking at siblings in two- and three-person groupings, one can speculate about how those same groupings would be experienced in a larger family. Siblings from larger families may have struggled with a heightened sense that resources—emotional and financial—were overly diluted, and older siblings may have been called upon to do more child care. Nevertheless, this is a matter of scale, for certainly some of the brothers and sisters who described their connections and histories for me had also dealt with these same issues. In addition, the larger families of the past are on the wane. Family size continues to decline nationwide; the tendency now is to have smaller families, with children spaced more closely together. Over time, speculate some researchers, both these factors may further increase the intensity and importance of the individual sibling relationship.

Narrowing the focus of *The Accidental Bond* to two- and three-sibling relationships allowed each one who was interviewed to describe his or her story fully in these pages, so that a richer portrait of the family—past and present—could emerge. Furthermore, since sibling-oriented psychologists routinely acknowledge that these relationships develop in paired sets, alliances in a larger family develop along similar lines to those in a smaller one: In a "normal" situation, sisters and brothers tend to view themselves as organized into twosomes, or dyads, that have both positive and negative aspects.

In general, according to psychologists Stephen P. Bank and Michael D. Kahn, authors of the groundbreaking 1982 book *The Sibling Bond,* "There is no neutrality or indifference in this sibling world; [for each brother or sister,] a particular sibling is the one who really 'counts.' " Bank and Kahn note that in families with three children, one pair always becomes more intensely involved, leaving the extra child to establish his or her identity without the intensity of such a sibling connection. While gender, age spacing, and birth order must play some role in the process by which two siblings choose to ally, such influences and affinities are far from predictable, the result of the unique circumstances and personalities within a particular family. For each child, "one sibling is always more prominent, eliciting passionate feelings of hate or love," Bank and Kahn comment, "rarely are such feelings distributed evenly. . . . Two people will inevitably seek closeness, even fusion, leaving the third person to fend for himself or herself." It isn't merely membership inside the pair which has developmental significance; being the party on the outside obviously matters at least as much.

Who Is "EverySibling"?

In 1984 a sketch appeared in *The Atlantic Monthly* titled "And Give My Father Here Whatever He Wants." In this piece, a fledgling author named Howard Kaplan described how he'd taken a bartending job in order to immerse himself in material for his writing. Here was the truth of life, the most basic reality, the chance to learn about everyday mysteries as they tumbled, fully revealed, from the unguarded mouths of the salts of the earth. What he learned rapidly, however, was that there are in fact only two dozen tired comments that comprise the entire repertoire of bar patrons, be they brain surgeons or factory workers. Among these pearls of original comedy: Two friends come up to the bar and one says, "I'll have a beer. *And give my father here whatever he wants.*" Or, after ordering a round of drinks, a happy patron confides to the bartender, *"They're not all for me."* Then there's the teetotaler who smiles broadly after ordering a club soda for herself, and then proudly proclaims, *"I'm a big drinker!"*

My experience when broaching the topic of siblings quickly began to resonate in a similar manner. No matter whether I was talking with siblings themselves or with psychologists, psychiatrists, doctors, editors, friends at dinner parties, even two pleasant women I met on an interminable line to take our kids to see Santa Claus, I came to understand that there are only a very few ways in which adult brothers and sisters actually muse about their relationships with one another. The themes that entangle the sibling bond, holding it together despite remarkable levels of stress and strain, are similar for almost everyone, despite apparently drastic dissimilarities or unusually complicated relationships.

People begin—as I did when I first started to research this topic—by becoming overwhelmed at the potential complexity of the sibling connection. A thirty-year-old man may have two older sisters or one; a half brother who is ten years old or one who is fifty; six siblings; one sibling; a sibling who died at the age of three, or one who committed suicide at the age of eighteen; one who is mentally ill, or two who aren't; or an identical or fraternal twin. There are millions of possible permutations, each with a very different influence on how the man sees himself in relation to others in the world. How can one begin to have an orderly grasp of a connection that is so variable, so unpredictable, so unlike those bonds with mother, father, or love partner that people usually ponder in order to better understand themselves in relation to others?

The answer is that we are coming at the topic from the wrong scale of reference. It would be difficult to make sense of a huge rhinoceros if one were looking through the eyepiece of a microscope. If we looked at love relationships using that same lens, we'd have the same trouble making predictable rules. People have different personalities and needs; they come from different families of origin, vary in their sexual inclinations, their need for closeness, readiness for commitment, impulsivity, their willingness to endure the difficult phases, their desire for children or affairs or professional success—and their partners' acceptance or rejection of the same. If every woman was attracted to exactly the same man, or vice versa, we'd have an extremely tense situation on our hands, at best. A multiplicity of factors make every love relationship unique. But we *can* define certain basic principles of what makes relationships work and when and why, in the aggregate, which will help us understand our own individual situations. We interpret our own lives in relation to *what everyone does*. Of course, we know that "everyone" is not someone we have met. "Everyone" means the average.

There are major themes that run through all sibling relationships as well. Over and over again, throughout the course of writing this book, I found that siblings raised the same issues about one another. Even though their particular family trees had a given number of branches, or they came from certain ethnic backgrounds, or a parent had died, or they were estranged from one another, each brother and sister had shared certain common experiences and undergone similar watershed moments. There is no "EverySibling," per se, but there are certainly issues—particularly the "Three C's" of Competition, Cooperation, and Comparison—with which every sibling wrestles in his or her own unique manner.

Sibling Themes

It cannot be possible to be raised in a household with someone else and not be affected by who he or she is, how that person treats you, what he or she looks like and acts like—and what that person manages to give and get from you and from the other people around you.

Our siblings, in fact, affect us from earliest childhood onward in a variety of ways: We share space in the family with them, we learn from them and teach them, we divide up parental loyalties with them, we envy them, admire them, dominate them, hate them, love them.

In fact, a goodly percentage of the groundwork for later intimate relationships is laid during early life interactions with our siblings.

Our sisters and brothers play leading roles in the day-to-day reality of our childhood experience—as our competitors, true, but also as our peers, our first real partners in life. With our siblings, to some extent, we actually play out our first "marriages": We experience conflicting yearnings for enmeshment and independence; we learn how to argue, negotiate, and compromise; how to express affection and to balance our need for privacy with our need for closeness. We learn what behavior is appropriate with peers, and what is not. And as we interact, react, and develop, the essential elements of our personalities evolve as well. All of us, we hope, eventually outgrow the childlike nature of our earliest relationships, but just as our first complex attachments to our mothers and fathers continue to affect the choices we make in adulthood, so also do the ties with our sisters and brothers.

Why, then, do even the most sophisticated psychological thinkers continue to focus on the early relationships with parents—and primarily the fusion with the mother—as if these ties were formed in a vacuum, the only significant bonds of early life? As social worker Janna Malamud Smith wrote in a beautiful 1990 *New York Times Magazine* article called "*Mothers: Tired of Taking the Rap,*" mothers continue to be thought of as the central determinant of a child's failure or success at developing into a functioning adult. When things go wrong, argues Smith, Mom is the "convenient missing link. . . . If it is not viral or bacterial, it must be maternal."

Common sense frankly confirms that other people play significant parts in our personality development: fathers, siblings, grandparents, teachers, other caretakers, even friends. We're simply so used to looking directly at Mother—and then perhaps glancing at Father—that we often neglect to tease out the complicated threads of other relationships that are enormously important as we grow up. Take a few steps backward. Now can you see that rhinoceros?

Although in our society, the overriding belief—rightly or wrongly —is that primary care by the mother is *the* critical factor in determining whether or not a youngster becomes a fully functioning adult, vast numbers of children are being raised by a combination of caretakers—day care, baby-sitters, siblings, grandparents, mothers and fathers in separate households, stepparents. The formula is as varied as the possible household arrangements. Although one caretaker may have primary responsibility for a child's well-being, all those other caring presences play substantive roles: A sister may be the first person to witness a baby's toddle, a baby-sitter may supervise toilet training, and a stepparent or grandparent may be the one who introduces a little child to his ABC's, his first day of school, or his first visit to the dentist. Without passing judgment on the positive or negative effect that these amalgamated rearing situations may have, one is forced to acknowledge that they are occurring all around us. Thus, with the future in mind, there is an even greater need to examine what role others, including a brother or sister, actually play in a child's personality development. We need to know what kind of long-term, lifelong impact these relationships can have. Once again, altering the lens through which we view ourselves can provide a completely new level of insight.

The task here is to come to a greater understanding of just one tie, that among brothers and sisters, and to learn how those relationships formed in childhood continue to have an effect long into adulthood. All the "accidental" factors of luck and chance play out with one another in a complicated manner that can best be understood on a case-by-case basis. Someone once said that there are as many psychological theories as there are psychologists; it seems also true that there are as many variations on human psychology as there are humans.

Nevertheless, the sibling connection as a broad factor contributing to a sense of self is so deeply rooted that when people say, "My sibling doesn't matter, we have nothing in common," what they often mean is that the polarization—the angry feelings, the dividing up of characteristics, the claims of "I'm like this; he's like that," the shutting down of empathy—began very early. These siblings may be entirely unlike one another, may not even like one another, may prefer to avoid each other—but have nothing in common?

Be serious.

Siblings have the most significant feature of all in common, in most cases: They sprang from the same loins and they grew up in the same households. Brothers and sisters who think they share nothing might benefit from a little reflection. When did the divisions begin and why? Don't some of those same distant, angry feelings recur in similar situations, with spouses, co-workers, children—even now? We are not condemned to repeat our early history as long as we are willing to grapple with the past.

The early interplay of self with siblings—played out within the powerful confines of the relationships one has with mother and father —continues to affect one's personality and self-image into adulthood. In one way, everyone knows this: People often claim that they do particular things because they are youngest or oldest or middle children. Each person has convictions about what those positions within the family mean (based, of course, on his or her own unique and specific early experiences). Furthermore, many parents unconsciously respond to their own children according to sibling-based expectations: A mother who is the older of two daughters may have little sympathy with her younger daughter's eagerness to trail after her big sister. Without realizing it, she has a more empathetic response to the needs of the child in her same sibling position. That mother's differential empathy, a remnant of her particular sibling experience but now a factor of luck and chance for her two children, will certainly make its mark on the way in which each of those two young women perceives the world.

In the same vein, a father who had competitive relationships with his own brothers and sisters may react in a hostile and competitive manner to the birth of his first child and the consequent intrusion into his exclusive relationship with his wife. This can even happen with later children: One young father whom I interviewed, a first child himself, had a very close relationship with his daughter Samantha. When his son was born, this man felt awkward about showing affection to him, mindful of the difficulties firstborn Samantha was experiencing. Two years later, when I first met with him, his relationship with his son was ambivalent and distant. This initial disturbance may well have its impact upon the later relationship between father and child, and might even place strains upon the lifelong bond between the young sister and brother. Thus, if not dealt with, such reenactments of, and reactions to, a parent's sibling experiences can continue to reverberate into the next generation.

As you read this book, certain basic rules of siblingdom should become apparent. It will be demonstrated that sibling experiences, which were long regarded as mere developmental leftovers, continue to affect how we function as adults, in the workplace, in friendship, and in love relationships. Some people are very close to their siblings; some quite removed and unfriendly, but this—surprisingly perhaps —does not change the fundamental importance of the connection.

Within each of us there exists a hidden "other"; a person who is as selfish as we are generous, as aggressive as we are passive, or as accomplished and self-confident as we yearn to be. This secret self is the repository of negative traits we cannot acknowledge in ourselves, and it is also the cave in which we bury the positive potential we fear to explore. One very human use of the sibling relationship in adulthood is to, unconsciously, learn to view a brother or sister as that hidden self. We perceive him or her as the selfish one, the angry one, the failure, or the grand success, as if by giving away the label, we can destroy that aspect of ourselves. Often the ascribed characteristics *do* exist in our siblings, but they exist in us as well. How else can we be so certain of such traits and inclinations, were they not shared? We may be working harder to suppress them, but we *know* such impulses very well.

Siblings also can become the psychological vessels in which to place any resentful, embittered feelings we might otherwise have toward our parents and our upbringing, or, worse yet, toward impulses, failures, and yearnings of our own. Of course, a sister or brother can really *be* a source of tangible malice, or of legitimate support, but often the symbolic relationship seems to be as important as the actual one.

This book is about the sibling bond, the least appreciated of all family and emotional connections, and (given the likelihood that we will outlive our parents) the longest-lasting. Our brothers and sisters are there with us from the dawn of our personal stories to the inevitable dusk. If we begin at the beginning, we find them, immutable presences in childhood existence. Imps and angels simultaneously, they hover on the sidelines of all the other choices and connections— spouses, professions, children, friendships—that we make, sometimes lending a hand or ear but often simply taken for granted as carved totems, static presences with limited and very clear dimensions. We define them in the simplest of terms: I'm this, ergo, she's that. Although in adulthood it is rare that they take center stage in our life dramas, our brothers and sisters retain both a symbolic and a functional importance. When we are lucky, they actually reemerge from the storage vault, not as unidimensional symbols but as actual people with a rich variety of difference and similarity to share with us. Our siblings become fluid, real humans, much more than just the touchstones that link us to what was important and sustaining in our earliest lives.

The Relationship Without Rules

The leaves of an oak change color as part of the tree's life course, entirely unrelated to human needs. Yet despite the leaves' indifference, we are moved: sheltered and cooled under the wealth of summer greens and then exposed by the stark absence of covering in winter. Our siblings grow and change with the same seemingly indifferent alacrity, the seasons altering them in just the same slow manner that turns leaves from bud to green leaf to brown. We are angry (or secretly pleased) when their marriages falter, proud (or jealous) when their children do well or they attain a certain professional success, intimidated (or impressed) by their investment acumen, ashamed of (or sympathetic to) their alcohol problems.

From birth to death, the sibling relationship undergoes an amazing amount of change and development, all because the players involved continue to evolve and grow. It is hardly possible for a relationship to remain the same over a period that can be as long as eighty years, or even longer. The volatile emotional quality of a single relationship can look like a cardiac patient's EKG reading, with peaks and valleys, even flat plateaus in which one or both players are calmly at rest, paying no attention to one another, or even indifferent to the value of the relationship.

Furthermore, just as marital and family therapists acknowledge that in any single marital connection there are always two marriages, his and hers, so we must begin this inquiry by emphasizing the fact that there are—with any pair of siblings—two relationships, his and hers, or hers and hers, or his and his. Because siblings essentially live in related but not parallel universes to one another, they may or may

not have the same need for the larger commitment of connection—
or, conversely, for distance—at the same time. For any number of
financial, marital, or other reasons, siblings may at different points
in their lives be better or worse at being each other's friend and
supporter.

With sisters and brothers, we can ignore, create distance, celebrate,
or assist but, above all, in our culture, *we can make the rules.*

There are simply no guidelines for being an adult sibling in this
society. Brothers and sisters have no culturally proscribed joint obligation, except perhaps to care for their aging parents. Given the lack
of societal focus on this relationship, we expect that it must provide
a certain amount of pleasure or satisfaction for us to devote any
energy to it. It must be worth it. Still, despite its open-endedness,
people are rarely able to think of a sibling relationship without experiencing a certain depth of emotional reaction. Unlike any other kin
or friendship tie that I can think of, the prototypical sister-sister,
sister-brother, or brother-brother bond in our middle-class culture is
at once involved and fundamentally disconnected.

The relationship between two siblings is perhaps more like a cactus
than an oak, for it requires less watering than other friendships in
order to survive. We go through stages of connection, indifference or
resentful competition, loyal support or generous sacrifice. No matter
what the previous history of understanding and misunderstanding
has been, growing older tends to involve coming to terms with one's
origins, particularly one's siblings. The urge to reconnect with brothers and sisters does seem to come upon one later in life, almost as if
it were another biological predisposition. Certainly the older we get,
the more our life phases are likely to run in synchrony, a situation
conducive to active and involved friendship.

It may be that we do not select our siblings, or any other aspect of
the world we are born into, but we owe it to ourselves to try to
understand and to manage the advantages and disadvantages we have
been given. We can learn to appreciate, even celebrate, the positive
aspects of sibling relationships; we can also become able to accept
and to integrate into our sense of self the existence of unchangeable
negatives.

A closer consideration of this multifaceted tie can help us to know ourselves better. The first step is accepting that our sibling relationship is not simply a connection mediated by our parents. Most critical to our past and present sibling bond is figuring out how *each of us* has developed a personal, and unique, view of our brothers and sisters. Then we can come to terms with what these flesh-and-blood people really mean to us.

CHAPTER TWO

Justine Arkady

"Edith Has Always Been There for Me"

On a humid June afternoon, just ten minutes after an abrupt downpour had deluged her graduation processional, Justine Arkady seemed, by a miracle, to be retaining her dignity. Even though her drenched gown was surely hot and uncomfortable as she stood on display before a large crowd of sodden listeners—parents, friends, and relatives of her several hundred fellow high school graduates—she spoke with a confidence generally lacking in adolescent communication. She began with a quote from Albert Camus, then went on to give her own interpretation of his thinking: "No art can completely reject reality," she said, "but every time an artist makes a decision to capture a particular place, at a particular time, in a certain light, he is claiming that one moment can be the essence of what is real."

She leaned over the podium, her curly blond hair starting to splay exuberantly over her shoulders and down her back as it dried. Most of the other seniors graduating from this Connecticut high school were quiet, tenting drenched robes off their knees, waving their programs back and forth in an effort to move the dank air. Here and there, Justine's classmates nudged one another, pointing out friends in the huge crowd.

Justine continued valiantly. "This moment is, for us, the essence of reality," she declared. "All of our memories of this particular place, this particular life, of what we have shared, can be distilled down to this last time together. Let us go out into the world, each of us, from here. Let us make lives as wonderful and meaningful, and real, as art."

She smiled at the crowd, a huge grin that was visible even in the farthest rows, where I had finally been lucky enough to find a damp seat on which to perch. Silence fell, and then the crowd began a furious clapping. I wondered doubtfully how many of her enthusiastically applauding classmates understood what she was exhorting them to do.

Then, a small thing happened that altered my angle of view; for just a blink of a moment, I had a perfect grasp upon an extremely important facet of Justine Arkady.

There is an instant in every adult's life when it suddenly becomes clear that adolescence has discreetly slipped away, that one is completely and irrevocably adult. I recognized that sensation, a little sadly, as I watched Justine and her classmates revert at a moment's notice to childlike exuberance; they ran, hooting and hurrahing, between the rows of seated viewers to meet in a large group at the back of the football field. Sodden black graduation robes made slapping noises against their legs as they passed. Justine, in what were very likely a pair of unfamiliarly high heels, slipped from the head of the pack to the middle. Then, suddenly, she wobbled to the pavement with one ankle twisted beneath her. The heel of her shoe came off in her hand. She grimaced with embarrassment but quickly recovered, donning once more that familiar, stouthearted smile.

A few hundred yards away, her classmates were throwing their mortarboards in the air, shouting and hugging and laughing. Although she was surrounded in an instant by outstretched hands, Justine sat, as if temporarily paralyzed, on the concrete path. Edith, her fifteen-year-old sister, suddenly materialized at her side. She quickly pulled off her flat brown sandals. Justine grabbed the shoes without a moment's hesitation, looking up at her sister gratefully. In a matter of seconds, she was shod and jumping happily in a crowd of her classmates. Edith stood, barefoot and motionless, the discarded high heels hooked delicately on the index and middle fingers of her right hand.

And, in fact, at that moment, Justine and Edith's relationship was revealed in its perfect essence. Here was the reality of the sister-sister bond for these two teenagers, at this time and place in their lives. Later in life, no matter what happened to them, such a moment of generosity and understanding—of being known and appreciated— would always be between them.

In Dorothy Allison's 1992 novel *Bastard Out of Carolina*, one character describes just such an instant in young adulthood, capturing the sense of being perched on the edge of life:

> Seems like after that we were all grown up and everything was different. It's the way of things. One day you're all family together, fighting and hugging from one moment to the next, and then it's all gone. You're off making your own family, scared of what's coming next, and Lord, things have a way of running faster and faster all the time.

I had wanted to meet with a set of adolescents for just that reason, because "things have a way of running faster and faster all the time." When I first made that long drive to meet with Justine and Edith, I could no longer remember what it felt like to be a young sister with siblings.

It had been a long time since I had been a junior member of a family in its primacy. At this stage of my life, as a wife and mother, I was well aware of what it is like to be one of the experts sitting at the control panels of the family ship. I was harder put to recall, however, what it actually felt like to be part of my original family, knowing only one way of living in the world. For, of course, that is one of the grandest mental leaps one makes in the course of growing up—the realization that there are many, many lives one can live, each eminently reasonable and equally feasible. Once the potential for variety is really understood, it is just about impossible to recapture that child's sense of safety and security, of the one true way.

For the Arkady sisters, I suspect, the one true way had never really existed; even early on, life had been somewhat complicated and confusing, for neither girl could remember a time when they hadn't known their family life to be unusual. In our first two interviews, I learned that they were three years apart in age, born during the decade that their parents had spent as part of a sixty-member commune. This extended "family" was not created as a religious organization, but rather was founded upon ideals about shared living, vegetarianism, and a disregard for material goods. The group supported itself by operating a health food store and restaurant. As two of very few children born in the commune, Justine and Edith's early memories were a pleasant jumble of benevolent caretakers and playful adults; at the same time, both girls recall a goodly share of arguing, of dirt and disorder. When Justine was six and Edith three, their parents decided that the group living situation lacked a needed measure of privacy. Also, although the girls were not aware of it for another five years, the fragmenting state of the Arkadys' marriage had contributed to the decision to leave the commune. Certainly as much was lost by the move as was gained: One of Edith's earliest memories was that the Arkadys were obliged to abandon their few possessions at the farm, including even the ragged stuffed bear the little girl carried around for comfort.

Although Edith had lost the reassurance of her teddy bear, she never doubted that she would always have her sister Justine. From their very earliest days, the older sister habitually included the younger one in her activities. They colored together, wrote stories, made castles in their closet, and acted out fantasy games with one another.

"I had lots of friends, we both did. It wasn't even that I always liked her so much," Justine told me cheerfully, while her sister rolled her eyes in mock anger. "And we fought all the time, about everything."

"We still do," Edith said.

"What do you mean?" I asked.

"We can fight about anything, at the drop of a hat," Justine said, and Edith nodded in vigorous agreement. "Furious fights, where we're screaming and rolling around on the floor pummeling each other. The thing is, it's over in five minutes. We'd never hold a grudge, or not be friends."

Edith shook her head from side to side. "Never," she said.

"When we were little, if I wanted to be the doctor, Edie would always be the patient. Or she would be the princess who needed to be rescued. I was Sir Edward, the world-famous knight, and you were Lady—" She turned to face her sister.

"Rosa," Edith said.

"Remember your faithful stallion?" Both sisters chuckled, and then Justine turned to me. "It was this great big gray and white cat, we fed him, and he hung around. She tried to ride him. Our mother was furious, she thought it was cruel."

"I was, what, four or five years old, maybe," Edith said quietly. "I was all scratched up."

"I told Mom I made her do it, but then we both got in trouble because I lied," the older girl said. Her sister smiled in sympathy.

"It wasn't as though we were unhappy," Justine continued. "I mean, I remember our father used to play with us a lot and our parents had friends and we had fun. We used to take huge cardboard boxes and make houses out of them, and we all ate together. I guess our parents were unhappy together, but we didn't know it."

"No, we didn't," Edie said, looking down at the table.

"Do you remember realizing they were getting divorced?"

"I've thought about that a lot," Justine said, "and I don't think I remember any particular moment. It took such a long time, it happened so slowly. First he was just not there once in a while, and nobody ever said anything, and then slowly it got to be more. And when they said they were getting divorced, I guess I already knew it was going to happen.

"When Mom and Dad split up, it was us who stayed together, you know. I mean, our parents talked to us, and they tried really hard to make sure we were okay. But. I mean, we weren't always fine and sometimes we really needed to be able to talk about it. Sometimes I just wanted someone to hang around with, to know I wouldn't be alone," Justine said, her voice more deliberate now that she was making her point. "Edith has always, always been there for me."

<hr />

"Edie Is Vanilla"

On the sultry June afternoon of Justine's high school graduation, perhaps neither she nor Edith could yet understand what was about to change in their lives, including the relationship that they had, for the most part, enjoyed with each other. They had vaguely contemplated the fact of Justine's imminent departure for college, promising each other that there would be many visits and phone calls and letters.

It was Justine who had realized for herself what psychologists know to be true as well: that their relationship, as they knew it, was about to undergo a major upheaval. From now on each sister would likely focus more exclusively on establishing her own self as an adult in "real" life. The need to foster stability, to help maintain each other within the family, would begin to dissipate as the need to create a new and independent life began to grow. Oddly enough, Justine, the departing sister, seemed more worried that her sister would make distance in the relationship than the other way around.

"Sometimes I think I love her more than she loves me," Justine had told me frankly, only a few mornings before graduation. "She keeps everything to herself. It's hard to know what she feels."

Although Edith blushed pinkly with pleasure to hear herself so described, she said nothing. We were seated at their mother's scarred enamel-topped kitchen table, which was heaped high with advertising flyers for the organic vegetables grown on the Arkadys' farm, as well as a sloppy stack of newspapers, a camera, and a worn canvas book bag. An assortment of old-fashioned and more modern garden tools were thrown together in a dirty heap on a fourth chair, the dirt-encrusted claws of one small hand fork hooked dangerously through the circular end of a scuffle hoe.

It was no later than nine o'clock on a Saturday morning; the two girls were eating guacamole from an earthenware bowl set casually atop a stack of magazines. They drew tortilla chips from an open bag.

Justine etched a line through the thick green dip with the edge of a broken tortilla, scooping up an oversized clump. Her voice was higher than her sister's, and she spoke much more quickly. She spoke more frequently as well, covering up Edith's strong-willed silences as if she were a volunteer firefighter dousing a tiny burst of flames with an elephantine spray of water. I had begun the interview by asking Edith how she and her sister were different; no silence had been allowed to fall before Justine eagerly asserted herself. "Edie never wants to stand out, never wants to be noticed," she said. "She's vanilla."

I chuckled uncomfortably.

Edith nodded in agreement. "That's right," she said.

"What does that mean, 'vanilla'?" I asked.

Edith looked across at her sister, not exactly shyly, but perhaps hoping that her sister would finish the thought for her. "I like to blend in, I guess," she said, hesitating again before continuing. "I mean, I used to wish we had a normal house, and lived in a normal neighborhood, you know, in town, like all my friends do. But then I figured that if we did, well, then everyone would know how weird my mother is, I mean, how she only sets out the new plants when the moon is in the right phase, and all the strange things she believes. She meditates out there, with the zucchini. So I'm glad we live out here by ourselves, where no one can see us." She smoothed her careful pageboy. In the ensuing silence, she curved her hips, lifting slightly up from her seat as she pinched the heavy cotton of her white shorts to crisp the neat creases.

Justine said, "You won't always be like that. I used to wish I was like everyone else. Now I'm really glad I'm different."

Edith blushed and shrugged at the same time. She didn't speak, but in the instant that her eyes met her sister's, it was clear that a communication had been sent and received. I watched them, marveling at the efficiency, and the intimacy, of their connection.

For the first time, it occurred to me that, in terms of appearance at least, the contrast between the Arkady sisters was so overt as to be amusing. Edith was as neat and pulled together as a young executive on summer vacation, her hair perfectly combed, her cotton blouse ironed. On the other hand, Justine's paint-stained T-shirt was huge, crumpled, and so worn it was nearly transparent. She had created her own red-and-white striped shorts from a pair of flannel pajama bottoms. Noticing my interest, Justine pointed to her shorts cheerfully and remarked, "You see, I'm the weird one. I'm like Mom and Dad. And Edie saw how much trouble I had when we moved here, how everyone laughed at me. She didn't want to go through that."

Justine had been almost eleven—just entering puberty—when they moved from the New Jersey college town where her parents had spent four years after leaving the commune, to this rural Connecticut area in which her father hoped to create a cooperative organic farm. The girls were bused ten miles each way to attend school in a neighboring village. As Justine reported it, she "missed the boat" in terms of understanding how conservative the community was. "I was pretty hurt for a few years. I mean, I got teased all the time for my clothes, and my opinions. I was too old when we moved, I don't think I could have blended in if I tried."

I was struck by Justine's maturity, her clear sense of the rightness of her position, of the self-confidence and strength it must have taken to remain so singular an individual in such a conservative community. "I was pretty unhappy," Justine said, "but I never wanted to be like everyone else. I never wanted to blend in."

Edith chimed in, suddenly eager. She'd sat quietly through much of our previous meetings, contributing rarely and usually monosyllabically, as if she were holding back some critical piece of information. I'd grown very curious about her reticence; now it seemed that we'd finally stumbled upon a topic she would willingly contribute to. "But it isn't just that I wanted to fit in, I *do* fit in. Mommy's embarrassing. She talks too much, she's strange. I like to be neat. I like to look nice." The enthusiastic speech ran out of steam as abruptly as it had begun. Edith mumbled, "I mean, sometimes I wish I had the courage to be more like Justine, different, but . . ."

She laughed nervously.

Justine took another tortilla chip and scooped up a generous glob of guacamole. Edith held out her hand to take it, an uneasy proprietary gesture that the older girl did not seem to see. The younger one giggled again, reaching across the table to grab the bag of chips in a flurry of self-conscious motion. I noticed that her fingernails were ragged, gnawed down to the quicks.

The Imaginary Audience and the Personal Fable

Adolescence is a fantastic witch's brew, concocted from a wild and unpredictable mess of ingredients. The adolescent's given personality, the timing of hormonal changes, the child's assigned role within the family, and his or her feelings about that particular label are all part of the mix. So are school relationships, intellectual and physical competence, and a host of other seemingly random components. These elements are tossed together with a healthy dollop of self-righteous confusion about the world and others; the results are well documented in their infinite variety, the stuff of literature and music, and, of course, of parental legend.

The issue of identity—of defining precisely *who* one is—is the central psychological task of adolescence. And in fact Edith Arkady's confusion about herself, and about who she might eventually become, is quite typical of the stage of life in which she was engrossed. Early adolescence is marked by a compelling urge for conformity, a desire to blend in with one's peers.

In adolescence a child is truly able to understand for the first time that other people have thoughts and beliefs of their own. Still, although the teenager grasps that others are capable of cognition, she is as yet unable to differentiate between her own concerns and other people's. As a result, because *she* is overwhelmingly concerned with her own self—and the physiological and emotional changes taking place within her—she assumes that the thoughts of each person are just like hers. Thus, she naturally believes that others *must be* as obsessed by her actions and looks as she is.

As a result, according to developmental psychologist Dr. David Elkind, the adolescent is "continually constructing, or reacting to, an imaginary audience." When a group of teenagers get together, each truly believes that he or she is the focus of intense scrutiny by others. "Each is more concerned with being the observed than with being the observer," writes Dr. Elkind. "Gatherings of young adolescents are unique in the sense that each young person is simultaneously an actor to himself and an audience to others."

An adolescent holds tenaciously to the bizarre and counterintuitive conviction that she is the most prominent member of her particular social milieu, despite clear and constant evidence to the contrary. Although each teenager *does* eventually come to understand that he is not the center of the known universe, such a simple leap of comprehension is surprisingly difficult to make.

Think of Justine's conviction that Edith would outgrow her desire to be "vanilla": Despite her mature manner, what Justine was really saying was that one day Edith would be more like *her*. Edith, according to her sister, was only going through a phase *on the road to becoming more flavorful, more like Justine*. Such a conviction is in and of itself a sign of being eighteen years old. Each young adult assumes that the way of being eighteen, and being grown up, is to be like himself or herself. It's hard to believe that the other person may simply turn out to be someone entirely different.

This is partly due to one other preoccupation of adolescence, the "personal fable," or the belief that one's own particular story is exceptionally rich, unusual, and fundamentally important. Thus, one's interests and traits are deemed superior, and worthy of imitation by others. "Only [the teenager] can suffer with such agonized intensity, or experience such exquisite rapture," as Dr. Elkind writes. And, when well told, the dramas of adolescence often comprise the most appealing tales in our literary canon: A perfect illustration is J. D. Salinger's *Catcher in the Rye*. Holden Caulfield's turmoil remains relevant to new generations of readers precisely because it is the kind of brilliantly quirky personal fable that each of us imagines for our own selves.

Later in adolescence, as Justine at eighteen was just beginning to realize, the importance of the personal fable diminishes. The young adult begins to establish truly mutual relationships. Recently, when Justine and her best friend shared the details of their actual and inner lives, each one felt less unique. They also obviously felt less alone. As this phase takes hold of an adolescent, the highs and lows of emotional experience become more moderate, and a certain reasonableness begins to prevail. The personal fable has been modified and integrated into the self, and the young adult is able to appreciate— and empathize with—the other players in her life story.

In another way, however, the personal fable continues unabated, giving meaning to our lives. Without some sense that our individual struggles are important within the greater scheme of things, our aspirations and dreams would gradually come to seem depressingly irrelevant. Even as we evolve into more mature and confident beings, most of us carry around at least a remnant of our confused, self-centered, and emotionally unpredictable adolescent selves. In adulthood the personal fable becomes a source of inner inspiration and courage, a motivating force we use to bolster that somewhat elusive sense we describe as self-esteem, to energize ourselves into taking risks. For it is often a belief in one's unique ability to contribute that propels one to accomplishment.

"She Isn't a Mother"

At this point, I had met with each of the Arkady sisters several times, and I had met with them twice, together, for extended interviews. I had inadvertently had several long telephone calls with their mother as well. Whenever I'd gotten her on the phone, she'd been quite forthcoming with information about the kids, whether I asked or not. All the while, despite her helpfulness, she continued to insist that I might prefer to interview her and *her* sister. I explained that I didn't think I could interview her while I was meeting with her daughters and, with difficulty, I managed to postpone that question. Still, it became clear in those interactions how much Justine and Edith functioned on a peer level with their divorced mother: They were all involved in one another's romantic lives, the house and meal planning were all managed communally and in a fairly scattershot manner, and, above all, the mother clearly resented that her daughters were having the opportunity to talk about their relationship while she was denied the same pleasure. Cora Arkady was always friendly and eager to help, but she frequently made excuses to enter the room when I was meeting with the kids, drawing attention to her presence like a neglected child. Although I liked her, and found her as charming and intelligent as her daughters, I wondered what kind of mother she must be.

"She isn't a mother," Justine told me flatly when I asked. "If anything, we are the parents, not her."

"Oh?" I said.

"But, you know, my friends are always feeling sorry for me because I don't have a curfew and no one watches when I come in. I like it though. I think she respects us. She has always treated us like equals." Justine's voice was as defensive as her posture on this Friday afternoon as we sat on the steps of her high school waiting for Edith to join us. School was over for the year, but Edith was tutoring in the summer school, and Justine had suggested that I meet them there. One had to wonder if she was already feeling a certain nostalgia for high school.

The steps were of uncomfortably grainy, gray cement, wide and low, and Justine sat curled over her knees, her entire torso bent, her head down so that her hair brushed the pavement. She was playing with the buckle on the top of her calf-high boot, pulling the black strap just to the edge of the metal prong and then pushing it back in. She had bent over like this the moment I mentioned her mother; now I watched as her slim frame stretched further and further, like a

tortoise's head, into a position of obvious discomfort. I leaned closer
in order to hear her as she directed her dialogue toward her ankles.
"All my friends' mothers, they're just mothers. Mine is different."
She pushed the strap into the buckle again and turned to me. I edged
back slightly, trying not to crowd her. "It's good," she said, "to have
a mother like ours. It is."

Justine felt sure that her mother's methods with them were benign.
Since both young women were intelligent and attractive people with
strong peer relationships, it was very tempting to believe, as Justine
did, that they were uniquely lucky. However, the Arkady sisters were
certainly coping with untraditional family circumstances, and while
some of the consequences appeared positive to them, the potential
for negative aspects was present as well. In their effort to live in
personally fulfilling situations, the Arkadys had developed a family
structure in which all women of any age function as peers and equals.
This is often the case following a divorce, as Judith Wallerstein and
Sandra Blakeslee point out in their best-selling book *Second Chances:
Men, Women and Children a Decade after Divorce.*

It is, however, acutely anxiety-producing, Wallerstein believes, for
young people to see their parents as peers with similar sexual problems and urges just at the moment when "they are trying to cope with
their own emerging sexuality." Young adults find divorce particularly
upsetting, she writes, because they have a particularly "strong need
for family structure to help them set limits on their own sexual and
aggressive impulses."

I wondered how much ambivalence Justine was hiding from me—
and, of course, from her mother. I waited, hoping that Justine would
continue, but she was determined to say nothing more on the subject
of Cora Arkady.

"Tell me about Edith," I said. "What is she like?"

It was almost funny to watch the comfortable way that Justine
unfurled to lean against the steps, torso resting on elbows. In an
instant, she seemed completely relaxed and open; could she, an aspir-
ing actress, possibly be unaware of the difference in her posture when
she discussed each of her two housemates?

"Edith is great," Justine said. "She's such a complete person. I
mean, she's very smart, I think she's smarter than me although we
both do well in school. And she's pretty and she gets along with

people. She has lots and lots of friends, I've never been like that. See, I'm always the same person, wherever I am and whoever I'm with. Sometimes I'm moody or difficult, I stand up for what I believe in. I get in trouble a lot. I have disagreements with people. But Edie is straightforward."

"I would think that meant she gets into disagreements, too."

"No, she doesn't," Justine said, shaking her head in wonder. "She just says no, and people listen to her. She won't go out with a guy unless she really likes him. She'd rather stay home. She doesn't do dumb things."

"Do you?"

"Oh, God! I've done so many dumb things, you could write a whole book about me!"

I laughed, as did she. Just then, Edith ran gracefully up the long flight of steps toward us. "You're late," Justine said.

"I know," her younger sister replied. She settled herself on the green railing, and smiled expectantly down upon us.

"It Would Be So Sad Not to Have a Sister"

"What," I asked Edith, "is the best thing about your relationship with Justine?" She had to answer this time, for we were alone, sitting dreamily by the edge of a charming creek that trickled through one of the fields her parents still farmed together, despite their divorce three years previously. The rows of green arugula and ruby-edged mustard marched neatly up to the sandy bank and then broke into scrubby sworls intermingling with wild vegetation right down to the creek, and, in some cases, even into the water, where a few tiny plants were visible, clinging to moss-covered rocks.

Later, when I replayed the tape of our conversation, I heard the twitters of the birds that arched and dove above us; but at the time that I asked the question, all I could hear was the silence of Edith's reticence, her unwillingness to be revealed. I sat next to her very calmly, trying by my quietness to put her at ease. Eventually, she began an awkward, hesitating speech.

"My parents are still best friends," she said. "I mean, since they got divorced, my dad still spends the night a lot. I don't know why they got divorced; it just seemed to happen. I mean, nobody ever really said what was going on. He just wasn't around so much, but they were still best friends, and I guess I don't remember them telling us anything.

"I don't know," she continued, "I think maybe my mom had a boyfriend. She always has someone. So, when it happened, I mean, when my dad wasn't around so much, well, Justine would come into my room at night when she couldn't sleep, and it just helped to have her there."

Edith's words now began to flow more easily. "I mean, I hate when my mom asks me about my life. She's weird. And I just don't like anyone to know my business. I would hate it if my mother read my diary or anything, but I guess I can talk to my sister, I can ask her stuff.

"My mom is fifty years old, and she talks to *her* sister practically every day," Edith said, and then she turned toward me abruptly. "It would be so sad if your parents were mean to you, or something awful happened or whatever, and you didn't have a sister to talk to."

Edith stopped speaking as suddenly as she'd begun. We continued to sit, more companionably now. I reflected that even a self-described "vanilla" type like Edie had thoughts that felt too private—too dangerous—to share with her mother. She had "business" she didn't want anyone to know. To an adolescent, even a vanilla one, one's inner life is rich in risky, potent dreams that are in fact more "flavorful" than even the most open-minded mother could stomach.

The Road and the Woods

Shortly after graduation, Justine broke up with her boyfriend, the first serious sexual relationship of her life—and one conducted under her mother's approving eye. I asked Edith how she had felt about Alec, whether she'd been sorry to see her sister's romance end. At Edie's suggestion, we were in the woods that edged their huge fields, strolling comfortably side by side on a dirt path that barged with determination through the maze of firs and spindly oaks. It was cool there, despite the damp summer heat. When I asked Edie about Alec, she said two things, quite matter-of-factly, and then lapsed back into silence. The first comment she made was that she'd liked him a great deal. "He was really cool," she said. "I mean, he didn't wash and that was gross; my sister always made him take a shower when he came over. But he wasn't afraid of what anybody thought. Justine says she really loved him, it was the first time she ever felt like that."

She took several huge strides, so that without realizing it she'd walked ahead of me. Suddenly, she slowed and half-turned just at the waist, so that her legs continued to move forward even as she inclined herself awkwardly toward me. "But you know," Edie said, "he wasn't making Justine happy. So I'm glad they broke up."

"You want her to be happy, don't you?"

"Well, yeah, I do. Of course." She didn't even seem to comprehend the question; it was as if wanting one another to do well was the automatic assumption under which the Arkady sisters functioned. They weren't conscious of envy and didn't seem compelled to act on the unconscious feelings. Somehow, these young women didn't have any real comprehension of the fact that many sets of sisters and brothers existed in a competitive or envy-ridden environment, I thought, as we walked on in silent companionship.

Then Edie, in her abrupt way, began to tell me about a night when she and Justine had walked through these very same woods on the way to visit a friend. "Our mother was having a grown-up party, all her weird friends, and it was so boring. So we just decided, hey, let's go visit Amy, who's a friend we've both known since we moved here. And I don't know, we decided to walk even though it was like five miles to Amy's house."

She stopped and held her hand up so that I would stand still as well. "Hear that sound?" she said. "A fox heard me start to talk, that's a fox scrambling away, there are lots of them in here."

"Are they dangerous?"

"They're more scared of us than we are of them. It's safe in here, that's the best part about the woods," she said, smiling at me as if I were fifteen and she were thirty-five.

"I'm never scared in the woods," she said. "There aren't any people in here, just animals. Animals won't hurt you ever, they just want the same privacy that you do. I hate walking on the roads out here, though. I'm so much more scared of some weird guy in a truck stopping and making me go with him than I am of any animal."

She started to walk more quickly. I had the feeling she was speaking now from the very depths of her fifteen-year-old soul. Our footfalls made dull thuds on the ground, which set the wildlife in flight from us before our quiet conversation even reached them. "You think about what could happen, there's so many horrible things." She giggled uncomfortably.

"Justine always likes to walk on the road," she said. "That's what I wanted to tell you, that she was terrified on the way to Amy's house that night. She worries about things jumping out from nowhere. But I'm afraid of cars that will stop. I'm more scared of people. I think they're so much more dangerous than any little animal."

"That was pretty poetic," I said. "I thought you weren't the artistic one."

Edith shrugged, and smiled. "Justine is a really good actress," she said.

When we got back to the house, I made my good-byes and hurried to my car. I had just learned that one sister was happiest on the road and the other in the woods. They were exactly like the town mouse and country mouse, it seemed, so neatly opposite that neither ever had to worry about invading her sister's turf.

Sibling Deidentification

Researchers have long marveled at the manner in which family members divide up personality characteristics so that competition between any two children is eliminated, or at least reduced to manageable levels. Certainly, Justine and Edith shared this experience of "deidentification" with every other sibling duo I encountered during research for this book. While Justine was wild, artistic, and flamboyant, Edith was predictable, quiet, and "vanilla." Justine had taken all the untraditional behavioral traits, and Edith retained for herself the less flashy characteristics that remained. Edith was compulsively neat, scientific, and virginal; Justine messy, aggressively creative, and sexually active.

Deidentification is, in essence, a process of labeling and defining the self. The term was coined by child psychologist Frances Fuchs Schachter, Ph.D., to describe a phenomenon that occurs most dramatically between same-sex siblings, particularly when they are the first two children in the family. Schachter's hypothesis is that siblings "deidentify" in order to defuse the intensity of sibling rivalry. The relationship between the first two children in a family has the potential to be more competitive and full of conflict because the turf war is undiluted by the presence of others (for later-born siblings, according to Schachter, competitive feelings are mitigated and diluted by the constant presence of more than one older child). And siblings of the same sex are more likely to be competitive because they share a common core of sex-linked traits and desires. They are, by nature, more alike.

Deidentification is a socially acceptable manner in which to cope with early feelings of rivalry. This polarizing of characteristics allows each sibling to feel good about himself or herself. Thus, an unconventional sister can feel superior because of her unpredictable, interesting nature. The other, more responsible sister may not be aware that her sibling finds her boring or rigid; in fact, she, too, may feel superior because she is not wild or explosive. Deidentification, believes Schachter, fosters harmony within a family; it allows siblings a certain distance so that they can feel affection and love for one another. "By expressing themselves in different ways and in different spheres," she writes, "siblings are spared the necessity of constantly defending their turf against incursions from each other."

On the one hand, defining oneself as opposite to another is a useful, adaptive manner in which to coexist during a shared childhood. On the other hand, however, this deidentification can become self-defeating over the long haul. At some point in life, each of us needs to take stock of the polarized inventory of our self-definitions. Which of us truly wants to be labeled so completely by—or only by —a few specific characteristics? Will Edith Arkady always want to be vanilla? Unlikely. Will Justine ever wish to do anything conventional in her entire life? Of course she will. Self-defining labels imply that personality is fixed and immutable, and that the world is black and white with no mediating shades in between. As useful as it is to use such terms in describing a person, nobody is all one trait and lacking its opposite.

███████

Finding the Other in Ourselves

In adulthood the utility of an "I'm this, you're that" approach to
defining our siblings is that it allows us to discard those characteristics
we are uncomfortable with, be they bad or good. For example, I
have always defined my own two older sisters as strong, intelligent,
and ambitious, and myself as gentle, sweet, and passive (when I recently
mentioned this to a close friend, she was dumbfounded and
dissolved into laughter, showing me just how accurate my self-
labeling has been). This vision, with its flattering and its hampering
aspects, has been consonant with who I thought myself to be in
relation to my parents and sisters. Such an inner "image of me"
derives from the personality I was born with. My unique character
traits also developed because certain traits and behaviors were encouraged and discouraged within my family as I grew up; and—along
a certain spectrum—I have continued to change in reaction to those
attributes that my husband, friends, and co-workers appreciate or
dislike.

"Love is not love which alters when it alteration finds," Shakespeare wrote. In fact, part of love—part of a continuing relationship
with others—is respecting the freedom of those we love to grow and
change. We react to their evolving selves, and in the process we begin
to change as well. The perfect analogy here is of Ginger Rogers and
Fred Astaire, those ultimate dancing partners, for as we shape the
world around us, we are constantly molded by our experiences of
others as well. One step apart, two steps together, and turn. When it
works, it looks beautiful.

Not so oddly, writing this book has brought me face-to-face with
some inner demons. I have had to acknowledge other aspects of me,
the dark side of the moon, those parts of myself that I had denied
because they were—in my view—really parts of my sisters. These
"not me" characteristics were always present, and yet I was unable
to *see* them. I am not alone in this; there is some "not me" lying
dormant in all of us. This is far from claiming that we are exactly like
our siblings. Rather, with our brothers and sisters, we share portions
of what makes each of us an individual, and we share those table-
spoons and quarter-cups of personality across the board, for every

characteristic. One of my sisters may have a tablespoon (or a full cup) of a trait; my portion may be greater or smaller, but it exists—in some measure.

Growing up requires us to differentiate not only from our parents, but also from our siblings. Once we reach adulthood, however, it behooves us to look back and try to accept the more subtle mix which is a truer portrait of our individual natures. As grown-ups, despite our uniqueness, we tilt much more toward the average than we imagined in our dramatic, turbulent adolescent dreams. And we are more complex than a simple listing of character traits might imply. As Christine Downing, professor of religious studies at San Diego State University, wrote of her own self in the cult classic *Psyche's Sisters: ReImagining the Meaning of Sisterhood:* "I'm an achiever and a nonachiever, conventional and unconventional, courageous and cowardly, bright and sometimes painfully dumb." One of our life tasks, in fact, believes Downing, is the integration of those attributes initially given over to our siblings, along with those we already believe to be our own.

If we ignore this phase of potential psychological growth, we do so at the risk of shortchanging our adult relationships. For no person —sibling or spouse or child—can bear the burden of being another person's "not me." An alter ego is self-generated: If I believe that my sister is "the smart one," *I am the one doing that believing.* Thus, when personality traits remain polarized in adulthood, it is as if the "not me" sibling represents a part of the self which has split off and not been acknowledged. The "not me" that we see in our loved ones are those parts of ourselves we have not been able to integrate into our self-image. *The reason we can identify those traits so easily is that they come from within us, are part of us.*

In my own case, the wish that led me to become interested in this topic—the desire for a deeper connection with my siblings—has most definitely turned out to be a search for such unacknowledged aspects of my own self. The exploration began from a need to change myself or, as Downing describes it, to claim aspects of my own potential that I had long believed were the sole province of my big sisters. I am smarter, stronger, more ambitious, tougher than I had ever believed I could be. I am also less gentle, less sweet, and less passive than I had understood myself to be (my friend was right to laugh!). My view of what is me, and what is not me, was always mine alone, based on my sense of self and my interpretations of other people's reactions to my behavior—and, of course, my sense of who my sisters are was mine alone, too. Confronting this vision of reality has been exhilarating. Surprisingly, because challenging myself to be more like my sisters and less like what I imagined was me has sometimes been frightening, I find that I am more contented, surer of myself, and a more reliable and less overburdened wife and mother, friend and daughter. I have become a better sister as well. "The deidentification that was appropriate in childhood becomes anachronistic," says Downing. "We do not forever have to divide the world into her sphere and my sphere."

Are the Parents the Problem?

A family therapist once said to me, in a firm, brook-no-discussion voice, "When difficulties arise among adult siblings, you have got to look to the parents to find the problem. Sibling troubles are triangular in nature, and the battles are always about parental love. It comes down to competition." Frankly, many people would agree with the idea that in order to understand and, one hopes, improve upon the relationship between two siblings, you must first look at what role a third party, the parent, continues to play. Obviously, in many cases, this is true.

I do, however, quibble with two aspects of this therapist's definitive statement. In the first place, such a remark frequently ignores the fact that life is not simple. Reductionist thinking helps us to make sense of what happens to us, and provides convenient models for thinking about our problems. On the other hand, it rarely helps us to find long-term solutions for our difficulties. Rather than affixing blame, it seems to me that if one has a problem relationship with a sibling, it is more important to figure out precisely what options exist for coping.

Even as we think about the past, it is important to keep in mind that the relationships that exist for us—in the here and now—are what we have to work with. Of course, they are the result of interplay between given personality types, the particular structure of one's social relationships, and the unpredictability of life events. They are also, in some measure, the manifestation of our internal need to enjoy and suffer in certain very particular ways. Why is this?

All of our bonds with significant others have long been assumed by psychoanalysts to be based on our own individual mind-sets, on preconceptions formed very early in life as part of each person's basic need to see the world as a specific and particular place. Within each person, Freudian theory goes, different internal forces work together to allow us to get along as our particular, individual selves in the world. The id is the place where there are no rules, where feelings roil together, pleasure mixing with aggression, sexuality with anger, all in a peculiar brew unique to each person. This childlike inner circle is restrained from free expression by the superego, which is the prohibitory aspect of the self. The superego is the part of our internal structure that clamps down on freedom, *and it does so very early in our lives.*

As Manhattan psychoanalyst Dr. David Ertel points out, the superego is part of our infantile selves; it is the ego, the center of reasoning, that is the last part of the psychological "control center" to develop. The superego is a childlike internal police force that is harsher, in general, than a parent could possibly be. Thus, one real danger that arises when, as Justine and Edith Arkady's mother did, a parent encourages the development of instinctual aspects, or "id life," without sufficiently policing her children, is that the child's superego can *over*develop. When parents abdicate responsibility for policing their offspring, the kids themselves may become extremely harsh policers of their own behavior at a very early age. If children can be cruel to one another, and we all know that they can, imagine how much harder they can be on themselves.

In any case, what the mind seems to do is to *organize* the known world, to create conscious beliefs—subconsciously, of course—that one can accept as reality. This individual reality can include character traits, symptoms, fantasies, sense of identity, self-esteem, and other aspects of the self, too. Generally speaking, our minds allow us to pay attention only to information we are psychologically able to believe.

Here's a simple way of looking at this: Liberals read liberal newspapers; conservatives read conservative ones. People use the information they receive to solidify their own intellectual or emotional stances. We take positions in life that allow us to maintain the status quo, that free us to continue believing in what is already familiar to us. And these stances are based upon the preconceptions that the individual has developed to cope with his or her most basic urges and anxieties.

Not surprisingly, one of the primitive pains one prefers to avoid feeling is the fear of the loss of love. Whose? The love of mother and father, or even call it the love of the caretaker, in order to include those who look after dependent youngsters in every known culture and species. This fear is obviously self-protective, for survival depends on the development of a mutual attachment—caretaker to child, and vice versa. And the fact that the fear of abandonment is not, in general, realistic, since most caretakers desire to stay and not flee, does not prevent it. "Man, like other animals, responds with fear to certain situations, not because they carry a *high* risk of pain or danger, but because they signal an *increase* of risk," as the preeminent theorist John Bowlby has written. "Thus, just as animals of many species, including man, are disposed to respond with fear to sudden movement or a marked change in level of sound or light because to do so has survival value, so are many species, including man, disposed to respond to separation from a potentially caregiving figure and for the same reasons."

The threat of abandonment, Bowlby goes on to say, creates intense anxiety and anger. Thus, we can speculate that when Edith was born, not-yet-three-year-old Justine probably felt anxiety and anger, and was afraid that her sister's arrival meant the loss of her own position as beloved child of her parents. At the same time, of course, she probably also had many positive expectations of pleasure; she was about to have a new companion, her own family partner. It would be nice to be bigger than someone, to have an empathetic ear within the family, to have the edge over someone smaller. Momentous events are always ambivalent, in truth, for with every loss, something is gained, just as with every achievement, some other possibility must be renounced.

All of this ambivalent fear and expectation is likely to have occurred at the unconscious level—in a place so primal that Justine herself could not access the information. We will return, time and time again, to the fact that psychological issues are *always* stimulated by the birth of a sibling; the particular issues that are raised at the time of the birth have to do with the child's already formed view of the world.

A three-year-old child may not have mastered the vocabulary with which to describe it, but nevertheless she already has a view of what marriage or adult union is, what family means, what is important in the world, how to make people love her. These beliefs may alter over her life cycle, taking on a more sophisticated veneer, but they will always be recognizable as natural evolutions from the child's early understanding of her world.

Even though her parents probably did whatever they could to reassure her that this would never happen, we can easily surmise that when Edith was born, Justine became afraid she would lose her parents' love. This feeling would have been compounded by the way in which the expectation and arrival of a second child stirred up her mother's and father's own sibling concerns. When parents have their first child, they are primarily involved in repeating and improving upon their own childhood experiences. For a woman, identification with her own mother (now the grandmother) is very intense around this time, for a new mother has the opportunity to re-create and reexamine her own early life. However, when a mother-father-child triad prepares to greet a new sibling, family history is stimulated in an even more complex manner. In preparing their firstborn to greet the newcomer, both the mother's and the father's efforts will be colored by their own perceptions of what the issues will be for the older child. Thus, two separate original families end up mingling their own histories and expectations: A mother who is an oldest child may have much greater anxiety about, or empathy with, her firstborn's upcoming disenfranchisement. A father who is a youngest child, on the other hand, may experience a certain unconscious sense of victory about the dethronement. And the intertwining of these two sensibilities with the child's own psychological structure and emotional well-being (as well as those same aspects of the newborn) will help form the basis of the two siblings' particular relationship.

A firstborn typically experiences angry, aggressive urges toward the newborn interloper. The older child feels that he or she has to get rid of the younger child in order to feel safe again. Rapidly realizing that hostility toward the infant only makes her parents angry with her, the child may make the choice that even angry attention is better than distraction and go through a troublemaking phase. Conversely, she may join with the parent in caring for the child; reasoning that if you can't beat 'em, you might as well join 'em. . . . Whatever choice the young toddler makes, the fact remains that the early, primal fear of loss of love is stimulated by the birth of a sibling, and some remnant of that high stimulus informs aspects of one's behavior throughout life.

Thus, the aggressive feelings that Justine doubtless had for her infant sister may be expressed even now, at the age of eighteen, when she says, "I don't know if Edith loves me." What she may really mean—at an entirely unconscious level—is, "I don't know *how* Edith could love me if she actually knew what I felt about her, way deep down inside." Love and hate coexist in all of us, toward all the people we care about most in our lives. In fact, the more we identify with a loved one, the more difficult it is to acknowledge that ambivalence, for it is tantamount to accepting the unlikable parts of our own selves.

Now, even though it is tempting to look at Justine and Edith's relationship as mediated by competition for parental favor, that can never be the end of the story. The roots of the bond must be understood, but then it is time to move on. Just because Justine and Edith's relationship perhaps began with that primal hatred, its present manifestation—today's friendship—is the result of some fifteen years of mutual experience. There is a relationship that exists between them, in the here and now, that exists *only* between them and provides unique gratification and pain.

Acknowledging the past is important, but once that is done, the present must be contended with. One subject this book will continually return to is the fact that sibling relationships always begin in an anguish of loss and resentment. Children contend with that, early in their lives; nevertheless, the disenfranchised oldest child does not remain in a state of horrified shock forever. At the same time, the never-able-to-catch-up youngest eventually does do just that, and reaches the finish line of childhood to enter adulthood with assets and deficits all his or her own.

Thus, for the Arkady sisters (and all siblings, for that matter), the present is the key to the connection. The present involves the parents, without question, but it also involves another ongoing, supportive, loving, destructive, active, passive, ambivalent, and important rela-tionship: theirs.

For the Arkady sisters, adolescence has been a time of great emo-tional closeness, of helping each other cope with the typical experi-ences of this period. They have enjoyed a very *real* connection, with room for ambivalence and affection, for angry fights and loving sup-port. Now that Justine is about to leave for college, things are likely to change. The tie between Justine and Edith has provided them with a great deal of the juice they've needed to reach adulthood, but it is about to be subjected to the strains and pummeling of grown-up life. Physical distance will have an effect, as will the inevitable emotional distance that develops along with the formation of new families. These sisters are quite likely to become less close for a period of time, which may even be as long as several decades. Whatever choices they make in future years about the sibling bond—and however they learn to think about that tie when they leave home, establish careers, find romantic partners, have children of their own—this sister relation-ship exists by itself as well as within the context of their past and future families, careers, and friends. While their sisterhood won't endure in a vacuum, it will remain an entity unto itself.

Over and over again, when I was writing this book, people de-scribed their siblings to me in sentimental terms, as a port in a storm or a safe harbor. Frequently, the feeling that one sibling would be there for another one, no matter what, was an untested fantasy that provided each with a dubious sense of security. My suspicion was that many of these people were unsure if their siblings would fulfill even the poet Robert Frost's frankly utilitarian position, "Home is the place where, when you go there, they have to take you in."

When it came down to it, few adult siblings seemed eager to discover whether their brothers and sisters would actually raise the sails on the boat to help them out. Or, in terms of another fond phrase I frequently heard, one's brothers and sisters help create the illusion of a safety net; I suspect, however, that many adults spin remarkable rationalizations rather than risking the leap to discover the reality.

It was not until I met with Justine and Edith that I truly began to

understand some of the practical importance of siblingdom. When
Edith Arkady said that it would be terrible if something bad happened and she didn't have a sister to talk about it with, she wasn't
just speculating. For, of course, an awful event *had* occurred in the
Arkady family, as little as anyone seemed willing to acknowledge
it in those terms: Despite the parents' ongoing friendship and the
apparently harmonious current in the family, a marriage had died.
That little house I visited on the outskirts of town was a place where
three women lived; but in functional terms, the Arkady sisters have
been each other's home more than any physical location could be.
Their bond has not been unambivalent, by any means, but it has been
of critical importance.

For these two young women, the best assistance they have had in
growing and separating from the confusion of their early family life
has been their willingness to do for each other—to provide each
other with shoes to run in at a moment's notice. The Arkady sisters
have helped each other transform difficulty into possibility. Their
relationship has been such that indulging in the sentimental does not
feel maudlin but appropriate; and so the words that best describe
Justine and Edith, as they perch on the brink of adulthood, are the
poet Christina Rossetti's: "For there is no friend like a sister, in calm
or stormy weather."

CHAPTER THREE

―――

Jack Morrison

A Brother Who Lives Alone

―――

Jack Morrison and his sister Amanda live no more than twelve miles from each other; yet the towns, the homes, even the bodies that they inhabit could not be less alike. Jack is all excess, a dark, wild-haired, thirty-year-old bruiser who appears even taller than he is because of the muscles that swell his arms, the solid flesh of his drinking man's belly, his robust thighs. The word his delicately boned older sister Amanda once used to describe him was "lusty"—as if he were a latter-day Henry the Eighth. In fact, at our first meeting, it took little effort to imagine him in a king's bejeweled doublet, sprawled at the Tudor table, cheerfully devouring a haunch of game and guzzling tumblerfuls of wine.

We were seated in the dining area of Jack's new house in a working-class village located just outside a well-known resort area along the Massachusetts coast. The few "luxury" properties in this rugged little community are buried far from one another down bumpy dirt trails, giving wealthy owners the chance to fancy themselves, briefly —until the wail of a neighbor's car alarm destroys the illusion—as homesteaders isolated in an unexplored forest. Jack's modern bungalow, surrounded by sturdy maple and pine trees, was a perfect example of such a private mecca, with a long, wooded run and access to a lake rich with snapping turtles and flying fish to entertain Pilate, his friendly Malamute puppy. The house itself was carefully built into the slope of the hill leading down to the lake, with an oak-paneled master suite on the top floor, a kitchen and L-shaped living room on the middle floor, and two small, plain bedrooms stashed at the base. It was, Jack told me proudly—at our first meeting, shortly after he moved in—the ideal house for a man who lives alone.

For a man who lives alone, I joked, there were an awful lot of people around. We were sandwiched amid packing boxes, perched on flimsy black folding chairs at an ancient oak table. I had to keep turning up the volume on my tiny tape recorder to catch Jack's words in the bustle. Painters toiled in the hallway. Outside, two young men laughed with one another as they set slabs of bluestone to form a pathway to the door. Not twenty feet from us in the living area, a friend of Jack's lay on the couch, asleep. Greg had passed out there the previous night, Jack told me, after an evening of bar-hopping. Pilate wandered back and forth, sniffing at Greg's stillness, nuzzling his master affectionately, ignoring the workmen. Clearly, at least from a dog's perspective, such chaos was usual.

For a moment, Jack seemed annoyed—was I suggesting that circumstances were not ideal for this interview? He was doing me a favor by meeting with me at all, and he let me know it with one glancing patrician stare. Then he smiled, and shrugged. "I'm a relaxed person," he said, as if he were reminding both of us. "I let things happen."

He leaned back, raising the front two legs of his chair. I could hear the creak of his weight on the thin back supports. He lit a cigarette and, without warning, dove headlong into our topic for the day. "Now, Amanda, my sister, she's a different story," he said. He expelled a stream of smoke. "We're absolutely the opposite personalities. She's extremely uptight. Anal-retentive. And those two personalities just do not get along.

"Trying to get Amanda's approval is a joke," he asserted in a quick, flat tone, as if he were a criminal confessing to some heinous crime, eager to get the words out and over with, but slightly proud of himself all the same. "She's a complete bitch. She's so incredibly insecure, you see, that's why she romps all over my life."

The dog lay at Jack's feet, staring up at us with a bemused expression. On the couch Greg was breathing deeply in sleep, and the workmen were, for the moment, not speaking with one another. We had stumbled into an odd and unexpected coincidence of near-total silence. I could barely make out the whisper of paintbrushes stroking in the hallway behind me. Jack's vehement remarks had upset my rhythm: I was originally referred to Amanda and Jack Morrison by a mutual acquaintance who had described a very different relationship from the one Jack was now outlining. I had been told that, despite Amanda's eight years of seniority, she and her little brother had been extremely close ever since their mother's death from leukemia in the late 1960s. Amanda was seventeen at the time, and Jack only nine. Their father, scion of an aristocratic Boston family, had embarked on a constant round of parties immediately following his wife's death, leaving the two children to cope with their grief as best they could. These "poor little rich kids" had been each other's only haven in a frightening and unloving world. It had been, I was told, largely due to Amanda's firm intervention that Jack had freed himself from a cocaine habit of several years' duration and been able to graduate from college. The bond between these two siblings was valued and unbreakable: That was why wild Jack had chosen to purchase his first home in this windblown little village just minutes from the exclusive community where his sister maintained a manicured, substantial oceanfront property. Or so my informant had reported.

Now I was hearing something entirely unexpected from this artless man. I said, "It doesn't sound as if you like her very much."

It was Jack's turn to look surprised; from his perspective, apparently, such angry feelings were no indication of any lack of affection. "No, I do. I do. It's just that I don't expect as much from myself as she does," he said slowly. "She's just brutal. She has this dream that other people will be perfect but she's so screwed up herself, she has no right to tell other people what to do."

"She wants to be the one in charge?" I asked.

Jack gave a sarcastic bark, or was it laughter? "That's an understatement," he said, and picked up another cigarette. "Can I smoke?"

When I nodded, yes, he leaned back in his chair again, closing his eyes for a moment. "It's some kind of mother syndrome," he muttered. "She's got me stuck someplace. She won't let me grow up."

"How does she do that? What does she do?"

"Oh, commentary on when I come home at night, what I do, my motorcycle, my dog, how much I had to drink, whatever," Jack said tiredly. "Just constant bickering."

Jack explained that, for the six months prior to purchasing his new house, he and the dog had lived with Amanda, sharing her rigidly run home. For him, the experience had been unbearable: Amanda's Spartan cleanliness, her insistence on routine, her obsession with the healthiest of healthy living, all seemed to be traits and characteristics she'd acquired in order to torture him. He'd felt her critical eye judging every aspect of his life, from the behavior of his pet to his preferences in junk food. "I used to stay at a friend's house," he said, pointing to Greg still quietly asleep on the couch. "I just didn't want to come home, I couldn't stand it. I moved out of there the first hour I owned this house. Oh, my God, living with Amanda was the most strenuous experience I've ever had in my life."

If his words had failed to do so, the immoderate speed and excitement in Jack's voice would have alerted me immediately to the depth of emotion he felt for his sister Amanda. "Have you always had a difficult relationship?" I asked. "Tell me, what is your first memory of her?"

"Well, I don't know," he said abruptly, and then trailed off for a moment. When he began to speak again, his voice was gentler and his whole huge frame seemed suddenly to have relaxed. "I do remember her room when we were little. I used to sit in there in the mornings and watch her get dressed for school. We would talk—" His voice faded, and when he began to speak once more, I could almost *feel* the engines of his anxiety revving up again, could practically hear the doors slamming on the happy memory. "I remember the walls," he said, speeding up, his voice growing angrier. "Yeah, they were some god-awful pink. That's what I remember.

"Look, when our mother died, Amanda was in boarding school," Jack said, jumping forward several years without a pause, as if I would immediately understand the link between the two memories. He crushed the half-smoked cigarette into a chipped green ashtray, pressing hard with his thumb as if he were impervious to heat or fire. "I mean, Amanda just went on with her life. She wasn't around when I was ten years old and things were pretty rough. She has no damn right to tell me what to do now. She lost that right a long time ago."

The dog shifted forward with an uneasy roll of his haunches, to rest his square chin across his master's left foot. "She keeps trying to make it up with overkill," Jack said. "It drives me bloody crazy."

"How often do you see her?"

"Oh, once a week at least," Jack answered immediately, ruddy patches of anger mottling his cheeks and forehead. "She's always coming over here to tell me what to do, how to fix my house up or what I'm doing wrong. I don't call her, though, I never call. *She* calls me. I wish she'd leave me alone, get out of my life."

A huge flatbed truck filled with lumber began to beep-beep-beep as it backed down the driveway. "That's for the dock," Jack said. His expression relaxed into a child's enthusiastic smile almost as quickly as it had just erupted into ire. "We got approval to put in a dock, even though I wasn't zoned for it. Some guy fixed it with the village."

"How did you arrange that?"

"I don't know. Amanda found him, she loves getting people to do stuff, she can organize anything. I hate bureaucracy," he said, completely unaware of the way he continually betrayed his own blanket statements, of how his dependence and his resentment were so completely intertwined that he could contradict himself without any apparent discomfort.

"It's funny," I said, trying to choose my words carefully. "You talk about Amanda as if you'd like not to be around her. You say she's too involved with your life, and then you get her help with your dock." Jack stared blankly at me as I spoke, as if he were Superman and my words were made of Kryptonite, too dangerous to penetrate his skull. I was a little frightened that if I pushed the subject he might explode with anger or melt into tears. His emotions seemed so immediate, so close to the surface and uncontrolled that I had no idea what he might do next. All throughout my interviews with Jack Morrison, I remained conscious of this barely controlled anger. He never appeared to become used to the process of question and answer; it was as if he experienced each new question as yet another invasion of his barely hidden soul. While he wanted to be known (he had agreed to be interviewed, after all), he simply couldn't cross the barrier of revelation without feeling enormously compromised. I stumbled on. "Why did you move here, to this town so close to where she lives?"

"I like the ocean," Jack said, his voice firm, even defiant. He had, perhaps, understood what I was saying but he was not going to deal with it. I got the point. If Jack Morrison wanted to see himself as a man who lived alone, apart from everyone, that was his absolute right. In many ways, Jack seemed indeed to be as alone in the world as he claimed, with no one to care about him except his overinvolved older sister.

"Do you have a girlfriend?" I asked.

Raising the issue of women seemed to agitate him a great deal. He reddened, and emitted a surprised series of three snorts. "Sure I do," he said angrily, clipping each word. "Celeste."

I was silent, waiting for him to continue.

"For three years now," he said.

"Does she live near here?"

"That bitch? No way." He was sputtering slightly as he spewed forth his story. "Last night, on the phone, she was bitching at me about how I never see her, but, you know, she's always busy. Whenever I say I'm coming into Boston to see her, she makes an excuse. Like she's always too busy for me, but then the bitch turns around and complains I don't do enough for her."

I stared at him as he raged on; he hadn't met my gaze from the beginning of this monologue.

"You know what she wants?" he asked, looking down at his huge hands as they kneaded his strong, rounded thighs. "I know what she wants."

"What?"

He sputtered again, and I realized he reminded me of a caricature of a Victorian gentleman, unflappable in a real crisis yet moved to outrage by some outcast's ignorance of an obscure ritual surrounding the pouring of tea. It was odd to reconcile his inherent dignity and his well-bred speaking voice with the inappropriate quality of his words. "She just wants to come to spend the summer here. She's just using me, that's all. She just wants to go on vacation."

"Really?"

"Oh, yes. I know her, I know her very well." His eyes, now that he was looking up, were sparkling with tears of frustration.

"How often does she come out here?"

"Oh, never, I guess. She likes the city more, she won't come out here."

"Never?"

"Yeah, well, she's always busy when I want to come in. And she won't come out here, she says it's because she hates Amanda and Amanda hates her."

"Is that right?"

"Yeah, well, I think it infuriates Amanda that Celeste is her age and she has a much better body. I think it drives Amanda crazy." He snorted, leaning back proudly to balance on the back legs of his chair again.

"Is that what Amanda says?"

"Well, no. She thinks Celeste is using me, that she just takes my money."

I was beginning to feel extremely sorry for him. "Do you agree with Amanda?"

"Well, yeah. I mean, I pay for her apartment and then she won't even let me come in and see her. Then she gets mad at me and plays all kinds of games as if *I'm* the one that won't visit her, but that's bullshit."

"Why don't you break it off? Why do you continue to see her?"

"What?" Once again, he seemed stunned, even disoriented, by my interpretation of his comments. "What do you mean? She's my girlfriend. We have a great time when we get together. She likes to stay out and party, she can drink like a man.

"She's my girlfriend," he repeated. He looked down at those formidable hands again. "I love the bitch."

Here was a thirty-year-old man with a history of drug problems, enmeshed in a love affair notable mainly for its absence of compassion and affection. Furthermore, his work record was nonexistent. Although trust income meant that he had had little need to find gainful employment, I felt far from envious of the "carefree" way Jack was able to live. Was Amanda's involvement saving him from utter despair, I wondered, or was she standing in the way of his self-fulfillment?

"There Was Another Child, You Know"

The fact that Amanda appeared to have taken responsibility for keeping Jack's life on track—and that he was, despite his verbal protestations, not visibly fighting it but instead living as physically and emotionally adjacent to his sister as he could bear—was something that deserved a second look. To begin understanding the course of Jack's life, a closer look at the entire Morrison family seemed imperative. What role had infant Jack been assigned within his family circle? By being who he was and where he was, arriving at a particular time in the life of his family, what effect had the baby had on those around him as he grew?

Although she'd never really thought about these issues, thirty-eight-year-old Amanda was eager, even enthusiastic, to discuss her relationship with her brother. She felt sure that there was something to be learned about the bond she had with Jack, something significant that could help explain some of her own problems and difficulties. Amanda was herself in an optimistic phase, teetering on the verge of a major life change: She was trying to decide whether to marry a divorced artist whom she'd met two years before, when their paintings had hung side by side at a large group show. It had been the first public exhibition of Amanda's mixed-media collages; she'd been flattered at Tony's positive response to her work. In terms of passion, though, Amanda felt their affair had never really gotten off the ground. She was, however, well aware that her taste in men had guided her poorly in the past; moreover, she genuinely liked Tony's companionship. In fact, during the same nippy September week that we began our interviews, Amanda and Tony had agreed that he would move his belongings into her rambling oceanfront mansion. Encouraged by Tony—and Jack—to consider an even more "official" relationship, Amanda found herself surprisingly willing to think about marriage.

As Amanda discussed "the Tony situation," she appeared calm and warm, even happy, an odd contrast to the doubting feelings she'd claimed to be experiencing. She was visibly relaxed, or so it seemed, as she sat on a worn, black club chair in my office, long legs crossed in perfect yoga fashion. As a matter of fact, it was not until she began to describe Jack's enthusiastic support of the potential marriage that she untwined one leg to rest her left foot on the floor, leaning toward the tape recorder on the coffee table between us. Watching her maintain that oddly unbalanced posture, I, too, felt my tension level rising.

"I guess that Jack would love it if I married Tony," she said, speaking in the same disaffected staccato I'd heard her brother use. "He thinks I'd get off his case." She laughed sharply, turning her head at the same time to glare at me sidelong, a look that compelled me to nod in agreement, without considering my own point of view. For a moment, just the length of the hawkish stare, I understood the uncomfortable pressure Jack endured. I most assuredly did not like the sensation of having Amanda Morrison on *my* case.

I looked down at the sheet of questions before me. "What is your first memory of Jack?" I asked.

"Well, you know," she said and paused, as if I were about to be told a very shocking secret. I waited.

"Well," she said again, "there was another child, named for my father, Carl. A little boy. He died of crib death; he lived, oh, for two weeks."

"When was he born?"

"I was two, almost three." Amanda looked down at the slim suede shoe that she'd managed to work off her right heel as she spoke. Her elegant frame was now involved in a variety of awkward balancing acts—arm propped to maintain her forward stance, left leg slicing down to the floor, right leg jutting across her other knee, foot cantilevered north. We both watched her pale green flat dangle from one stockinged toe.

The First Renunciation of Paradise

"There was never a child who did not need an adult," wrote the psychiatrist Gregory Rochlin, "nor was there a child who did not fear losing an adult he had. It is axiomatic that this contention is the human condition."

For decades, most psychological thinkers believed that, at birth, a child has no concept of separateness: The infant believes herself to be as one with the universe, her entire cosmology composed of self and the mother's breast. This is a phase of total fusion with the mother, and with that symbiosis comes what many psychoanalytic theorists have described as the rapturous bliss of perfect satiation: The infant's needs are simple and basic, and her caretaker is able—and biologically predisposed—to gratify them.

In recent years, however, the work of the psychiatrist Daniel N. Stern and other developmental psychologists has pointed the way toward an interesting alternative hypothesis: that, in fact, the infant is born with a nascent sense of itself as an individual, and that the primary task of early life is to learn not how to be separate and autonomous, but how to interact with and relate to other people.

The question of whether the infant enters the world in fear of losing the perfect oneness it has enjoyed up until then with its mother, or whether that infant begins life prewired to interact as a separate individual eager to have relationships has been studied from many different points of view. The first psychoanalysts relied on the reconstructed memories of their adult patients to formulate theories of earliest experience. Later groundbreakers, such as Anna Freud, Melanie Klein, and Margaret Mahler, concentrated on observations of children and analytic sessions with them, in an effort to understand what the children themselves were undergoing as they saw it in real time. Now, however, developmental psychologists have constructed experimental means of measuring what appear to be the actual responses of even the youngest infants to a variety of situations, including maternal overstimulation and deprivation. As a result, many psychologists now believe in the theory that infants are born with a certain ability to mold the way in which others interact with them.

This ability may better be understood as an ability to respond lovingly to loving behavior, to turn away when overstimulated, to elicit love by reacting. Nevertheless, no matter how much control the average infant has of the way in which its caretakers respond to him or her, the infant remains, as Dr. Rochlin implies, entirely dependent on others for survival. The infant—unsootheable with a stomach upset, or forced to wait some minutes for the breast to be provided —must realize early that the all-powerful provider is not omnipotent and perfect. Is this the first snake in the Garden of Eden?

As a result of this early realization, the child comes to accept that she—and her mother—are separate, imperfect, though loving, beings. According to psychotherapist Hannah Fox, a family and marital therapist in Manhattan, who is now the director of the Metropolitan Center for Object Relations Theory and Practice, "If the infant can negotiate through this phase properly, other losses later in life, although painful, will be manageable."

Thus, very early in life, a child learns to endure the uncomfortable coexistence of love and hatred, both in herself and in others. This integration of affection and rage sets the stage for the adult ability to tolerate mixed feelings about a loved one: As psychiatrist Otto Kernberg has written, "It implies the capacity for ambivalence."

Accepting this ambivalence—and the fact that gratification is not always possible, no matter how passionate and enduring the love of a mother and father, of siblings, of grandparents and baby-sitters— does not, for most children, mean growing used to chaos. A certain bearable, comfortable, predictable fluctuation of frustration and pleasure becomes the norm for the toddler as she begins enjoying her increasing mastery of the world, her growing ability to speak and walk and play. A new, less idyllic ideal has been accepted, and the structure of the child's life becomes constant and predictable again. Until, that is, the impending birth of a new family member sends even the most well-adjusted child's equilibrium straight off course.

With this shocking jolt, nothing the child has understood to be true in the world holds up to investigation. For if the very structure of the family nest can alter, so can every other aspect of life. The world, that comfortable and fairly predictable place, is simply no longer safe.

Despite the initial tremors it causes, the birth of a sibling, in the long run, can become a positive event for the shaky, newly disenfranchised dictator. Generally, the arrival of a new child into the family propels an older sibling to begin investigating, thinking, and questioning in a manner that only helps him or her to become more sophisticated and knowledgeable. As Freud wrote, "The threat to the bases of a child's existence offered by the discovery or the suspicion of the arrival of a new baby and the fear that he may, as a result of it, cease to be cared for and loved, make him thoughtful and clearsighted." Freud believed that part of the instinct for research—the impulse to understand—develops in response to the incipience of this early interloper.

However, whatever the benefits, the arrival of a new sister or brother *feels*, in a word, awful. A child realizes swiftly, as the British psychotherapist Joseph H. Berke has observed, that the sibling's birth "announces a state of permanent deprivation coupled with an acute blow to self-esteem. The dethroned sib is no longer first and foremost in his mother's life." Natalie, a two-and-a-half-year-old, cheerfully pats and plays with her new brother Reuben during the day. But starting about a week after Reuben's arrival, the little girl has begun to wake each night crying, screaming desperately for "Mommy's boobies." These sacred suppliers of nurturing, which used to be hers alone, are no longer even available; they are the sole possessions of Reuben, the invader.

Not surprisingly, most "dethroned monarchs" react with a combination of guilt and fury: *I should love the new baby, everyone expects me to. I hate the new baby, I can't help it. Why won't they take it back?* An immediate negative reaction to the birth is the norm, not the exception. Studies have found that older siblings often develop sleeping difficulties, either trouble falling asleep or waking unexpectedly during the night. They have more frequent temper tantrums. They often "forget" learned social behaviors such as bowel and urine control, or how to eat with a spoon and fork. Children can become more aggressive or more withdrawn. Although the reaction itself can vary widely and unpredictably, it is clear that the changes are related to changes in the relationship between the mother and the older child. Such calls upon the patience, attention, and love of the child's parents are expressions of the complete tizzy created by the newborn's arrival —and the unmitigated, incomprehensible willingness of Mommy and Daddy to meet the baby's needs.

According to prominent sibling researcher Judy Dunn at London's Institute for Psychiatry, the firstborn takes a terrible body blow when the next child is born. "It's clear that firstborns go through a change in their lives that no other kids in the family endure," Dunn comments. "The first transformation from a one-child family to a two-child family is a big deal for everyone."

The eldest child, in general, is demonstrably more upset when the second child is born than the second child is at the birth of the third one. Such distress—or lack of it—quite obviously colors the type of relationship that develops between the siblings. It is, however, the *relationship itself* that is likely to suffer, far more than any individual: Over the long haul, firstborn children are no less well adjusted than their younger brothers and sisters. They don't tend to suffer from psychological problems more than other kids in the family. Says

Dunn, "That folk belief has not stood up to the rigorous tests of science."

No matter how careful and concerned a parent is, nonetheless, jealousy of the attention and affection given to the newborn can reach truly epic proportions in the immediate aftermath of the birth. During the 1920s, the psychoanalyst Alfred Adler described the admittedly over-the-top case of an eight-year-old girl who, over a period of time, drowned three little girls from the village where she lived. This older sister, Adler believed, was attempting through murderous acts to get her revenge for the parental neglect she felt she'd endured in the two years since her adorable younger sister was born.

While this case obviously takes matters to the extreme, the little girl's feelings of homicidal rage are not actually so unusual. Moreover, fantasies of killing the sibling—or of a fluke of nature accidentally relieving the older sibling of the burden of the newborn, shall we say?—are a natural, and normal, expression of resentment over the shocking and unexpected rearrangement of the child's universe.

Magical Thinking

Amanda Morrison no doubt experienced the devastating sense of "dethronement" siblings go through when a second child is born. Thus, if the envious rage of a young child can feel murderous, what must poor three-year-old Amanda have thought when her rivalrous fantasies became reality and her brother Carl quietly died in his crib during the night? Rather than having the opportunity to get to know the newborn and work through her powerful feelings, she likely believed on some level that she had actually succeeded in fulfilling her secret, hateful wish! To a little child, it must have seemed as if she'd magically killed her baby brother.

Amanda's sense of "magical power" derives from the manner in which very young children process information. Our wishes, we believe, can make it so. Family therapist Claudia Jewett reminds us of the childhood rhyme "Step on a crack, break your mother's back." How many countless sidewalks have each of us carefully negotiated, sure that we were capable of doing great harm with a misstep? Later in life, in fact, this childlike belief that our wishes can control events is the source of those "If I'd only" thoughts that haunt us when a job is lost, or a romance breaks up, or a tragic accident occurs. "Magical thinking is never completely eradicated in any of us, and it tends to recur in times of crisis, even in adulthood," according to Jewett.

Furthermore, certain losses, including stillbirths, miscarriages, and abortions, often remain unresolved and undiscussed, because these events are imbued with a peculiar kind of pain. Societal expectation seems to be that because "one never knew" the infant, the grief cycle will run its course fairly rapidly: Where there has been no actual hello, bidding farewell should not take too long. This means that predictably painful feelings of failure, inadequacy, even embarrassment are all too often quickly glossed over. Thus, the entire family system can feel compelled to cover up its grief and confusion over a stillbirth or miscarriage.

Compounding this urge to ignore the pain is the unique sense of loss involved when a child dies before a mutual relationship is established. None of the family members' expectations and fantasies for the child are ever chastened by the unruly reality of an actual child with its own personality, behavior, and appearance. Fantasies about the child may continue unabated, unless efforts are made to talk about and face the grief involved in the loss. How had Amanda faced this challenge?

"I Considered Him My Child"

Amanda spoke quickly now, as if having told me the bad news, she was eager to get to the good. "I had been praying for another brother, and she kept having miscarriages, you know?" I nodded. "It seemed as if she was always pregnant, always sick and then no baby. I remember that I felt just desperate for another child.

"And then, finally, she became pregnant with Jack, and everyone kept wondering if it was a boy or a girl, but *I knew*. I thought they were all crazy, because I knew it was a boy to replace little Carl." She tapped the heel of her hand on my knee. In her enthusiasm, she seemed to think it was her own. "I was sure it was my wanting it that had produced him, not anything my parents did. And when Jack was born," she finished triumphantly, "I considered him my child!"

"So you never really resented him then?"

"Oh, no. Oh, never. I would have laid my life down for him, anything. He was The One, as far as I was concerned." Amanda smiled happily at the memory, as if her redemption had been complete.

And given the emotional journey that little Amanda traveled—from baby Carl's death through years of watching her mother's seemingly futile efforts to reproduce, and then finally after five long years to be absolved from any guilty feelings she may have consciously or unconsciously harbored—it is far from surprising that Amanda developed such an enormous sense of responsibility toward her baby brother. Why, were she to relax her vigilance for just one instant, he might disappear, just like Carl did. And Jack, for his part, has provided his big sister with lots of reassuring anxieties to fuss about over the years, eagerly risking his life at bungee jumping, motorcycle racing, and drug involvements—anything, in fact, to keep her interested. If family life is a dance, this one has become a real rhumba.

Of course, we cannot look at Jack and Amanda's relationship with each other as if the lockstep of their attachment developed in a vacuum: We must consider the traumatic effect of the loss of their mother so early in their lives. Nor can we ignore the way Carl Morrison Senior so completely abnegated his parental responsibilities. A sibling relationship evolves along with all the other interpersonal ties a person develops; thus, the form of the bond not only has to do with the two personalities involved, but also with the substance, commitment, and quality of myriad other influences and connections. From a strictly "number crunching" point of view, many sibling experts would claim that the eight years that separate Jack and Amanda make them an unlikely pair to be so mutually involved. In general, siblings who are born more than three or four years apart are thought to play less influential roles in one another's development, *unless* a crisis (first the infant's death, and then the mother's) or parental insufficiency (the father's inappropriate behavior during the mourning year and thereafter) brings them together in the search for nurturing that is largely unavailable elsewhere.

"The more available parents are both emotionally and physically, the less intense is the attachment between siblings," write the foremost sibling researchers Stephen Bank and Michael Kahn in *The*

Sibling Bond. Conversely, to the extent that parents are absent or unavailable in childhood, siblings tend to lean on one another that much more. According to Bank and Kahn, parental overinvolvement can actually diminish loyalty among siblings; while parental under-involvement tends to increase sibling attachment, loyalty, and support.

Let me note here that some well-respected sibling researchers are beginning to report experimental results that appear to contradict Bank and Kahn's blanket claim. At least one recent report has found that in childhood happier relationships with parents were associated with more supportive sibling ties. One possible reason for these contradictory claims is that this newer research, unlike that of Bank and Kahn, is based upon studies of "normal" children, that is, those who are not in therapy. What seems most clear is that the temperament of the individual child—and his or her "fit" with the personalities of the other children in the family—plays a critical role in determining who helps whom, and when, and why.

Still, brothers and sisters can function like the emergency backup system of an airplane or train: Throughout their lives, when relationships with parents, spouses, children, or friends fail to give them what they want and need, the sibling button is there to be pushed. The backup system is activated and, although often in ways that are far from perfect, siblings can step in to provide the necessary assistance: financial, emotional, and physical. In the Morrisons' case, while Amanda appears to be doing all such work, Jack also plays an important role, for he provides his big sister with a primary occupation. In fact, he also can be seen as having made an enormous sacrifice of his own potential in order to provide his sister with a sense of meaning and self-worth. For, in truth, the strong ties that can develop between such bereft siblings may not be completely positive and helpful; they can become so overwhelming, so involving and stifling that they preclude the development of other intimate relationships.

Life Without Mother

It can hardly be claimed that there is ever a good time in which to lose a mother or father; even in adulthood the death of a parent can be devastating. In fact, adjusting to death is believed to be more difficult for family members than any other life transition. For young children, who need their parents for physical and emotional protection, such a loss is frighteningly enormous and extremely likely to have a negative, even paralyzing impact on their normal development. A teenager, who should be busy establishing his or her own independence from the family, can be shocked back into the nest in reaction to such an "abandonment" by a parent. The quality of parenting rarely makes a difference: No matter what kind of a mother Ellen Morrison was, losing her was emotionally overwhelming for Amanda and Jack. When she died of leukemia at the age of forty-two, her son was nine years old and her daughter was seventeen; for both children, Ellen's death was a watershed moment that defined much of the quality of their lives. Neither Amanda nor Jack has yet been able to regroup from the emotional shock wave resounding through the family since their mother's death.

In particular, it is Jack who still appears to be frozen in place, a devastated little nine-year-old boy. Early in our interviews, I asked him how old his mother would have been if she had lived. He became quite agitated, even a little angry, and then replied, "Oh, I don't know. I don't remember. I was so young when she died. *She'd be forty-two, I guess.*" That his mother would have aged in twenty-two years did not occur to him apparently, nor did he seem to notice the thirty-year disparity in age between his imagined mother and his now seventy-two-year-old father.

Psychologists often note this "freezing" of positions as a sign of unresolved mourning. It is as if the developmental clock simply stopped short for Jack when his mother died. In many ways, he remains a child trapped in a man's body, still looking for that trustworthy someone to care and nurture him properly, so that he can be freed to grow up.

At the time when forty-two-year-old Ellen Morrison exited the family stage, the whole synchrony of her little troupe was jeopardized: Ellen and Amanda had already embarked angrily on the major job of adolescence, weaning one another from the dependencies of childhood. After her mother's death, the teenager Amanda, suddenly thwarted in her ability to rebel and develop a focus outside the home, became mired in the emotional remains of her original family. Unable to extricate herself, she eventually found herself acting as a quasi-parent for Jack—much resented on the surface perhaps, but, in another sense, desperately appreciated, too.

Furthermore, as the parent in charge of day-to-day household activity, Ellen had been Jack's most influential guide to learning about the world; she provided him with immediate emotional and physical protection as well. The loss of that critical sense of security is perhaps at the root of much of Jack's later difficulties. For nine-year-old Jack, left to rattle around a six-bedroom townhouse so large he described it as "an aircraft carrier," the loss of his mother was compounded by the near-total emotional—and physical—absence of his grieving father. According to his son, Carl Morrison was rarely home for even an hour a day during the year following Ellen's death. "His friends rallied around him, he was out to dinner every night. I was brought up by the maid," Jack said almost proudly, as if his ability to survive such loneliness was the triumph of his childhood.

"Do you still know her?" I asked. I was curious, true, but beyond that, I was eager to hear that someone, anyone, had been around to give this child some affection and love.

"A series of maids," Jack amended. "Many of them."

Jack's abandonment following the death of his mother was, in a word, complete. His father was busy drowning his own sorrows in a round of social gaiety, scarcely dropping in each evening to say hello. His sister was away at boarding school, awash in her own feelings of grief and loss, but able to funnel much of her anxiety into preparing for college. Even the maids who cared for him didn't last long enough in the household to become real figures of caring.

<hr>

"You're the Only Person I Love, and You're Not Here"

When Amanda thinks back on the period after Ellen's death, her primary sense is that she failed her brother. "It's horrible, really. I have terrible guilt," she said one sunny fall morning as we talked in her intimidatingly neat private study. Amanda's angular shoulders and neatly featured face were beautifully framed by the dark ocean waves that crashed silently on the beach, visible through the large picture window behind her. We were seated on comfortable rose chintz chairs; we sipped at mugs of tea in an effort to fend off the first real chill of autumn.

Amanda spoke precisely, as if she were attempting to find the perfect words to describe what happened to Jack when their mother died. "I was away, so I would talk to him on the phone, but I wasn't around very much. I remember that he went from being a bubbly kid who did well in school and had many friends, to being a kid who got sent home for picking fights and punching people out."

Amanda told me a story about her last semester at boarding school. She recalled hearing that Jack had begun to lock himself in his room every afternoon when he came home from school. He played the radio constantly and refused to speak with anyone. When Amanda came home for Easter vacation, she tried to talk to her little brother. Each time she asked him what the matter was, he just shrugged and ignored her.

He had, reported Amanda, been pretending to read at his desk. Finally, he'd sat down on the edge of his bed, refusing to look at her, and said, "Nothing's wrong."

Amanda had said, "Tell me, come on. What's going on?"

Without warning, Jack had burst into tears. He'd gripped his sister's arms in a tight hug, sobbing in big, whistling gasps. When he'd finally stopped wheezing long enough that he was able to speak, he'd sat up, sniffling, and said, "I wish I were dead. You're the only person in the world that I still love, and you're not here."

At the time of his tearful outburst, Jack Morrison was only ten years old.

When Amanda described this conversation to me, she said, "I didn't know what to do. I was just eighteen, and I was trying to cope with going to college, and it never occurred to me that I could not do what I was supposed to do. I was stuck feeling a responsibility to him and another one to the demands of my own life."

She put her mug down and looked straight at me, as if I could provide absolution. "I'm sure I was very selfish at that stage, because I felt for him, but I didn't do anything about it. I didn't really know how."

So Amanda felt that she'd been not just a parent for Jack, but a *bad* parent. Indeed, like her father Carl but with more appropriate justification, Amanda was unable to be there for her younger brother.

She needed (her opinion to the contrary) to go out into the world
and establish an adult life, with her own relationships and career.
That she was somehow sidetracked from this venture to become her
brother's heroic rescuer only a few years later should by no means
be taken as a contradiction of that inalienable right.

Overall, however, what was most lacking in the Morrison family
seems to have been an outlet for all the understandably painful feelings of grief arising unavoidably from the loss of Ellen. The most
important activity for helping each of the Morrisons to cope with
Ellen's death would have been simply to tackle the forbidden topic,
to talk about what they felt. That they could not, or would not, do
so seems to be at the root of Jack's obvious psychological stuckness,
his ambivalence over whether he loves his sister or hates her, and
above all, his simultaneous existence as a little boy and a grown man.
For on the emotional plateau where the two Morrison kids interact,
Jack is still nine and his sister is still seventeen. Like players in the
child's game of Statues, nobody is free to move from the position in
which he or she was left at Ellen's death; they are caught in a place
where the past is the present.

As several of the psychotherapists whom I interviewed about the
Morrisons speculated, Jack's risk-taking seems like one manifestation
of his remaining frozen as a nine-year-old boy. This age is hardly one
characterized by terrific judgment, a time at which a youngster might
play baseball while sporting a cast on a broken wrist under the assumption that the cast will protect him from further injury.

Older sister Amanda seems frozen in *her* first mourning position
as well, as a seventeen-year-old girl. She continues to date, yet feels
ambivalent about committing to a more serious relationship and having children of her own. In some way, she has taken the place of her
mother in relationship to Jack *instead* of becoming a member of
a new family. Amanda Morrison is keeping her mother alive by becoming her mother, and Jack Morrison is eagerly helping her to
do so.

The Morrison children seem painfully unable to acknowledge
what therapists believe are natural feelings of anger toward their
mother for abandoning them in death, instead deflecting all the rage
onto Carl, the father who'd abandoned them in a more selfish manner. As a result, they seem to have become boxed into a relationship

in which they are alone, all the family each has. Appropriately, adolescent Amanda would have grieved for her mother, and left home to form her own relationships and family. Instead, the only long-term intimate tie she and Jack have been able to maintain thus far is the one between them. Stuck together as each other's only safe life partner, neither is free to grow up and leave. If Amanda were to marry Tony, she would be abandoning Jack, which up until now has been the one impossible thing for her to do. In sum, Amanda and Jack function for all the world as if *they* were married: Although they talk behind each other's backs, and say they yearn to be apart, they routinely continue to fight and make up. They are exclusively involved with one another in some very basic way.

Jack claims frequently—and loudly—that he wishes that Amanda would just marry Tony and get off his back, but he manages to claim her attention each time she begins to take Tony seriously. For example, not three weeks after Tony moved into Amanda's house, Jack broke his leg in a freak skiing accident in Switzerland. Amanda hopped onto a plane the next morning, in order to make sure that "the doctors were taking care of him properly. God forbid someone starts giving him all kinds of pain-killers and he gets in trouble with drugs again."

Each therapist with whom I consulted about the Morrisons, no matter their theoretical orientation, speculated along similar lines about this brother and sister pair. This is a sibling duo that needs each other to feel useful and functional. Were Amanda to marry Tony, what would Jack do? Where would he go? Who would fight with him? Who would take care of him? Who would, in fact, *remember* for him? For Amanda to enter wholeheartedly into another relationship, she would need her little brother's permission. And the real question is, why would he possibly want to give it to her?

In a sibling relationship like Jack and Amanda's, the participants are kept locked into the positions that saved them in childhood; now these once succoring bonds prevent them from changing and growing. Irritating, annoying, infuriating as they may find each other, they are also the most comfortable, most familiar, and most trusted helpmeets: Jack and Amanda Morrison, for better—and more often, for worse—are one another's most weathered and treasured life partner.

CHAPTER FOUR

The Francis Twins

"We Were One Being Who Separated into Two"

It isn't possible to think about siblings without considering twins, identical and fraternal. Much of the most important research on siblings as a whole derives from the study of twins in particular. We tend to think of twins as special, the ultimate siblings, those with the most to gain or lose from their connection. To a certain extent, we make assumptions about them in the same manner that we do about the very beautiful or wealthy or accomplished: Such beings are blessed by a certain quality that sets them above the run of common mortals; as a result, their lives are enhanced, perhaps made easier or more enjoyable. They are born covered with a fairy dust that eludes us common singletons.

The truth of the matter is that from the average to the deviant, to the accomplished and special, twins run the gamut of human types. And the experience of twindom can run the scale from extremely intimate to hostile to indifferent, just like the experience of sibling-dom—and variations can even exist in the same set of twins at different phases of their lives.

Aside from their twinship, Penelope and Paula Francis are about as average as they come, genuine and open women with little experience of life outside the world of family and friends in which they grew up, and little interest in exploring the unfamiliar. Born and raised in a northern Michigan town, neither sister has ever traveled farther than Chicago, and although Paula speaks of going to New York City or visiting the Grand Canyon, it is possible that she will never reach either place. Their world is a clean and comfortable one, peopled with family, friends, and neighbors with whom they feel completely at ease. Within that community of neatly mowed lawns and carefully maintained homes, the Francis sisters have grown quite naturally into their separate adult lives. Nobody, anywhere in the world, goes through life without some questioning and some experience of pain, loss, and doubt, and certainly Penelope and Paula have undergone their share of troubles. Yet, to some extent, these sisters *have* manufactured a kind of fairy dust: They have learned to use their twinship to make their lives less ordinary. It isn't always the size of the pond that matters; more important is the pleasure derived from swimming there.

From the first, Penelope and Paula Francis seemed to know how to play to a crowd: They were born on July 4, 1954, a complete surprise to their parents, who until the moment of birth had not suspected that they'd created two children. To be sure, twenty-three-year-old Anita had grown extremely large during her pregnancy; nonetheless, her obstetrician had never heard more than one heartbeat. Both Anita and her thirty-three-year-old husband, Otto, a factory laborer, were eager for a daughter. When a seven-pound baby girl was delivered at 2:42 in the morning, the Francises already knew that she would be called Paula. At 2:45, instead of the afterbirth, a second baby girl emerged. This little girl—who after some bemused, exhilarated moments was named Penelope by her exhausted parents —weighed just five pounds, and so was too small to take home from the hospital.

What happened next was something that I, as a non-twin, found fairly surprising, but that the Francis twins shrugged off as merely an amusing anecdote.

Apparently, Anita and Otto Francis were more than a little disoriented when they went home from the hospital with the elder of their twin girls. The unexpected bonus prize had left them a bit confused. What they did was to bring seven-pound Paula home, all the while calling her Penelope. When Penelope was released from the hospital two weeks later, they realized what they'd done. By then, they felt so comfortable with the elder twin as Penelope that they just started calling girl number two Paula, and the names stuck. On their birth certificates, Penelope is Paula and Paula is Penelope. In real life, nobody but the family knows that they are switched, and no one cares beyond making this an entertaining story.

"How did it happen?" I asked Paula, on the telephone.

Her voice was matter-of-fact as she answered, "I think they were just terribly confused. I was marked Baby B and she was marked Baby A, I guess they were just confused by it—" She paused for a moment, and then she quickly added, "It's not like we were switched at birth or anything like that. Our birth certificates are wrong, that's all."

I came to suspect that this was a metaphor for a fairly basic acceptance of all the complex elements of their circumstance. They know that each of them is a separate and unique person, and yet at the same time they are so frequently perceived as interchangeable units that each woman's self-definition has to be in reference to the other. While the Francis twins enjoy a relationship that is basically free of conflict and provides them with a major measure of satisfaction in life, the very strength of their twinship—and the degree of their physical, psychological, and emotional similarities—also sets them apart from the general population in a very fundamental way.

The freedom to be different and to experience life individually is an implicit aspect of their connection; nevertheless, the existence of that mirror self makes the very definition of the word "individual" almost incomprehensible to either of them. When, in our separate interviews, I asked each of them what it was like to be a twin, I received identical responses. Each sister laughed, a little uncomfortably, and then said, "What is it like not to be? We don't know anything else."

In a certain essential manner, it didn't seem to matter which of the Francis sisters was Penelope and which was Paula: They were so easy with each other that it seemed they really did not care which of them began life as whom. What was difficult to comprehend was how completely irrelevant such a distinction seemed to them in the first place.

Tracking Down Twins

Toads lay thirty thousand eggs at a time. Cats usually have at least five or six kittens at a shot. Armadillos routinely give birth to quadruplets. And whooping cranes almost always produce sets of twins. But we humans—like whales, dolphins, chimps, and horses—tend to have only one child at a time. Our children stand a good chance of making it to adulthood, so Mother Nature doesn't need to improve the odds that a family line will continue, the way she would for members of a species that is constantly threatened.

Nevertheless, multiple births—twins in particular—are evidenced in the earliest recorded history: Cain and Abel were twins; Romulus, the founder of Rome, had a twin brother named Remus. Even as far back as four thousand years ago, sailors used to sail their ships "by Gemini": guided by the twin stars, Castor and Pollux, who before ascending to the heavens had traveled with Jason and the Argonauts to secure the Golden Fleece.

If the incidence of twins is rare—they occur just once in every ninety births—finding a set to interview offered even slimmer odds. Although I was referred to several dozen pairs, I was never able to get them both to commit to helping with the project. On several occasions, one of a set of twins stood me up for a scheduled meeting. I started to wonder if twins were, as a whole, not eager to answer the kinds of questions that might separate them, even in theory. I have absolutely no proof at all for this suspicion, that twins who don't get along seem more ashamed of it than regular siblings in the same situation; and that twins who do get along seem to have an awful lot invested in that connection, enough so that they may not want to risk rocking the boat by scrutinizing their relationship.

In a certain way, this supposition was borne out in my interviews with Paula and Penelope Francis, although they did make a generous amount of time available to speak with me. I had managed to track them down through one of the other twin pairs with whom I'd tried—without success—to schedule interviews. Paula and Penelope agreed to be interviewed, in part because they'd been consciously emphasizing their twindom in a more complete way in the previous five years. Although this appeared to be somewhat of a sea change to other members of their families and to their friends, Paula and Penelope regarded it as part of a natural evolution. They'd always been close, but now they were trying to make a career of their similarities. The forty-year-old women had begun doing advertising and commercial work together. They'd had some real successes, having recently won roles in an industrial film produced by a Chicago ad agency. They had also begun to dress alike again, after nearly twenty-five years of attempting to maintain different appearances. Now they made sure to have their hair cut on the same day, by the same hairdresser, and whenever one twin shopped, she would buy two of whatever outfit she'd selected. Penelope explained this over the phone before I had had the chance to meet with them in person, and I asked her why they strove to look so much alike.

Penelope chuckled. She said, "I think a lot of the way Paula and I enjoy each other has to do with upbringing, because our parents never compared us. I think conflicts between twins develop when they are constantly being measured against one another."

"That was a big gift they gave to you," I said.

"Yes," Penelope continued. "They never said, oh, Paula's smarter or Penelope's prettier, or why can't she be as nice as you. They never pitted us against each other, so we never felt that we were competing against each other."

"That's wonderful."

"Absolutely. Because for twins that's where the problems lie, with people always comparing you. So that's why we dress alike, so people don't compare us. They compare us *less* when we're dressed alike, because then we look the same."

"I don't understand. Do you mean it's better *not* to be separate individuals?"

"It's not that exactly," she said, and then corrected herself. "Well, it is, sort of. Otherwise, it's, oh, she looks so nice and the other could look better. Or that outfit makes the one twin look a little fat, and the other one looks so wonderful. This way, we either both look wonderful or we both look awful. So we are not compared."

We had not yet met in person at that point, and so I had no idea how similar they looked. "Are people always walking up to you and asking, 'Which twin are you'?"

"Yeah. Say, if we're at a big party or something, even our closest friends won't know. Unless I'm hanging on Matthew and Paula is on

Joe, then if the person knows whose husband is whose . . ." Penelope paused for a moment, and then chuckled again, adding, "And of course, if we haven't switched in the middle of the evening to play a joke on our husbands."

"They really can't tell you apart?" My tone, at this point, must have sounded disbelieving.

She laughed out loud. "Last Thanksgiving, Paula was sitting on my bed filing down a chipped nail. My husband, Matt, walked in and started snuggling up against her. He was rubbing her knee and telling her how great the meal had been, how terrific she was, how much he loved her. She let him go on and on until he started kissing her neck. That's when she goes, 'Wrong twin, Matt.' He was so embarrassed all afternoon, he could barely look at either of us."

"How could your own husband not be able to tell you apart? How long have you been married?"

"Twenty years," Penelope said, her voice clearly betraying how much she enjoyed this story.

Penelope told me that she and Paula had entered a look-alike contest the previous summer, and had been voted the most identical out of three thousand sets of twins. Although their lives were very different—Paula worked as a store manager while Penelope was a homemaker; each of them was married with a family of her own; and each had many friends who were not shared—the resemblance was, she assured me, startling. "Wait till you see us. Just wait."

I'd come to Penelope's house prepared to do a double take—and I was not denied it. The sight of these two forty-year-old women in their identical pink turtlenecks and black jeans was dumbfounding. Paula answered the door; she was a handsome woman with dark-brown hair worn shoulder length. A tortoiseshell comb held a length of hair in a swoop above her ear, so as to reveal a row of three tiny diamond studs traveling up the lobe. She was quite tall, perhaps five foot nine, with a broad, friendly grin.

As soon as I entered the house, I saw Penelope waiting in the living room to the left. She was standing, one leg slightly forward as if she were about to move to greet me but wanted me to get the full effect first. Her grin was, if anything, just a tiny edge wider than her twin's. I burst out laughing when I saw her. "We're the Doublemint Twins, aren't we?" she said.

Penelope wore a barrette on the right; Paula's hair comb was on the left. Penelope's earrings were long and silver; Paula wore the three little diamonds. Their bodies appeared identical; their outfits certainly were. Looking into first one's eyes and then the other's, I hoped to see something unique, as if their essential souls would be revealed as distinct, but there was no visible difference, just the same frank and agreeable gaze. Each face was identical, down to the laugh lines. Now Penelope said, "You'd think we called each other this morning to decide what to wear, wouldn't you?"

I nodded.

"Sometimes we do that, but today we really didn't," she said. "And these are obviously not our best shirts or anything. We just decided the same, it happens all the time."

Behind me, Paula offered to put on a pot of coffee. When I turned to say yes, it was disorienting—had the room moved with me as I swiveled? They were more alike, physically, than my brain could comprehend, from the way the legs flared slightly outward at the knee joint, to the identical manner in which their shoulders curved forward. More disturbing, however, I came to feel, were the unconscious gestures that echoed from one to the other, such as the shared habit of drawing an elbow in close with the other hand, or cocking the lower lip just so at the identical moment before taking a sip of coffee, or the way in which each woman bent one arm onto the armrest of their very different sofas during later interviews. Their brains seemed to be directing their limbs to make the same movements at moments of high involvement, and when they grew tired as well. While most of their gestures were somewhat universal in one sense—for example, shifting slightly before answering an uncomfortable question—the exact manifestation was so precisely theirs that nobody else, even their younger brother, could have imitated the full range as they did. Each sister had the habit of crossing a leg akimbo, at the identical place on the thigh. Each pointed a forefinger and then inscribed a quick half-circle in the air when emphasizing a point. Their laughs were identical, as were the ways in which they tilted their heads as they giggled. Even the phrases they used and the stories they chose to tell when interviewed separately were, for the most part, the same. It was exhausting to try and keep them straight. Over the hours that we spoke, that feeling would fade and return; my mind was playing games, as if the Francis sisters were part of a funhouse trick, doubling, then singling, then doubling again.

Paula's voice was slightly deeper than Penelope's; she smoked quite heavily, although her sister had given up the habit more than a decade before. My initial private conversation was with her, and then I met with Penelope, so I heard their stories from Paula's point of view first. Fairly soon in my conversations with the twins, however, I was struck by an odd realization: Their life experiences had been entirely different, and yet somehow their memories were filled with almost identical information. When Paula told me how Penelope had given birth to a stillborn son thirteen years previously, it was clear that she was fighting back tears; she could *feel* what her sister had gone through as if she had lived the tragedy herself. Later, when Penelope described the horrible custody battle Paula had endured with her son's father, a struggle that lasted for seven years, her anger was as palpably heartfelt as Paula's had been in telling the tale at the earlier meeting. She used almost the same words, in fact, to describe how Paula had finally decided to relinquish her nine-year-old son, Richard, aware that the little boy had become a pawn in a power struggle.

The Francis twins were so deeply connected that, in telling each other's life stories, each sister would provide the same perspective on events whether she was talking about herself or about her sister. It was as if they were two distinct people with one shared memory bank. Their lives moved forward on parallel tracks, but then closed behind them like a zipper.

And yet—and this is the difficult part to comprehend—the Francis twins had absolutely *no* sense of themselves as undifferentiated beings. In an odd way, they dressed alike not to showcase how similar they were, but to make life easier for themselves. If other people treated them as one person, it simply didn't matter; what mattered was that blurring their borders saved a great deal of wasted emotional time and needless comparison. They knew they were separate people, and had always known it, but they weren't interested in studying one another constantly. It was those of us on the outside looking in who had a problem understanding how two such physically similar women could have, for want of a simpler description, separate and individual souls.

To date, Penelope had led a fairly even and stable life. She had been married to Matt, her former high school boyfriend, for the past twenty years; she was raising two sons, and she managed her household with competence and skill. She'd never desired a career of her own (although she certainly was enjoying the fact that they'd both recently won parts in a TV commercial). Despite this disinclination for the workplace, everyone in her family acknowledged that she was a born manager—of events, of people, of her life. "I always wanted to be a wife and mother," Penelope told me. "I'm more like my mother, more conventional. Paula wanted a career from the get-go, she was ambitious, she didn't have the same feelings for children that I did. All the same, she's less organized and more impulsive. Look," she said, shifting several of the embroidered throw pillows on her blue Victorian couch so as to lean toward me, "I would never have moved in with Matthew, not without being married. Paula, though, left home when she was seventeen to move in with Ed. She didn't care what it looked like, she just followed her heart. Paula is headstrong and she's independent, and she always has been."

"I get the impression that her life has been harder because of those traits."

"It has," she said. "I honestly think it has." According to Penelope, Ed was already married to someone else at the time he took up with her sister. Paula had remained with him for six years, had a son with him, and been abandoned when baby Richard was only a year old. Although she'd worked up until Richard's birth, she hadn't intended to go back to the store full time for a few years. After Ed left, however, she had to support herself and Richard. The little boy was placed in day care and Paula returned to the clothing store where she'd had her very first job (and where she continues to work to this day). "If she didn't want to work, why didn't she turn to you, or to your parents, for help?" I asked.

"It's not her way, I guess." Penelope's open gaze did not shift in the slightest. "That's why she's had more ups and downs, she's risked more than I did. She could never have settled down so early, not like me."

In the next room, Penelope's two sons, fifteen-year-old Gary and twelve-year-old Phil, began squabbling over the Nintendo game they were playing. Their mother did not move or speak as the boys' voices began to rise; her attention had shifted completely and immediately. A minute later, when the boys began playing again, having apparently resolved the difference by themselves, her expression became animated once again. "Where were we?" Penelope asked. "I'm sorry, I've lost what we were talking about."

We were silent for a moment until she finally looked at me, smiled, shaking her head slightly to one side so that her brown hair brushed the edge of the couch, and returned to our earlier topic. "Oh, I know, I remember. Paula. I think Paula always wanted to work, a career was very important to her," said Penelope. "And she wasn't as interested in being a mother as I was. She loves Richard, and she always tries to do the best for him, but she isn't inclined that way. I am." Penelope shrugged, almost ruefully. She leaned back against the couch, lifting her chin so that the back of her head rested on the top of the cushion. "Also, Paula's the most stubborn person you ever met. She just wouldn't give in if she made up her mind to do it herself. If you ask me, it wasn't my parents she was trying to prove it to, it was Ed. As bad as she felt, she didn't want him to know how hurt she was."

Later, Paula confirmed that her first love affair had ended in a devastating manner. "One day, Ed was there and the next he was gone. Sure, I knew he would never be faithful to me, I knew what he was. The worse he acted, the more I tried to hold on to him. I was more obsessed than in love, I think. I would have tolerated anything that rat did. It's better that he left, I know that now. But it was just awful at the time."

"What did Penelope think of him?"

Paula was silent, stroking the red silk pillow she had placed on her lap during this conversation. At last, she said, "My sister didn't like him."

"Did she tell you not to move in with him?"

"I'm sure she did, though I can't remember it. My family was so upset when I left. My little brother Charles did not speak to me for the whole time I was living with Ed. For six years, he'd walk out of the room every time I walked in."

"Did you ever ask him why? Try to talk to him?"

"I guess so. It's hard to remember back so many years. Maybe I was so focused on my own problems I didn't pay much attention. But I do know that Charles was furious about Ed. Ask him about it, I don't mind."

"I will," I promised, scribbling the question into my notebook. Charles, the twins' younger brother by seven years, had grown up in the shadow of this strongly bonded set of women. The impact on him had to have been interesting; although I wasn't to get a chance to speak with him for several more weeks, I was already becoming very curious about him. For now, however, it seemed a priority to focus on the twins themselves.

Acting Like Twins

"Tell me about the twin stuff," I asked Penelope. "You know, the dressing alike and all. Did you always do that?"

"Up until we were twelve or so, we used to dress alike all the time. Then I guess we realized that if we wore different clothes, we'd have twice as many outfits, so that's when that stopped." Penelope spoke in a firm, blunt tone, as if there could have been no other explanation; as if, for example, a predictable adolescent desire for a degree of independence from the family—and each other—had not played even the most minor part.

"Did you like dressing similarly?"

"We didn't dislike it or like it. It was just the way it was. So it didn't mean anything." She paused briefly, looking down at her hands again, and then back up without acknowledging that her next words would be in direct contradiction to what she'd just stated. "It's funny, I think when I was in high school, if I met somebody new, I don't think I'd have mentioned that I was a twin. I wasn't thinking about it back then. She was my sister and my best friend and all, but I think we are each more conscious of being a twin now. We enjoy it more. Now we can appreciate the fact of being twins."

"You were trying harder to be different from one another back then?"

She was silent for a moment, listening to the more peaceful tones of conversation emanating from the den in which her sons were playing. "Yeah, I guess so. But that's not really it. We've had more

fun playing up being twins in the past five years or so. We really wish
we'd gotten involved in twin things earlier, gotten to know other
twins, done some more modeling when we were younger and likelier
to get better-paying jobs. It wasn't until we turned thirty-five that
we started focusing on our twin-ness, and we've had so much fun, I
just wish we'd done it sooner."

"What happened when you turned thirty-five? What made you
decide to change your focus?"

She laughed uncomfortably, pulling one knee up to cross it over
the other, outstretched leg. "What happened when we turned thirty-
five was that we turned thirty-five. We were both depressed about
getting older, and then Paula ran across this ad. I think it was in the
Reader's Digest, for a research firm that was looking for twins to
study. We decided to do it for a lark. We got an all-expense-paid trip,
with hotel and everything. It was a blast. When we were there, we
met these other twins, sisters who actually lived just a few towns
away from us. It was great to talk to them, we had so much in
common. They felt the same way about us. These two sisters told us
about a twin convention, and we decided to all go together. It was
mind-boggling, it was so great. That's when we realized how much
fun it was to play up being twins, to spend time with other twins. It
kept snowballing from there."

"How did your families react when you started going to all these
twin events?"

She stopped smiling abruptly. This seemed to be somewhat sensitive turf. Then she said, "I wouldn't care if it bothered my husband,
or my parents, because it's too much fun. But the truth is, I think it's
good, I think they enjoy it when we come home with all our stories."
There was a note of stridency in her voice; clearly, *someone* resented
their "return" to twindom. With my next question, I inadvertently
stumbled upon the identity of the critic.

"How does your brother feel, do you know? How did he like
growing up in a family with twin sisters?"

"I guess he probably sees us as different people," she began
slowly. "To my knowledge, if someone asked him if he had siblings,
he would say, 'Yes, I have sisters.' I'm not so sure he would say, 'I
have twin sisters.' "

"He would say he has older sisters."

"Yes. Sisters who are seven years older. Then he might mention that we are twins."

"So he can tell you apart?"

"Always. Isn't that funny? Because he's really the only person we've never been able to fool, including our parents."

Once again, it seemed as if Charles was going to provide a very interesting perspective on his elder sisters. He would not be able to see me for two more weeks, he'd said, postponing our meeting for a second time. It was beginning to seem that he wasn't eager to talk about his childhood memories. In the meantime, I began to focus on his sisters' earliest experiences.

Twin Childhoods

Certainly, even twins who try, as Penelope and Paula did when younger, not to "focus on their twin-ness," grow up under unusual circumstances. It is believed that because twins create a higher level of pressure for their parents in that it is simply more difficult to raise two simultaneously than one, they may be raised in a more stressful environment. Raising twins may also require that responsibilities be shared among a variety of caretakers, simply in order to perform all the normal tasks of daily life. The British psychiatrist Michael Rutter has written, "We do not know whether this constitutes a beneficial or adverse influence, but clearly it constitutes a difference that might have some implications for the psychological development of twins."

One of the clearest differences in early environment for a twin is that patterns of interaction seem to be less focused on the individual. In order to respond to each child's needs throughout the day, the parents must frequently shift the highlight of attention from one to the other. Thus, each child may receive briefer bursts of a parent's concentration. Also, research has noted a tendency for the parents of twins to speak with them as if they are a set rather than individuals. Parents are also thought to use shorter, more directive phrases in speaking with their twin youngsters, and to speak with them less overall. The expectation is that the twins have each other as a major source of stimulation, and the parents are reluctant to interfere in the developing twin bond. This may in some way be connected with the widely accepted finding that twins lag behind singletons in speech and language development. According to Dr. Rutter, who is a professor of child psychiatry at the University of London's Institute of Psychiatry, "Twins have an extensive body of common knowledge and mutual experience and it may be that, when the relationship within the twin pair is unusually close, this may be associated with a reduced pressure to communicate with others in a manner that is more generally understandable."

The stress inherent in having two children at the identical developmental phase at the same time may greatly heighten the parents' need either to treat the children as a unit or to differentiate among them and set them up as distinct individuals. Thus, the children may be pushed harder to do everything together than a more regularly spaced set of kids would be. Or, conversely, they may be forced apart more than they would like. The Francis twins reported, in fact, that the latter had been their experience. From the first, their mother had had to concentrate in order to distinguish them. Even though Anita Francis dressed her baby girls in identical clothing, emphasizing their twin status to the outside world, she also left their (switched) hospital bracelets on their wrists for several months. Anita and Otto most decidedly wanted to know which little girl was which.

Separate Rooms

"People always tell parents to separate twins, to help them forge their own identities," Paula explained to me. "But we never wanted to have separate rooms growing up. If Mom had put us in different bedrooms, we'd have ended up in the same one anyway. We wanted to be together." (Hours later, Penelope would tell me the identical story, down to the same words.)

When the girls entered the first grade, Paula continued, a school adviser insisted that they be placed in different classrooms for the year. He gave dire warnings to their mother about the likelihood that the twins would develop behavioral and academic problems if they were not separated. "I'm surprised that our mother agreed. This guy must have been really convincing, especially because it was so awful for us."

"You really missed each other then?"

"Oh, it was terrible," Paula said excitedly. "It was just awful. I don't think there was ever a day that I didn't feel like crying. Every morning, I would walk her to the door of her classroom and we would kiss and hug good-bye. And then she would pick me up at lunchtime, and we would walk home. After lunch, I would walk her to her door again, and we would kiss again. And I remember walking to my classroom, feeling so lonely my heart wanted to break."

"When you think back on it now, was it helpful in any way to be separated?"

"Definitely not. We missed each other so much it wasn't good. We would have been better students and happier if they had kept us together. I could barely concentrate."

"I guess they were trying to show you that you were separate people," I offered.

"Yes, but that's ridiculous," Paula said explosively, jabbing her cigarette up into the air to underscore the point (a gesture I would also see Penelope make, but with a pen). "We always knew we were separate, we always knew who was who! We just wanted to be with each other!"

According to Paula, she and her sister were always different under the skin. Penelope was, from the earliest days, more compulsive and organized, more likely to try to control events and people—in a word, bossier. And yet when the sisters were teenagers, it was the more easygoing Paula who emerged as the leader. "I was more outgoing, more interested in meeting new people and making friends. Now it's more like when we were little; she's more the leader again."

"Would Penelope say the same thing, do you think?"

"Oh, yes, no question about it. She'd agree if she were here. She knows what she's like. I always say she's a typical older sister," Paula said, chuckling.

Their parents, she added, had always been aware that it was important to focus on getting Penelope to relax her tendency to make stringent demands on herself and others. What had Otto and Anita worried about with Paula? I asked.

Paula uncrossed her leg and leaned forward, her hands clasped in her lap as if she were about to begin a prayer, an ironic contrast to what she began to say next. "I guess I was the wild one. I smoked pot. I tried other drugs. I was involved with many more guys than Penelope. I lived with Ed. I lived through a lot of ups and downs, I wasn't such a model person. But then, I was out in the world for a long time when she was settled down and married. I enjoyed myself, too. It wasn't like I was always miserable or anything." She sat back and closed her eyes briefly. "I have no regrets," she added. "It's just that my opportunities were different. My timing was different. You know?"

I nodded. "Is that why Richard went to live with his father?"

"No," she said shortly. "That's not it at all. I was a good mother to Richard, I always took care of him. I kept my social life very separate from parenting. What happened was that after Ed left me for another woman and lived with her for a year, he went back to his wife. You see, he'd been married when I started seeing him, and he never actually got divorced. Then a year or so later, I guess his wife found out she couldn't have kids, and they started coming after Richard. They wanted him to be theirs."

"How did you feel about that?"

"Well, it was awful, and I fought to hold on to Richard for a long time. Then one day I suddenly realized, hey, Richard has a dad who wants to be with him. Lots of kids in his situation don't even know their fathers. I knew he'd be loved and taken care of, and I was sure the fighting wasn't helping anyone. That's when I gave him up."

"He lives with you now, though, doesn't he?"

"That's the funny part," Paula said, shaking her head from side to side before pulling a cigarette from the pack on the coffee table. "Richard asked to come back here around five years ago, just when Joe and I decided to get married. He was having trouble in school, acting up. His grades were slipping. He really needed to be with his mom. After all those years I was alone, suddenly I had a husband and a full-time son again." She fell silent, half-smiling as she lit her cigarette.

"Can't you see," she said abruptly, "how very different my life has been from my sister's?"

I nodded.

"Look around this room," Paula commanded. Obediently, I scanned the living room in which we sat, taking note of the two black leather couches, the red area rug, the black varnished entertainment center. Shiny red and black curtains prevented the brilliant spring light from penetrating the room, topping off an overall effect that was at once harsh and dark. Even the family pictures hung in casual rows on the wall were framed in black and brass, or set off by red enameled wood. Before I could formulate a comment about the design, Paula said, "See, I'm modern, I like a contemporary, sophisticated look. Now think about Penelope's house, you know, it's kind of—" She broke off for a moment, and then continued. "I don't know, she likes blue, and Victorian, you know, old-fashioned?"

I nodded again.

"That's not for me," Paula said. "I mean, we're alike but we aren't. We like different furniture. That sounds like a small thing, but we have different friends as well, ones that are just mine or hers. We aren't exactly the same. We are separate people. We have always, always known that."

"Tell me about your friends."

Paula shrugged. "What do you mean? They're just people, friends. You know, to go to the movies with, or go dancing, or whatever."

"Do you have a best friend?"

"Well, obviously," she said, staring in disbelief. "My sister."

A Note About Friendship

One person's thoughts about friendship—its meaning, its importance, its function—can be as different from someone else's as those same two individuals' estimates of the quality and substance of their sibling relationships. Like the bonds we have with our brothers and sisters in adulthood, the rules of friendship are not common across all members of our patchwork culture. In fact, each of us uses the term "friendship" to ascribe a particular value to a relationship; we don't know exactly what our friend believes friendship to be, any more than we know what our sisters and brothers really muse about when they are seated alone in their living rooms, late at night.

Sociologist Sarah H. Matthews of Cleveland State University has observed that friendship styles tend to be fairly consistent throughout life. She has defined three specific varieties of people with certain friendship styles: the *independent*, who have a network of friendly bonds but no particularly special friend; the *discerning*, who have both intimate friends and a wider network of friendly acquaintances; and finally, the *acquisitive*, who adapt to new circumstances by making new friends to replace those lost by a move or other change.

Until very recently, society—and science—tended to dismiss women's friendships, while men's friendships were studied more seriously, according to Temple University sociologist Robert Bell, author of *Worlds of Friendship*. Writes Bell, "Kinship has long been believed to meet all the needs of the woman and the woman has been expected to find through her relatives the kinds of emotional relationships often associated with friendships. It has often been the case that friendship was seen to subvert kinship and by its very existence to threaten the values of kinship."

Professor Bell argues that the friendships women make are, in fact, more meaningful and involved, more self-revealing and accepting than those commonly found among men. A man's closest confidante actually tends to be his wife, while the wife is likely to confide as much in her husband as in a close female friend. Furthermore, women simply have more friends than men, Robert Bell has found; men, on average, name three friends apiece, while the average woman says she has nearer to five intimate friends. "One factor that is crucial to the friendships of many women is the willingness to share," he observes. "There is often a strength that can be gained by individuals based on having shared important feelings, thoughts, and experiences."

Friendship is thought to be in many ways an improvement over kinship, in that we can select our friends and not our siblings. We do tend to take our friendships seriously and expect them to be lifelong. Real friendship lasts, we believe, and survives the ebbs and flows of changing personal circumstances. Good friendship, believes Dr. Bell, "can absorb the more transient feelings of anger, resentment, or disappointment." We don't approach our friendships as casual connections; and when a friendship fails it can be extremely painful. Even when a relationship ends because two parties merely drift apart due to changing life circumstances, it can be very saddening. Like good sibling relationships, a healthy and enduring friendship may go through periods of great intimacy and contact, and then be followed by more fallow periods in which the emotional connections remain but regular day-to-day contact dwindles. Not surprisingly, good friendships thrive on a healthy combination of self-revelation, mutual acceptance, and support, just as good sibling relationships do.

Real friendship is in and of itself a form of self-selected kinship. For although we do pick our friends, we do not have total control over the repertoire of behaviors we will use with them. The range of possible friendship behavior is something we begin to learn very early, within the family home.

As a matter of fact, we learn how to be friends back in that early classroom of siblingdom. Salvador Minuchin, one of the pioneers in the field of family therapy, once wrote, "The sibling subsystem is the social laboratory in which children can experiment with peer relationships." With one's siblings, he strongly believed, children have the opportunity to "learn cooperation, competition, ways of avoiding or surrendering, how to gain or lose an ally, and other skills of living with peers." But the sibling subsystem cannot perform its socializing function unless the adults in the family give children enough freedom from supervision. Children need to "exercise their right to privacy, have their own areas of interest, and be free to fumble as they explore."

For their part, it appeared that the Francis twins thought little about friendship, for why would they need intimacy from other people when they had such perfect intimacy with one another? Oddly enough, when I subsequently met with their younger brother, Charles, it became clear that he had learned a similar lesson, for once he had a "twin" of his own, his adored wife, he, too, felt his life to be complete. All the Francis' siblings had friends to play golf with, to go to the movies, dancing, or dinner with. They didn't look to make friends of the heart, however, for it wasn't necessary. Neither Paula nor Penelope nor Charles needed more than one special friend, for that was the lesson they'd learned in their early sibling classroom. At this point, each of the Francises already *had* the only bosom buddy that he or she wanted.

The Angry Little Brother

The twins' brother Charles is seven years their junior, a handsome man who lives some thirty minutes from the town where the rest of the family still make their home. His wife of ten years, Dina, is a sweet-looking brunette who bears a strong resemblance to Penelope and Paula. She works in the insurance firm where he is a salesman. They have made a decision not to have children, Charles told me, because they like their lives as they are and aren't eager to make any changes. "We've discussed it and we've always come up with the same answers," he said with disarming honesty. "The only reason we would really have kids is because later in life we'd think, well, gee, maybe we should have. We're happy with the lives we have."

Before I had a chance to ask Charles anything about his sisters, he burst out, "You know, I know what you're going to ask and I can't really answer it. I can't tell you about twins. I mean, what it's like to be the brother of twins, because for one thing, I don't know anything else. And until they started making such a big deal about it, you know, in the last five years or so, I probably didn't even think of them as twins. They were my sisters, but they are such different people."

"They are?" I asked.

"They're extremely different," he repeated. "They're nothing alike. They're like day and night."

"And are you more like one than the other?"

"More like Paula," he replied immediately.

"What is she like?"

"Paula is easygoing, calm, and generous. She goes with the flow. Penelope is, well, hyper. She's harder to deal with, always has been."

"So they were really different all along?"

"I remember going up into their room when we were kids. They shared a room, and Penelope used to want me to leave, but Paula would always say, 'He can stay.'"

"So Paula was really a friend and Penelope wasn't?"

"Yes," Charles said. "I mean, let me explain Penelope. This is very simple. Okay. Penelope, when it's April first, she puts away her winter coat and puts on her spring coat. Because it's April first. This is Michigan; it could be thirteen degrees outside, and she'll freeze to death."

"But she would do it," I said.

"She would do it because it's spring and that's what you do in the spring. Where the logical people in the world would say, Gee, it's freezing, I've got to bundle up. But Penelope thinks things run on a calendar, and that's just the way it is. You have to be on a budget, you have to watch the clock. She's bound by rules."

Charles's tone was angry and aggressive. I wondered why it was so important to him that his sisters not be a matched set. Then I remembered that the psychologist Dorothy Burlingham—who had made perhaps the first formal observations of the phenomenon back in the 1940s—once commented that siblings of twins often feel like outsiders within their own families. Most people tend to feel that the companionship that twins provide each other is unique. As a whole, we suspect that they are happier than singletons in childhood, that they never experience loneliness because they are always lucky enough to have the other twin with whom to play. The sister or brother of a pair of twins is generally even more conscious of this. Twins, as Burlingham wrote, ". . . make an intimate pair just as the parents do. The [non-twin] child may believe that the world is made up of couples, feel left out, and decide that he is lacking something and at a great disadvantage in consequence."

Perhaps, I suddenly thought, that was why Charles was so adamantly against having children himself; now that he was finally part of a couple, he didn't want to share his beloved wife with anyone else.

"Let me tell you a story," Charles said. "When I started community college, I decided to move out of the house and get my own apartment. I was pretty wild back then, drinking a lot and going to bars and stuff. Irresponsible. Didn't know much about how to get along in the world. So after a few months, maybe it was November or December, I was in trouble because I hadn't been paying my rent or my bills. I got kicked out of my place."

Charles's tone sounded annoyed, as if I were pressuring him to tell this tale he'd volunteered to share with me.

He continued. "So that was just about the time that Ed walked out on Paula. She had Richard, and no place to live, and no job or anything, and she was a mess. We'd barely spoken for years. And when she found out that I was in trouble, she called me up and volunteered to lend me some money." His voice rose high as he said, "And she didn't *have* any! Penny did, she has tons of money! I'm still waiting to hear *her* make an offer like that."

"Did you take Paula up on her offer?"

"No."

"Why not?"

He was silent.

"Well, I moved back home," he admitted at last. "Mom and Dad helped me out. But the point is that she would have helped me, even though she had nothing to give. And Penelope wouldn't."

"So Penelope is more selfish?"

He didn't want to go that far. "No, it's not that. It's that she doesn't understand that life can be hard, because it's never been hard for her. She has no empathy. She has no clue."

"Were they always that different?" I asked.

"Oh, yeah. When I was little, Paula was a great sister. I really loved her."

"So," I asked, phrasing the question carefully, "why didn't you speak to her for six years while she was living with Ed?"

He seemed thrilled to hear that Paula had told me about their years of silence. "She told you that! She told you?"

"Yes," I said, puzzled.

"I'm glad she remembers. It was the worst time and I was so mad at her for leaving. Ed was such a jerk. I couldn't believe she would just leave like that. We'd been such close friends, and then she was gone, almost overnight. She never even told me she was moving out. So I figured, forget it. I was around eleven or so, and I remember I didn't really understand how she could leave, and I just refused to talk to her when she called. It went on for years. I thought, if that's how much she cares about me, then fine, there's no need to talk."

"So how did you get to be friends again?"

"I guess one day I realized how ridiculous it was. And so I called her up and we made a date to meet, and we were right back as good friends as we'd been before."

"When was that?"

"Oh, I guess right about the time that Ed left, maybe a week after," he said, his tone casual. I couldn't tell if he realized how competitive his feelings toward Ed must have been, for he could only be friendly with his sister once her lover was gone.

"Do you like Paula's husband, Joe?"

"Oh, yeah," he said immediately. "Joe's fine." Then he looked at me, and I saw that he knew what I was driving at. "I'm older, past that," he said. "I have the best marriage of anyone I know. It's different."

Maybe, I speculated, when they were young, Paula had needed Charles to alleviate the fusion of twindom, just as much as Charles needed to divide his sisters up into good twin and bad so that he could have one for himself. Now that each of the three siblings had made new families of his or her own, they could reduce the pressure on the bond among them to manageable levels. Most important, however, seemed to be the notion that being a sibling of twins was as psychologically critical as being an actual twin, at least for this threesome.

The Making of Twins

Of the twins who are born in one out of every ninety pregnancies, two thirds are fraternal sets and one third are identical. Interestingly, the rate of identical-twin births is constant around the world, while the rate of fraternal twins varies widely. In one Nigerian tribe, a set of fraternal twins occurs in every 42 births; in Japan, on the other hand, fraternal twins occur only once in every 160 births. Researchers suspect that these differences may be connected to the presence or absence of particular foods in the diet.

Identical twins are the result of the equal and complete division of one fertilized egg at a very early phase. These twins usually grow in separate amniotic sacs within the womb while sharing the same placenta; they are always genetically identical, and, of course, are of the same sex. Approximately half of all sets of identical twins are male and half are female.

Fraternal twins, on the other hand, are merely siblings born at the same time. They are the result of two separate sperm fertilizing two separate eggs, and, during development, each child has its own placenta. The genetic material is subject to the same variation that would be found in any other set of two siblings. Fraternal twins can be physically quite dissimilar and need not be of the same sex. It is even possible for fraternal twins to have different fathers! Roughly half of all fraternal twins are mixed-sex pairs, and half are same-sex pairs. Obviously, the timing of their lives is similar, so that they enter the family at the same moment in its history, and they never know a life without each other. Still, in terms of looks, personality, and perception of shared and unshared experience, fraternal twins will tend to be far less similar than a set of identical twins. Fraternal twins are more likely to be born to older women, those who have been frequently pregnant, or those who have a family history of twins. Fraternal twins are also more common in Asia and Africa. None of these predictive factors seem to apply to identical twins, and although scientists understand how such twins are made, they are still not sure why, what subtle quirk of nature actually initiates the process in a particular pregnancy.

Differences in Development

A woman's body did not evolve to carry more than one fetus at a time. As a result of the tighter quarters, twins have a slightly higher rate of birth defects, such as club feet and lower birth weights; and they are born an average of three weeks earlier than the average baby. According to Elizabeth Noble's *Having Twins,* about half of all twins weigh less than five pounds, eight ounces, which is the international standard for low birth weight. Identical twins tend to weigh less than fraternal twins, although one of the most interesting aspects of this is that—like the Francis sisters, who were born with a disparity of two pounds—genetically identical twins can have widely varying birth weights, for one may have had better access to the basic nutrients provided by the placenta.

Thus, even though twins begin development in the same prenatal environment, each is to some extent affected differently. Whether they are identical or fraternal, within the close walls of the womb, they already experience life uniquely, as individuals.

Identical twins have the same physical appearance, gender, blood type, and dental characteristics, but though their hand- and footprints are similar, their fingerprints are always unique. Often, one twin is left-handed and the other right-handed. One identical twin may have a mole or a different pattern of freckles, or a slightly more crooked smile. What this tells us is that even the very first moments of life *in utero* have a shaping effect on who we are.

And who we are continues to be shaped in relation to the people with whom we share our expanding world, of course. When researchers have studied identical twins who were separated at birth, one of the most amazing things they have found is that identicals raised together tend to be *more different* from one another than identicals raised separately! How can that be possible? Remember the concept of deidentification? These twins, raised with no knowledge of one another, who grew up miles or counties or even states apart, had no need to modify their behavior, for they weren't establishing themselves in relation to an "other." They were just being who they were, by nature. And, by nature, they were identical.

Nonshared Environment

It is the pioneering work of developmental psychologist Judy Dunn and behavioral geneticist Robert Plomin, both of the University of London's Institute of Psychiatry, that has spurred a huge shift in research into human personality development, dramatically moving forward our understanding of the origins of sibling differences. Drs. Dunn and Plomin, who joined forces some fifteen years ago, brought to the study of siblings the divergent perspectives of their two disciplines. By this convergence of Dunn's in-depth family studies and Plomin's large-scale comparisons of singleton, twin, adopted, and step-siblings, a remarkable discovery was made. Robert Plomin described it as a "figure-ground alteration," making the comparison to an M. C. Escher drawing: What he and Judy Dunn suddenly identified as critically important to the understanding of sibling relationships was something that many experts had known—and disregarded —for years.

What was this realization?

To understand the idea of nonshared environment, we must first understand that even though all siblings stand the chance to inherit and share the same characteristics, they never do—aside from identical twins, that is. What is more remarkable is that when adult identical twins are measured on personality and temperament scales, or for a propensity to illnesses or psychological difficulties, their chances of being alike are on average about 50 percent. Identical twins, therefore, are 50 percent *different* in terms of personality on most known measures. This means that even when genetics predisposes two people to be exactly the same, they still end up 50 percent different.

Now, if those same two siblings were not identical but were merely born into the same family, they would begin their relationship not 100 percent alike but 50 percent alike. As mentioned earlier, a child has, more or less, a 50 percent chance of inheriting the same chromosome as his or her sibling. That similarity is genetic in nature.

As I mentioned in the first chapter, the fascinating question that Dunn and Plomin isolated from this information is this: How come researchers keep finding that siblings are *much* more than 50 percent different? All the existing data show that siblings are often as dissimilar on standard measures as any two random members of the population.

Furthermore, even where similarity is found among sets of siblings, often it is the less interesting aspect of the figure-ground composition. For example, there is a surprising lack of connection among siblings in terms of predicting such common diseases as heart disease, cancer, or asthma. If having a sibling who has a certain disease increases one's risk for it, as it often does, isn't it equally worthwhile to consider how *un*likely one actually is to develop the same disease? For example, if the risk of depression is 5 percent to the general population, and the risk to a sibling of someone who suffers from depression is 30 percent if she is a woman and 13 percent if the sibling is a man, what does this tell us? That for every thirty sisters of depressed people who themselves become depressed, some seventy sisters of depressed people do not. Yes, the risk is much higher, but what explains the seventy women who do *not* become depressed?

By now, numerous studies have been done using twins in all variations—fraternal and identical, raised together or apart—to unravel the extent to which differences are genetic in origin. Other studies have compared adopted children raised in the same family to understand how the environment affects kids when there are no blood ties. Dunn and Plomin identified the fact that, while genetic inheritance makes children in a family both similar and different, environmental factors *mostly cause differences.* This means that children who grow up in the same family not only have different experiences of that family but also different experiences in the world—with parents and siblings, teachers and friends, by accident and on purpose—that ultimately make them even more dissimilar than they were by nature. Plomin and Dunn termed this influence that makes siblings so very different from one another, "nonshared environment."

Adjacent Lives

According to Plomin and Dunn, the overall message is not that family experience is unimportant, but rather that significant influences are specific to each child. "These findings suggest that instead of thinking about the environment on a family-by-family basis," as Robert Plomin recently wrote, "we need to think about the environment on an individual-by-individual basis."

When researchers ask mothers how they treat their children, whether singletons or multiples, their answers tend to be more consistent than the behavior itself. Parents are generally convinced that they are egalitarian in their handling of their children. The children, on the other hand, know better.

When children are asked if their parents treat them in the same way, their responses almost invariably indicate precisely the opposite, that parents treat individual children individually. Video recordings also demonstrate this to be true: One parent is better with a preverbal child than a talkative three-year-old, or more skilled at calming an excitable little girl, or happier to sit and read with a very calm boy. Another parent seems gifted in coping with her adolescent's conflicting urges toward independence and clinginess. Each parent is an individual with variable skills and preferences for certain kinds of interaction and activity. Frankly, this is the way it should be, for as Robert Plomin told me, "If you were somehow programmed to behave exactly the same to your two kids who are of different ages, it would have to come off as very inappropriate behavior."

Parents behave in distinctly different ways with each child partly because the children themselves are so different from one another. As Plomin's research colleague, psychiatrist David Reiss of George Washington University, explains it, "Individuals have some very distinctive features which are very stable over time and which have a powerful influence on the relationships in which they enter." Reiss,

Plomin, and the developmental psychologist E. Mavis Hetherington are working with more than seven hundred families across the nation to try to establish precisely what features of a child's environment have a formative influence on the development of personality traits, depressive and antisocial behavior, and other aspects of the eventual adult self. They are attempting to identify what features actually make up the nonshared environment that plays such a huge role in making adult siblings so different from one another.

Certain suppositions with which one might begin such a project have proven to be dead ends, such as the notion that the way in which certain children are pulled into parental fights while others are spared would eventually affect personality development. This is known as "triangling" in the family-therapy literature, and is often seen as a key way in which shaky family groupings stabilize themselves. Dr. Reiss found, to his surprise, that in this sample of more than seven hundred families drawn from the general population, many parents tended to work extremely hard to contain marital fights and to avoid bringing children into them. Also, the children themselves were extremely sensitive to even the finest distinction in treatment between one child and another, and drew the parents' attention to it immediately. In other words, the children played an enormous role in regulating the parents' behavior with them. "Parents so want to be fair to their children," explains Reiss, "that it only takes a modest complaint from the kids for the error to be corrected."

Dr. Reiss is a psychoanalyst by training. He began to study non-shared environment in the last decade because he was so persuaded by the strength of the data Plomin and others were developing. Reiss believes that a major source of difference in children's experience of their environments is actually genetic in origin. The children bring a particular orientation into their family systems and thus elicit different behaviors from the others with whom they interact. "Kids are treated differently because something they have in their genes produces a range of characteristics that elicit different reactions," he says, "not only from their parents, but from their teachers and peers, and best friends, and so on."

Within the huge sample now under study, for example, one of the differential or unshared-environment experiences that one of a pair of adolescent siblings might have is knowing a friend who has made a suicide attempt. Is there a gene for becoming friends with someone who may become suicidal? One doubts it. Yet it may be true that a youngster with a tendency toward depression might be more likely to make friends with another depressive adolescent; therefore the original predisposition would be genetic in origin. The loss of the friend to suicide, nevertheless, would constitute a major environmental event that could have an effect on ongoing personality development. In other words, genetic inheritance influences the environment.

Furthermore, the environment most likely has its own influences on genetic inheritance! Robert Plomin is presently examining features of the prenatal environment that might affect the way in which one's genetic inheritance is, as it were, disbursed. For example, genes themselves are subject to mutation (cancer is one clear indication of that), and the result of a genetic mutation might be Down's syndrome or an ability to invent incredibly complex and beautiful music. As Dr. Plomin told me, "When we talk about environment, it may not simply be psychosocial. It could be biological or nutritional. There could be a slow-acting virus that alters the DNA. What about accidents or illness? Anything can happen to an organism, human or not."

The genetic program that is laid down by nature may be altered at the most fine-grained level, believes Plomin. Chance plays a notable part in this. Such seemingly minute early alterations "have snowballing effects that make bigger and bigger differences as you go through life. Even within pairs of twins who are genetically identical."

Thus, we begin as different people, and we grow more and more distinctly ourselves throughout life.

This was, in fact, the odd paradox exhibited by the way in which Penelope and Paula Francis actually lived very individual lives, and the efforts they made toward emphasizing their similarities. From that first separation into different elementary school classrooms all the way to their very divergent tastes in furniture, husbands, modes of life, and approaches to risk-taking, outside influences and internal impulses had clearly worked to make them as different from each other as their brother Charles insisted that they were.

And yet their physical similarity was so disturbingly powerful that, in a certain way, they were constantly encouraged to think of themselves as one and the same. Once, when Paula's son was about four years old, she was unable to leave work on time to pick him up. Since only a parent was allowed to pick up a child from this particular day-care center, Paula asked her sister to "pull a switch." Penelope easily substituted for her sister and retrieved her nephew. As they were walking to the parking lot, Richard looked up at her, saying, "Mommy, why do you have Aunt Penny's car?" Even Paula's son couldn't tell one from the other. And this, Paula pointed out, was during the years when they weren't actively trying to look alike.

Throughout our discussions, I continued to mull over what could possibly be propelling the sisters toward a greater sense of twinship as they aged. It is true that all of us experience a greater pull toward our families of origin once the "empty nest" phase begins. To a certain extent, as our children become more independent, we begin to look back toward our early families as a first step in trying to understand what our lives have become. And yet, five years earlier, when Penelope and Paula began to focus consciously on their twinship, they were certainly quite young to be beginning such "retrospective" work. At that time, Penelope had a ten-year-old and a seven-year-old, a marriage that was beginning its sixteenth year, and, perhaps, a growing sense that she was ceding center stage to the younger generation. Paula's thirteen-year-old son Richard had just moved back in with her and her new husband, Joe, and she was struggling to adapt to the rigors of motherhood and a new marriage all at once, after years of single life and part-time parenthood. What a lifeline that ad in the *Reader's Digest* must have seemed, for where else but with that other twin could the sisters so easily feel themselves to be special and fundamentally understood? In turning back to one another, the Francis sisters were turning to the one place where they could always cope, where they were always center stage and worthy of notice: their twinship.

Twin Envy

To a certain extent, twins take center stage to all of us: Most people experience wonder and envy at the thought of such perfect fusion, at the notion of having another half who so closely resembles oneself that perfect understanding is actually possible. The fantasy of having a twin is thought to be a very common childhood daydream, in which one revels in the thought of a constant companion who can relieve one's loneliness. A child can dream of another self who is more skilled in math or English, or with whom one can play innumerable tricks on teachers and parents. The twin fantasy also has its narcissistic aspects, as the psychologist Dorothy Burlingham points out, because in creating a dream "other" who is identical to oneself, a child is setting a seal of approval on his own being. As Emily Dickinson wrote: "I'm Nobody! Who are you?/Are you—Nobody—Too?/ Then there's a pair of us?/Don't tell! they'd advertise—you know!"

At the other extreme, as in Thomas Tryon's novel *The Other*, a fantasied twin (in this case, a dead one) can be the repository of the other twin's unbearably negative feelings and actions. If the other embodies all the evil, then the child himself can continue performing his murderous deeds with impunity, for he need not face his own rage and guilt.

In Thornton Wilder's *The Bridge of San Luis Rey*, the twins Esteban and Manuel feel "a curious shame in regard to their resemblance. They had to live in a world where it was the subject of continual comment and joking. It was never funny to them and they suffered the eternal pleasantries with stolid patience." And yet, despite the growing difficulties of their connection, when Manuel dies, twenty-two-year-old Esteban can find no reason to go on living. After he is foiled in an attempt to hang himself, he falls to the floor, crying, "I am alone, alone, alone." His subsequent death on the bridge seems almost fortuitous, the only possible outcome after such complete and perfect fusion with another.

A pair of twins is fascinating to look at. One immediately begins to scrutinize and compare them, and they always seem more attractive than they might if there were only one. For the parents of twins, some of the stress and strain of coping with two at once is alleviated by the pleasure of the flattering attention that the children garner. To encourage this, parents may dress the children alike, cut their hair similarly, even give them twin names like Bessie and Jessie. Psychologist Burlingham noted that some mothers (fathers' experiences were not described in this study) responded to comments about differences in their young twins as if the children were being insulted or disparaged. Both identical and fraternal twins tend to be treated this way when very young. However, as fraternal twins grow, their parents are likely to treat them more individually. Parents may take far longer to look for distinguishable traits between identical twins.

Nevertheless, there is a strong motivation for parents to come to know their identical twins as separate individuals. In Burlingham's study, she noted that mothers were often sure that they could tell their twins apart even when they were unable to. When a mother realized she had mistaken one twin for the other, she was mortified. "It is as if she feels that a mother should be able to distinguish between her babies," Burlingham writes, "and that it is a serious failing on her part when she cannot do that—it shows a lack of love."

Burlingham believes that until the mother was able to distinguish between her twins, she was unable to feel truly connected to either of them. (Thus, Penelope and Paula's mother kept their identity bracelets on for months until she felt certain that she could tell them apart.) One has to *know* who someone is, Burlingham theorized, to feel an identification in some basic sense, in order to feel the emotion of love for a particular child. Several of the mothers in her study stated this explicitly, saying that "it was impossible to love their twins until they had found a difference in them."

Though distinctions between twins are necessary to make, such differences are not typically very large, as the nineteenth-century genetic scientist Francis Galton observed. Galton claimed that when one is distinguishing personality characteristics in a set of identical twins, the distinctions must be considered simply a matter of intensity, for they do not "extend more deeply into the structure of the character. The difference [is] in the keynote, not in the melody."

Twins *do* get a great deal of pleasurable attention simply for being part of a duo. An identical twin may struggle with two conflicting ideas: the notion that he or she is more interesting or special than a regular child, and also the suspicion that each twin in the pair may be less a person than a nontwin. Twins may never really be sure that anyone knows them as particular selves, for even their parents struggle to identify them. Both Penelope and Paula described occasions when their own husbands had mistaken one for the other. Penelope told me that right before Paula's marriage to Joe, she'd stopped by their apartment and Joe started describing all the presents they had received, saying, "Honey, we got such nice stuff." She let him con-

tinue for just a minute, she said, before laughingly clueing him into
the fact that he was calling his future sister-in-law "honey." This
story was one both sisters enjoyed telling, along with other stories of
fooling teachers, employers, and dates. Funny as it was, the story
highlights the fact that an identical twin may only know one person
who can absolutely identify him or her without a moment's doubt.
That perceptive person is, of course, the other, the twin.

Even that isn't always the case: Paula told me that occasionally,
when she looks in the mirror, she thinks, "Gee, I look like Penelope
today." Penelope confessed, too, that sometimes when she plays back
her answering machine and hears her own voice leaving a message for
one of the kids, she thinks her sister has called to say hello. It was
Penelope also who told me that she was once riding up the escalator
in a department store when she saw her sister on the adjacent set of
moving stairs. "Hi!" she called, throwing up her arm to wave hello.
"Do you want to have lunch?" Suddenly Penelope realized, to her
complete embarrassment, that she was shouting at her own reflection
in a mirror.

That Private Inner Self

"I've spent hours with these women," I complained to Manhattan-
based marital and family therapist Hannah Fox. "They told me the
stories of their lives, but something was missing; it's almost as if I
can't get a picture of them as people."

Psychotherapist Fox had become one of my most important
guides to understanding what was actually taking place in the "under-
world" of my sibling case studies. We spoke almost weekly, and our
habit was this: I would present the family's stories to Fox, describing
not only the details they'd given me but also the emotional impressions I'd come away with. We would speculate about what possible
reasons a family member might have for feeling a certain way, or why
one sibling might behave one way and the other one, a different way.
We were both aware that the various explanations we arrived at were
only possibilities. Truth is a very flexible concept when it comes to
family interactions. Nothing is set in stone, and certainly all the family stories I presented to all the psychiatrists, psychologists, social

workers, and sociologists whom I interviewed were filtered through my own particular perceptions of the importance of certain events and my interpretation of apparent emotional states. Furthermore, I was altering certain details of my interviewees' lives to preserve their privacy, so ultimately, even if two people *could* analyze a third person's life story, it would have been completely impossible to determine where the siblings' true stories ended and my protective tale-telling began. Nevertheless, since I was trying to present these stories to reveal certain global aspects of siblingdom (rather than to assist the particular family, as a therapist would), the procedure seemed adequate for the purpose . . . until I tried to understand the lives of the Francis twins. For I truly seemed to be missing some important detail, some key aspect of who they were. Without that core sense, I felt, it would be impossible to write their life stories.

"They are really likable, nice women, and yet I found them disturbing," I admitted. "I think I've always fantasized that having a perfect other like that would be wonderful, but instead I now feel as if it must be an unpleasant way to live. Even though they seem perfectly content with it."

"Well, in this case, it seems as if having two people so alike is scary," Dr. Fox replied. "It's as if each one is always sharing herself with the other. Without a self which is your own, where could you ever go to be private, to be alone?"

"They may have shut down some aspects of themselves completely, because if they didn't, they would have to share it with one another," I agreed. "So it's better to ignore part of yourself than to let it out in the open and have it not be completely your own."

"If you are in a twinship and appear to have no inner life, perhaps it's because when you expose your feelings, the other twin gets them, too," Dr. Fox speculated. "So these emotions and urges aren't yours alone. The feelings belong to both of you."

"That was one thing they said to me, that they were both incredibly good sharers."

"Exactly. Neither of them owns anything of her own except her inner life, which she keeps so far inside in order to preserve it. Otherwise, she'd have to share it."

In other words, with either Paula or Penelope Francis, coming too close to knowing what she truly felt about herself and the world would have been tantamount to invading the only place where the private core of her being lay safe in its protected fortress, unexamined and unexposed. I recalled my early suspicion that twins were less willing to examine their relationships than other siblings. I now had the feeling that I was actually on to something. To some extent, the "fairy dust" of twindom might be available only to those who are willing, or able, to live under a particular set of psychological circumstances. No wonder I hadn't tapped into the inner core with Paula and Penelope Francis; it was no-man's-land.

Around her neck, Penelope Francis wears a gold chain. From the chain hangs the left side of a heart, edge jagged on the right where the other half has been cleaved. In neat printing, the word "twin" is engraved. Paula Francis has the right half around her neck, the side that reads "sister." Their plan is this: When the first sister dies, the second one will put the pieces together and wear the heart as a whole. When both sisters are dead, the necklace will be buried along with the second twin. Paula told me that she intended to spend eternity right next to her sister.

"What about Joe? And Penelope's Matthew? Will they be buried with you?"

"I guess so," Paula said, chuckling at the thought. "Joe will be watching football and Matt will be working on his car."

"What will you be doing?" I asked, laughing along with her.

"You know, we started as one person," Penelope interjected, her voice serious. "We were one being who separated into two, and I'm sure we'll end up that way again. One. You know?"

"Yes," agreed Paula, nodding slowly. "That's right." She reached over and took Penelope by the hand, as if with the gesture she could demonstrate how perfectly, despite their differences, she and her twin sister fit together.

CHAPTER FIVE

Catherine Pantera Guerra

"I Always Saw Her as My Roots"

Some people seem to nurture their early distresses, as if the tragedies of childhood had created scars that remain raised and red despite the passing of decades. Often, this is justified by a level of traumatic experience that simply cannot be put to rest easily. On the other hand, there are men and women who—after enduring unfathomably difficult ordeals—seem to stride through the world, resilient and undefeated. They are resolutely, perhaps defiantly, normal.

Even though Maria Pantera Albanese and her sister Catherine never actually hid the troubling details of their upbringing from me, it was nevertheless challenging to think of them as the survivors of an odd and difficult upbringing. There were two reasons for this view: First of all, both Maria and Cathy *looked* about as normal as they come, each a slim, well-groomed brunette in her late forties. Maria had several grown children, Cathy had a successful and well-compensated career; furthermore, each woman was in an enduring marriage and spoke about herself cheerfully. They were in regular contact with one another and with their elderly parents. It was counterintuitive to see them as risen from the ashes.

For a long time, I harbored a basic misunderstanding of what childhood had been like for Maria and Cathy. Each of the Pantera sisters spoke about their younger years with such good humor, as if what they described had been utterly unremarkable. And somehow, because our conversations lacked the affect of bitterness or, conversely, the blank dissociated quality of utter despair, I'd managed to miss the facts that had been presented to me.

Then, one afternoon, while listening once again to the tape of my initial interview with Maria, I suddenly understood how fundamentally traumatic the two sisters' childhood had been. Although I had listened to this section of the recording two or three times already, I had simply been unwilling or unable to hear the story she had told. This time, however, I fully grasped the impact of Maria's words.

On the tape Maria was laughing as she described their early life. "Oh, my father was at work from five in the morning until God knows when at night," she said cheerfully, "and my mother was out gambling, she just loved to gamble."

"Gambling?" I heard my voice asking on the tape. I was chuckling along with her.

"Oh, cards, you know. Bridge, canasta, anything. She would leave about three in the afternoon and play with her friends in the neighborhood until maybe three or four o'clock in the morning. So then she wouldn't be able to wake up in the morning to get us breakfast and, of course, our father would be gone."

"So what did you do?"

"Well, we lived in a neighborhood of row houses, and right next door there was this wonderful couple, Dick and Jane, just like the books. And his mother, her name was Britta, they were Dutch, I think. I remember them so well. From the time that I was, oh, four years old or even younger, every morning I would get up and run next door, still in my nightgown. I would have breakfast with them, they were my friends."

There was a long pause on the tape; in hindsight, I imagine I was retooling this story to fit it into my own concept of the Pantera childhood, for I have no recollection of feeling that there was a lack of parental involvement. Instead, I was drawing a parallel to the friendships I'd had with adults during my own childhood. In fact, however, having a mother who gambled all night and an absentee father was unusual, certainly very far from my own experience. I asked, "Were your parents paying them, Dick and Jane, to take care of you?"

"Oh, no, not at all," Maria said. "Things were different in those days, it was safer. I mean, nobody locked doors. Later, when we moved to an apartment, everyone in the building would sleep on the roof on hot nights. People were more trusting back then. I'm sure Dick and Jane were just being neighborly."

She continued. "In my own home, I remember thinking very early on that this was not my real family, that these people were not my parents. I hated the way they did things. I cared about all kinds of things that didn't matter to them. I always cared how I looked and how my room was arranged. The family was chaos, and I was organized. Most of my early memories were of Jane and Dick, and Britta, and being at their house. I admired them so much."

"They Were My Friends"

I had already flown south once to interview Maria and her sister Cathy; now, after reorienting myself to the new vision of their lives, which I'd finally acknowledged, I decided it was time to make another visit to their suburban Maryland community. It was clear that I had a great many more questions to ask them.

The answers were immediately forthcoming; probably both sisters had been puzzled initially at my failure to understand what they had been describing. As soon as we were seated in Cathy's sunny breakfast nook, Maria said, "I think I just felt that life was unfair from the beginning. Our mother was never home, our father made sure that someone fed us and all, but nobody cuddled us or hugged us or was affectionate."

"Well, that was true for you, I guess," Cathy said, "but my situation was different."

Maria's upper lip descended abruptly, halting the observation she had been about to make.

Cathy said, "You see, I had these friends, these neighbors, they were Dutch, and I used to spend every free minute with them. So I never really missed the lack of Mommy and Daddy, because I think I got so much loving from Britta and her kids."

For a moment, Maria appeared actually unable to speak. Cathy turned to look at her sister, surprised. "What?" she said. "What is it?"

"They were *my* friends, his name was Wouter but everybody called him—"

"Dick. I know, because she was Jane, his wife."

"They were *my* friends. I didn't know you even knew them. I never saw you there."

"That's impossible," Cathy said. "I was there all the time, every day. They were my family." She grinned at her sister. "I went there to get away from *you.*"

Maria turned to me, obviously bewildered. "This makes no sense," she said. "I mean, I was there all the time; how could she have been there?"

"I don't know," I said. "You mean you just don't remember seeing her there?"

"No. Never."

Cathy chuckled. "What was the name of their cat?"

"Benny." Maria sounded slightly angry, and I understood why. A piece of her childhood, perhaps the happiest part of it, was being appropriated by her little sister.

Cathy, on the other hand, seemed triumphant. "Well, I picked Benny. From a pet store. Jane and Britta took me to get him, and I picked him out."

Maria wore the dazed expression of a person who has been deeply shocked. I was, in fact, as puzzled as Maria by the manner in which these two sisters had cut each other out of their happiest childhood memories. There appeared to be some faulty wiring in what Proust called "the vast structure of recollection." Were they blocking a painful memory of some hostile or sexually tinged interaction? Several therapists whom I consulted raised this as a possibility, but after my fairly thorough description of the sisters' life stories, one expert pointed me to Sigmund Freud's essay on the family romance. In this short article, Freud describes the way in which a child who feels less than perfectly loved by his or her parents may resent having to share that love with a sibling. The resentful child may begin to fantasize about being a stepchild or adopted child, as if there were a more perfect family out there who would love him in the complete manner of which he dreams. If, as in this case, each of the Pantera girls developed the identical fantasy replacement family, why should each little girl's memory not permit her to bask in the unalloyed sunshine of Dick and Jane's love? For if the two most powerful forces are the needs for food and love and the Dutch neighbors were providing both, wouldn't happier memories be created by recalling these moments as unshared? A century ago, Sigmund Freud first wrote these important words:

> It may indeed be questioned whether we have any memories at all *from* our childhood: memories *relating to* our childhood may be all that we possess. Our childhood memories show us our earliest years not as they were but as they appeared at the later periods when the memories were revived. In these periods of revival, the childhood memories did not, as people are accustomed to say, *emerge;* they were *formed* at that time.

According to Freud, not only are our childhood memories formed later on in life, but they are formed as a result of that more mature self's current motives. In other words, memory is not about historical accuracy; rather, memory is about meeting a human need to know certain things and ignore others. While the role of Freudian thinking continues to be the subject of intense scrutiny and disagreement in the debates about recollection of childhood sexual abuse, Freud's position does seem appropriate in the case of the Pantera sisters. Maybe each of the girls simply needed to know that there was an adult out there in the world who cared enough about her to make sure she felt special and important. As unlucky as they had been in their "choice" of parents, it appeared that both Maria and Cathy had been fortunate that their parents selected a home on the particular Philadelphia block upon which Dick and Jane and Britta had also chosen a tiny row house.

"Our Mother Did Not Have a Happy Childhood"

I watched Maria and Cathy as they attempted to digest the information they had just stumbled upon, that they had shared an experience of love each had believed to be her own private one. I realized that the two sisters' driver's licenses probably contained the exact same information: height, five feet seven inches; weight, 130; hair, brown; eyes, brown. That was where the similarity ended, however, for they

looked—and sounded—nothing alike. Forty-nine-year-old Maria
was sharp and edgy, wide-eyed, pale and polished as the shiny interior of an oyster shell. Her dark brown hair was cropped in a Cleopa-
tralike bob. She spoke quickly and with ever-changing expression,
alert and excitable, her voice rising in dramatic surges to suit what
she described.

On the other hand, her sister Cathy, the younger by four years,
was one of those people who can actually be described as restful. She
was bigger-boned than Maria, all suntanned beiges and honey
browns, with shoulder-length hair, evenly made-up skin, smiling lips
the color of cappuccino; even her cotton sweater and leggings picked
up the same smooth, oatmeal tones. She spoke evenly, her voice
pleasant and her sentences measured and well thought out.

"Our mother did not have a happy childhood," Catherine said
then, as if she wanted me to know that she could empathize with
whatever difficulties her mother had undergone. "I don't think she
was ever enough for my grandmother; she could never do anything
so wonderful that it would make up for what the family had lost."

Cultures Are Slow to Die

As the late Irving Howe wrote, "Cultures are slow to die: When
they do, they bequeath large deposits of custom and value to their
successors; and sometimes they survive long after their more self-
conscious members suppose them to have vanished."

For example, as the noted expert on ethnicity and family relations
Monica McGoldrick explains, the reasons for migration to this country continue to influence a family's outlook for several generations.
Moreover, even well-assimilated families are affected; sometimes the
appearance of assimilation covers over a high degree of emotion and
ambivalence. In fact, it is suspected that the more a family represses
its cultural heritage, the more vulnerable the family will be to other
stresses in the present. A family that migrated, as the Panteras did, to
a primarily Italian section of Philadelphia, was under less pressure to
assimilate than the same family might have been had it landed in a
less ethnically diverse area. In fact, Luigi's and Anna Louisa's families
had emigrated from adjacent villages near Naples. A small circle of
relatives and neighbors hailing from the region formed their closest

social network, helping one another to maintain the traditions of the past even as the breadwinners in each family established themselves as American businessmen. (When questioned about why members of this more intimate circle had not been involved in their child care, both Maria and Cathy shrugged, unsure of the answer. Cathy subsequently speculated that perhaps her mother was ashamed of her gambling and wanted to keep the extent of her extrafamilial activities under wraps.)

One's cultural heritage has a significant effect on how the struggle to become a separate and autonomous adult will occur, and what family relationships will mean in adulthood. Ethnicity interacts with many other factors, including religion, social class, and the structure and experience of a particular family, but certain generalizations apply to many members of a specific cultural group. In an Italian family, when a young adult becomes separate and moves away—as both the Pantera sisters did—the family as a whole is perceived as having failed to raise its children properly. To traditional Italians, family is the most important support in times of trouble, the only legitimate place to turn. In effect, traditional Italian families maintain strong boundaries against the outside world, gathering together in times of trouble to eat, cry, and vent their emotions. Even in a more fragmented situation like that of the Panteras, these values were seen as important. Only family could be trusted to act in one's best interests. Traditional Greeks are also perceived as maintaining similarly strong ties to their families of origin.

According to psychologists David McGill and Dr. John K. Pearce, on the other hand, members of a traditional WASP family will feel they have failed if their progeny do *not* move away and establish themselves as independent individuals. In a typical WASP family, relatives are far from eager to "trouble" one another with confidences about personal troubles. In times of trouble, a WASP tends to withdraw, wanting to think the problem through alone. A traditional Jew in the same situation would want to analyze the difficulty with others, but for a WASP, to endure and maintain a stiff upper lip is the highest virtue; complaining is perceived as a self-indulgence that strains relationships. As a result, traditional WASP friendship among siblings and other close family members tends to center, for the most part, around shared activity.

As a whole, sibling relationships seem to be highly culturally valued among the Irish. According to McGoldrick, "Unlike parents and children, adult siblings function on a plane of general equality." Despite the lack of a societal obligation to care for unmarried brothers and sisters, and a tendency toward hostile or indifferent relations between men and women, ". . . brother-sister relationships constituted the only cross-gender relationships sanctioned by the society." One study found the Irish to be one of the few ethnic groups in which siblings are visited as often as parents are. The Irish, noted McGoldrick, tend to feel guilty if they fail to become friends with their siblings.

In African American families, female siblings can be of intense, lifelong importance, particularly in terms of child care and other forms of assistance. For African American women, according to Paulette Moore Hines and Nancy Boyd-Franklin of the Community Mental Health Center of Rutgers Medical School, the sister-sister relationship is generally not an optional one, for "relatives expect and accept reliance on one another in times of need and often live in close proximity. Various people interchange roles, jobs and family functions."

In an American Jewish family, adult sibling rivalry often manifests itself as competition over who has been the better child, been more successful, given more, married better, or raised better children. Because of the emphasis on emotional revelation in Jewish culture, a sibling can become involved in a vicious cycle of devaluing the others in order to feel better about him- or herself and subsequently responding to others' retaliatory needling. Although rivalrous feelings are often very strong among Jewish siblings, the sense of family is intense as well. In one 1978 study in the Chicago area, mothers were asked who would care for their children in the event that both father and mother were dead. Nearly 75 percent of the Jewish mothers chose one of their own relatives, while 48 percent of Catholics and only 31 percent of Protestants chose a family member.

Asians approach the family from an entirely different perspective, for traditionally the present family is perceived as only part of a long line extending generations into the past (and the future). Individual actions are not seen as personal matters, for they will impact a family for generations. The oldest son in a family remains the most important member of his generation, and he takes over leadership of the family when his father dies. This role is a mixed bag, for the eldest must serve as a role model and leader. Often, younger siblings are freer to evade traditional expectations of behavior that the eldest cannot. As traditional attitudes loosen, however, the role of an eldest *son* is becoming that of an eldest *child*, since women are increasingly viewed as being able to fill that position.

Inherited Patterns

Cultural patterns intermingle with family patterns and become normative habits of behavior that repeat and reverberate through the generations. Such repetitive modes of interaction may not be apparent to the naked eye, because one generation's response can be a reflection or a repudiation of a trait in the previous generation—or any reaction in between. Thus, an alcoholic's daughter becomes a teetotaler, or perhaps an overeater. One gambler's daughter (Maria) marries a man whose subsequent career transports her from struggle, to enormous wealth, to near poverty and back again, largely because of his inability to predict the consequences of impulsive actions. The gambler's other daughter (Cathy) not only maintains her own self-sufficient career but also marries a man who is even more risk-averse than she. The manifestation of the problem, and the solution, can be completely different, but the underlying issues of control of self and others, and compulsive behavior, remain of paramount importance.

In order to understand the lives and relationships of the Pantera sisters, it is critical to acknowledge the overall patterns of interacting that they have inherited. By examining the Pantera family's history and considering the impact of the cultural values they inherited, we can begin to trace the factors of chance and expectation in the evolution of who each sister has become, and what they mean to each other.

Maria and Catherine's mother, Anna Louisa, was herself the second child and first daughter of her immigrant parents. Anna Louisa's next sister, Carmela, was born with Down's syndrome. The next child, a boy, lived only nineteen months before he died unexpectedly from a ruptured appendix. As if this series of family devastations were not enough, Anna Louisa's last sister, Angela, born three years after the boy's death, was soon found to be severely mentally retarded.

No wonder Anna Louisa became such an avid cardplayer, I thought, when her daughters described her early history: While she had no doubt expected to rear a family of her own, the odds of finding happiness in raising children must have seemed well-nigh nonexistent. She must have seen simply getting pregnant as a serious gamble; is it a surprise that other games of chance came so easily to her?

To Anna Louisa's older brother, Ettore, came the only emotional rewards the family was capable of doling out. He was his mother's foremost pleasure in life, despite the fact that Anna Louisa handled the bulk of the work involved in caring for their elderly parent. In fact, Anna Louisa's lifelong focus of devotion was to her own mother and the Sisyphean task of trying to make her happy. Did the girls' father, Luigi, resent such a diversion of his wife's attentive devotion?

"Well, honestly, no, I don't think so," replied Cathy when I asked this question. "His older sister Adelina was the one he was busy fretting about. She was married to an alcoholic, always short of money, always ill and needing something. I can't remember when my dad didn't worry about Adelina."

Luigi and Anna Louisa were intolerant and unhappy with one another. They bickered all the time, complained about each other's traits and behaviors constantly, but would never have considered divorce or separation. "Nothing's done graciously between them, and we learned that from them," Cathy said. "Bantering, sometimes cruel discussions of family life are part of our *modus operandi*. It's often very funny, but it doesn't necessarily reflect the reality of the feelings."

"It sounds like *Fiddler on the Roof*," I said. "Remember the song 'Do You Love Me?' " I was thinking of the moment when Tevye gets his long-suffering wife to admit reluctantly that twenty-five years of shared children and home, of so many of life's troubles and joys, probably means that they *do* love one another.

"Yes," Cathy said with a laugh. "That's it exactly."

Cathy told me that her father, Luigi Pantera, had inherited a small distributorship, which he ran as a one-person shop until he sold it in order to retire; her mother confined her social life to a small circle of relatives and neighbors. The Panteras "practiced anonymity as if it were a high art form," according to their younger daughter, never even exercising the right to vote because they feared being called for jury duty. They feared many things that most of us consider to be inalienable rights, including change, ambition, and yearning; they were content to be part of the great mass of society.

"To our parents, it was dangerous to be known. If you were noticed, you could get hurt. Hey, maybe that's it," Catherine said slowly, as if she realized it for the first time. "Yes, I'm sure that's one reason they had so much trouble with you."

She turned to face Maria, who remained expressionless, and then she turned back toward me. "Maria was just so certain of what was right and wrong, so willing to stand up for herself."

Not only was Maria stubborn and full of conviction, but this firstborn child was also a girl. Anna Louisa had learned from her own mother that daughters were not rewarding, only sons. Sons "light up the room," as Anna Louisa's brother Ettore did; at their best, daughters are long-suffering, inadequate, and unhappy. At their worst, daughters are sickly and dependent, barely functioning human beings. In the mythology of this family, a daughter could never give enough or be enough. Thus, at the time of Maria's birth, Anna Louisa found her flawed, simply because she was not the expected son. "It wasn't as if our mother tried to hide her feelings," Cathy said. "She really didn't think girls were worth as much as boys."

Maria shrugged. "I really was difficult, you know."

In the silence that fell, I thought back to a telephone conversation I'd had with Cathy only a few days previously. She'd told me, "My mother always said I was a joy to take care of, happy and smiling all the time."

I didn't have to make a leap of faith in order to believe that this calm, measured person had never caused anyone any anxiety in her life. But even as edgy and witty as her sister Maria was, it wasn't easy to believe that she could have been the family demon. "Oh, no, it's true, but it was more than that." Maria rolled her eyes heavenward and groaned. "I was so unhappy at home that I didn't know what it was to be happy. I remember being annoyed and angry all the time. Life just wasn't joyful for me until I left home."

"Why?"

"Our mother," Maria said, looking toward her sister for confirmation. Cathy nodded. "She got married when she was nineteen. Just to get away from her own terrible home, and then the home she made was just as bad. Besides, she was too young when she had me, she really wasn't ready for a child. She was a baby herself."

Cathy chuckled. Maria and I turned to look at her. "She didn't have a child, she had you," Cathy said, grinning hugely. "Oh, my God, the poor woman." Both sisters burst out laughing; after a moment, I joined in.

Difficult Maria

The Pantera sisters were a perfect example of real sibling connection, two unique individuals who were the living personification of what Ralph Waldo Emerson once wrote: "Relation and connection are not somewhere and sometimes, but everywhere and always." The connection between siblings is based upon randomness and accident, but the fruits of such a bond are often rich in endowment.

I found their friendship even more interesting because their relationship had begun in such an unpromising fashion. That Maria really *was* a difficult child was reiterated time and again by both sisters. Over and over they told me that she had been isolated and moody, with few friends, that she had squabbled constantly with Anna Louisa, that she had been cruel to Cathy.

Maria used precisely the same words that Cathy had to paint a picture of herself as a child: "I was a miserable, mean kid," she said proudly, as if surviving such an early self was a badge of honor. "I was very unhappy and unsatisfied all the time, and I tried my best to make everyone else unhappy, too."

"Cathy? Did you like her?"

"We shared a bedroom, so she was always in the way."

The room, Maria said, was so tiny that Cathy's trundle had to be pulled out from underneath Maria's bed each evening. The trundle used up every available inch of space. Once Cathy got into bed, neither girl could leave the room again for the night. The door was completely blocked.

Cathy interrupted with a chuckle. "I tried to stay out of the room when she was in there."

"At best, I ignored her," Maria continued. "She was so different from me, she had lots of friends, she was always laughing and talking on the phone. Mostly I just pretended she wasn't there. But when she got in my way, watch out." She laughed again in that proud, even defiant, manner.

Cathy remembered one afternoon after school, when she was perhaps nine or ten years old. She and a friend were playing in the apartment, and at one point the friend sat on Maria's bed. "It was like Goldilocks and the Three Bears when Maria got home," Cathy said. "She was stomping around the house yelling, '*Who* was sitting on *my* bed?' I wasn't going to tell her. She wasn't frightening, she wasn't physical, but she was mean."

"Was there anything good about you," I asked Maria, "or were you just a completely horrible kid?"

Maria didn't miss a beat before answering, and Cathy smiled in confirmation. Clearly, the Pantera sisters understood their family legacy in precisely the same terms. "I was the family beauty, that was it. My mother used to joke that Cathy was so ugly when she was an infant that she would keep her face down on the couch. But Cathy was good, and friendly, and smart, and easy to get along with. I was just the pretty one. It was the only good thing about me, I think."

Cathy stood up. "If you ask me, these things, these ideas, they take on a life of their own," she said.

Siblings in Psychoanalytic History

The best resource for illuminating the details of current thinking about human personality development is undoubtedly Yale University professor of psychiatry Theodore Lidz's classic textbook *The Person*. The treatment of sibling relationships in this fascinating book is quite typical of mainstream psychological thinking on the topic. Overall, Dr. Lidz spends a few pages of this 600-page work acknowledging that the sibling bond is significant and important to the development of behavioral patterns and personality, even though he has chosen not to focus upon it in this work. He writes:

> Children establish life patterns not only through how their attachment to the
> parent of the opposite sex is resolved, but also through how they find or seek to

find a place within the family, with parents, siblings, and any other significant persons in the home.

[These children] are reacting in response not only to their own egocentric appreciation of the situation and their fantasies about it, but also to the way in which the other family members relate to them. . . .

. . . Sibling relationships can be almost as profoundly influential as the relationships with parents, and a person's relatedness to a brother or sister is often closer and more meaningful than the relationship to parents.

Dr. Lidz says it all, even though he doesn't go into detail. In a footnote he points to Sigmund Freud's *Totem and Taboo.* I followed Professor Lidz's guidance, and found myself embarked on an adventure of my own, a kind of magical mystery tour of sibling themes throughout psychoanalytic history.

Once I began to look for it, I saw that an undercurrent of sibling consciousness has run through psychological writings from Sigmund Freud onward. In 1909, for example, when Freud published his famous analysis of Little Hans's phobia of horses, he explicitly stated that the "most important influence upon the course of Hans's psychosexual development was the birth of a baby sister when he was three and a half years old. That event accentuated his relations to his parents and gave him insoluble problems to think about.

"This influence, too, is a typical one," wrote Freud, for "in an unexpectedly large number of life-histories, normal as well as pathological, we find ourselves obliged to take as our starting-point an outburst of sexual pleasure and sexual curiosity connected, like this one, with the birth of the next child."

In fact, an awareness of sibling themes runs rampant throughout psychological theory and discourse, always as the bridesmaid and never as the bride. Such themes continually surface as meaningful influences in the life histories of the field's most eminent thinkers, from Freud himself to Alfred Adler, Helene Deutsch, and Melanie Klein. Sibling issues are present everywhere, hiding behind Mom as she rushes around anxiously looking for the minister, or cowering in the corner where Grandpa is discreetly sipping his third scotch of the afternoon. They don't get the same attention as the Main Event, but everybody seems to remember how they behaved at the reception, even long after the party's end.

The Confused Bridesmaid

I came to the analogy of the bridesmaid and the bride because of a story that Cathy told me about her older sister's wedding. Cathy had been only fifteen when nineteen-year-old Maria married Arthur, her high school sweetheart. Cathy, more than thirty years later, still recalls the way her older sister looked walking down the aisle on their father's arm. "She was so beautiful, I couldn't stop staring, and I kept thinking if only I looked like her I could get away with anything."

"What would you have wanted to get away with?"

Cathy chuckled good-naturedly. "Well, you have to understand that Maria was just the most horrible, mean person in the world. The whole time we were growing up, I never spoke a word to her if I could help it. She terrified me."

She paused for a moment, as if the memory itself could raise a frightened feeling. Eventually she said, "We shared a bedroom, but we acted as if the other one didn't exist. To say we had no relationship is an understatement."

"Really?" I asked. It didn't seem possible to ignore someone that completely for such an extended period of years.

"If she went in the room, I went out. It was as simple as that. Oh, she was so selfish and unhappy even my parents complained about her. Then she got married and all of a sudden she wasn't cranky anymore. I remember I was panicked," Cathy said, smiling calmly as if the memory now amused her. "I mean, she'd always been the pretty sister but oh, was she mean. I'd always been the ugly one, but I was nice and everyone knew it. I remember at her wedding, she and Art were dancing and laughing and visiting every table to say hello. They were so perfect, and I remember thinking, well, if she's going to be nice from now on, then what happens to me?"

"What did you do? Did you dance on the tables, or start making nasty comments about your relatives?" I was joking, but I wondered what Cathy had actually done, for this event, thirty years ago, had marked the turning point in their relationship. I already knew that Cathy Pantera Guerra and Maria Pantera Albanese had gone on from the mutual standoff of their childhood hostilities to become the best of friends. How had this dramatic transition taken place?

"It's funny," Cathy said quietly, "but that was a hard moment for me. It was a conscious problem, who would I be now that nobody was mad at her, and I remember that I didn't know what to do so I just acted like myself. My normal self. And after the wedding, my mother was mad at me. She said I didn't dance enough, wasn't out there on the dance floor being happy for Maria. And it was so unfair; nobody even *asked* me to dance. What was I supposed to do?"

"So something changed that day?"

"Yes," Cathy said. "And after that day, things changed even more. I wasn't sitting in the catbird seat anymore. I seemed to get in trouble with my parents much more, I wasn't the good sister being compared to the bad one anymore."

"You must have been angry at Maria."

"Well, that's the funny thing. I'd always been angry at her, because she was so awful. And then when she started to be nicer, just at the same time that my mother began to be more critical of me, well, I just switched allegiances. She was easier to be around, and I began to prefer her. Now I think she's probably my best friend in the world.

"You see," Cathy said, leaning across her tiled breakfast bar eagerly, "it would be easy to be her bridesmaid now. Once she started to act like she liked me, it was the easiest thing to like her back, to want the best for her. I'd always wanted to be her friend, underneath all the hostilities."

"What happened to change that antagonistic childhood relationship into such a positive one?" I asked. "How did you become friends?"

The two sisters had different memories of exactly how their friendship developed. Catherine recalled painstakingly hand-painting each small bathroom tile in Maria and Art's first apartment, so that the blue bath towels received as wedding gifts wouldn't clash with the original decor. "The bathroom had real tiny tiles, and they were mostly white, but there were gold and yellow ones as well. And she'd been given these blue towels, so I spent several weekends hand-painting each of the little tiles blue to match."

"You did?" Forty-nine-year-old Maria had been listening intently as Catherine spoke, but now she interrupted, shaking her head from side to side. She said, "I have no memory of that. I remember that after the kids were born, you used to come around more, that's when I think I started to really enjoy your company."

Cathy shrugged. "Maybe."

Maria continued to shake her head, no.

Cathy leaned forward toward me, mock confidentially, and said, "I painted those tiles, believe me."

Maria said again, "I have no memory of that."

Cathy shrugged again, and they were silent.

Maria said, "If Arthur were here, doors would be slamming just about now." Both sisters laughed, letting me know that they were dismissing the topic without closing it, that they were agreeing to disagree, that for *them*, this was not an issue worth tangling over.

Neither woman actually remembers a specific day, thirty years ago, when their relationship suddenly became a good, active friendship. Perhaps, over time—and without that need to make distance and space which evolved out of sharing a tiny bedroom for so many years—the sisters had become less competitive, and realized that they actually *liked* each other.

Both sisters agreed that Maria had become a different, easier, much happier person once she was out of their parents' apartment and on her own. "I hadn't even known that Maria had a sense of humor. Now I think she's one of the funniest people I know," Cathy told me. "She and my mother were always fighting, as long as I can remember. They still fight, even now, but it's not the same. After Maria had her boys, my mother would have forgiven her anything."

Cathy explained her belief that she and her sister had each lived out half of their mother's fantasy of the perfect life. "My mother would have liked to have had several sons and no daughters, the way Maria did. My mother had such a terrible relationship with her own mother, and saw how nice a bond there was with her brother, my uncle." Maria's dramatic eyes narrowed angrily as her sister spoke, but she continued to nod in agreement. It clearly wasn't Cathy who enraged her.

Cathy continued. "Me, well, I had an independent life for many years. I married late, I was financially secure and had lived on my own. I had no children. We were the two sides of what my mother really wanted."

"She's Where I Come from in the World"

"It's funny now that we got along so badly as children," Cathy had told me in one of our early phone calls. I had a fantasy at this time about what she looked like, based on her evenly modulated voice, and the dry way in which she stated her opinions: I was sure that she was much taller and larger than she turned out to be, a woman with more of a physical presence. Cathy's voice is not loud or deep, but it implies such great reserves of warmth that one might imagine they could only be contained in a much bigger person. "For all that we didn't connect in childhood, once Maria got married and left the house, she instantly became the most important member of my family. I always saw her, not my parents, as the place I returned to. I always saw her as my roots."

"Your roots? What does that mean?"

"Maria is the person I complain to when things go wrong, the person I turn to when I need to know something," explained Cathy. "She's where I come from in the world, what centers me. I trust her to be there for me no matter what."

Now we were face-to-face in Cathy's kitchen. Maria had left to pick up a gift for her elder son's wife, who was pregnant. She would return in a few hours, but for now I was alone with Cathy. This afternoon would be my last in-person opportunity to talk with each sister solo.

I wanted to know more about the substance and history of Cathy's relationship with her sister. She smiled, as if simply thinking about her sister was pleasurable.

"We talk all the time, we're just there for one another. If we have an argument, we ignore it, or talk about it, but it doesn't linger. We get over it." Cathy shrugged, as if not precisely sure how to describe a relationship which was, for her, not optional, not a question—her bond with Maria was an immutable fact of life. "We're friends," she said. "Friends."

But what, I asked again, had Catherine meant by calling Maria her roots? What precisely did she mean by the word "roots"?

Cathy stopped for a moment, staring up at the simple white cabinets behind me. For the first time since we began our interviewing, she seemed to be stymied. It appeared that by asking this question again, I had finally by chance raised a sisterly issue that the two hadn't previously discussed. One thing that had become increasingly clear, as I interviewed the Pantera sisters, was that theirs was a very conscious relationship. Theirs was a connection that worked because its participants were willing to work on it. They *knew* about the bond between them, and they had, in the main, agreed to the terms of their friendship.

I looked around. Evidence to support Cathy's industrious nature was visible everywhere. She'd already explained that the large green and rose fruit bowl at my elbow was her work, as were two white-paper-shaded pottery lamps that hung over the table, suspended on thick electrical cord. She'd taken up pottery, she told me, after knee problems ended a decade of long-distance running. "I like to stick with things," she'd said, somewhat apologetically. "I'm not bored with the familiar, I feel comfortable with it."

I waited while she considered her answer, watching as several cheerful little brown birds dove and swooped, delicately selecting little yellow seeds from the feeder on the terrace. I could hear cars accelerating in the distance, the sound of their engines intermingling with the high, sweet chirping closer by. Cathy cleared her throat.

"It's funny," she said. "Roots don't simply mean making a solid base, or a history. They can strangle, I guess. But that's not it." Cathy told me that when she was in her mid-twenties, she'd been shocked to learn that Arthur and Maria were moving to Europe so that her brother-in-law could establish a new office of the consumer products firm for which he was working. It was a sudden and very important promotion; everyone was extremely proud and excited for him. Maria and Arthur left rapidly, after a great hysterical flurry of packing and planning, dramatic phone calls and crying. And then, after two exhausting weeks, Cathy's sister was gone. "I had never thought about them leaving, I guess. They were gone, and I really felt as if I had nowhere to turn," she told me, a half-empty cup turning round uneasily between her hands.

Cathy was working at a hospital in Philadelphia at the time, the first woman in her family to support herself, or to live alone in an apartment. She had not yet met Tony Guerra, who would become her husband. "I had lots of friends, my college roommates, people I worked with. But I missed Maria. It's no coincidence that I went into therapy right after she left."

She leaned forward to inspect my face, her pale brown eyes scanning mine to make sure that I understood. "That's what I mean by roots. I'd be more likely to run to her house with a problem than to a friend's. She was gone for four years, and I think more than anything, that's when I realized how much she mattered to me. When she was gone, I felt lonely, and like I needed someone to count on. I missed her a lot."

Was Anna Louisa this close to her elder brother Ettore? I asked because I was trying to find out what kind of example was set for Maria and Cathy by the previous generation. The answer was that they did learn from their elders, but in a slightly different manner from the one I had suspected. "It's not that Anna Louisa and Ettore don't like one another. They definitely do. But my mother's best friend was his wife, Gloria, from the time they were in high school until she died of cancer a few years ago."

For the Pantera women, friendship appeared to exist solely between women in the same generation. Mothers and daughters, in the family tradition, rarely brought each other happiness (except perhaps in the form of that exalted commodity, grandsons). Sisters provided comfort and affection. Sons were more important than anything else. And husbands, it appeared, were difficult, childlike, and to be disdained—but not discarded.

Coming of Age in 1968

"There's something else you need to understand," Cathy told me. "That four-year age difference between me and Maria made an enormous difference in terms of when we came of age, of what we expected from life. Maria got married in the early 1960s, and I was at Columbia during the student uprisings. We really grew up in different worlds."

It was true. In March 1968, more than a quarter-century before our conversation, when Cathy Pantera was just twenty, young people everywhere were yearning for lives full of originality and freedom. Youth, in fact, was what gave life meaning; only the young were willing to fight the system, to risk themselves to change the world.

"I think Maria's sense of me changed then, that she appreciated me as a kind of bridge to the real world. I helped her understand the way things were changing. She respected me more because I knew things she wanted to know."

Reminiscing several decades afterward, literary critic Morris Dickstein encapsulated the Sixties in the following note:

> Growing up, I had always been a good boy. It was hard to know what "good" meant anymore. Was killing people good? Was smoking dope good? Was group sex good? Was it good if it felt good . . . or only if it were conducive to the Good? The sixties were more given to the collective loss of inhibition, the assertion of group ethos and solidarity, than to collective law-breaking. Not since Prohibition had there developed such a gap between the stated norms of society and the actual behavior. In one way or another a large number of Americans learned to live outside the pale, as it were, in a separate state, an alternative culture.

And, as America emerged from the 1950s, living "outside the pale" took on so many forms that it could even be used to categorize those of the vast mass of university students who did not themselves elect to "tune in, turn on, drop out," or to become active in the peace movement, the civil rights movement, or the women's movement.

In April 1968, Cathy Pantera hovered at the edge of the alternative culture, curious and intrigued but far from eager to renounce the wage-earning life for which she had spent years studying diligently. She was still, in her own words, a "nice girl" who played by societal rules, and she was just about to graduate from the nursing program at Columbia University, the first member of her family ever to graduate from college. To Cathy's family, what she was doing was daring and unusual enough to be considered outside the pale. Unlike her older sister, and her mother before her, she had not married straight out of high school, but had instead elected to get an education.

This was a heady, dramatic, even dangerous time: Radical students had taken over several Columbia campus buildings to protest the university's sponsorship of war-related research and the school's plans to erect a gymnasium in the midst of a public park in Harlem. But for Cathy, and for many of her colleagues up at the medical school on 168th Street, far from the main campus, the revolution might have been taking place on another planet. "We were so different from them, we even still had a dress code," Cathy recalled. "I remember how surprised I was when one of my professors raised the idea that we could go down to the campus and get involved. It hadn't even occurred to me.

"Radicalized? Me?" Cathy chuckled softly, the corners of her golden-brown eyes crinkling into friendly and experienced creases when I asked her if she did head downtown to get involved? She shook her head from side to side, no, with some amusement. "I mean, I sympathized with the cause, I was against the war and all," she said. "But I never had a sense that I was part of history. I wasn't the type to be an activist or anything, although in my family's eyes I probably looked as daring as anyone. I did my share of wild things, those were the times to do crazy stuff, but I was never a joiner. I was always just me."

I could tell that Catherine was still "just me," pleasant to look at, a reasonable person in every way. Now, twenty-five years later, the decisions she made, or didn't, in 1968 seemed as plausible for her even-tempered character as they probably did back then. "In 1969, I was the only girl at Woodstock with a matching pocketbook and shoes," she told me, with that same light chuckle. "I spent the entire weekend looking for a clean bathroom."

"Why did you go?" I asked.

"Why did anyone go?" she answered. "We all went, everyone. It seemed so important at the time."

The War of the Husbands

"I could have another husband," Maria Albanese stated flatly, seemingly unaware of the dramatic impact of this statement, particularly in light of her thirty years of marriage, three sons, and the fact that she has never held a paying job. She was taking me on a grand tour of the small city where she lives, a place she has called home for ten years. It was late on a damp, hot afternoon. The thick urban air made breathing difficult. We sped down a multilaned road, past gray miles of strip mall after strip mall, without seeing people walking anywhere. The cars passing us were big, clean, and American; windows were always rolled up to keep the hot air out and the cool air in. We seemed to be part of a triumphant parade of chamois-polished vehicles, lacking only the happy bystanders waving flags who could have cheered us along our way.

Rumpled and exhausted, I glanced over at Maria. I realized, immediately and enviously, that she was as fresh as she had been earlier that morning, when we'd first met face-to-face. She drove expertly, clearly inured to the terrors of six-lane city roads. "I could have another husband," she said again, still watching the road, steering confidently. "He could die, we could divorce. But I will always have Cathy. She will always be my sister." A long pause followed, which was finally broken when Maria pointed out a gray elephant of a structure, a new sporting complex, which appeared on my right.

As I stared out the window at the huge cement malformation, Maria mentioned quite casually that her husband, Arthur, hadn't spoken to Cathy's husband, Tony, in three years.

"What? What do you mean?" I was amazed to hear this, largely because neither of the sisters had thought to mention such a significant piece of information to me previously during many hours of conversation over the telephone and in our in-person interviews.

The fight between Art and Tony had simmered for a long time before it actually exploded. Maria explained that she and Arthur had moved from Atlanta shortly after he'd lost his executive-level corporate job in a company restructuring. "He was one of the best in his business. Everyone knew that, but the company was doing so poorly. And Arthur is a short-tempered man, so he was a natural fall guy. In twenty years, he'd angered enough people to fill a book."

Arthur had been offered two jobs within a week of the layoff, but neither was at the level of his previous position. Their sons were finishing college and, although the financial risks were large, they decided to move nearer to Cathy and Tony and see what opportunities were available. "We thought he might start his own firm," Maria explained as she pulled the car into the turnaround in front of my hotel. "I was pretty naive about the risks. We both were."

Arthur's management consulting business ran at a loss for several years, and money was very tight. Tony, who owned a real estate appraisal firm, was able, even eager, to loan them money on a number of occasions. "We had a good deal of severance pay in the bank at first, but then it got hard for a while. I don't know if we could have paid our bills without Tony and Cathy," Maria said.

My hotel boasted a nondescript little bar in which I thought that we could sit awhile, undisturbed, in order to continue our conversation. Once we were settled at a small table, with glasses of soda water before us, Maria described the way in which Tony had changed after making the loans. Tony and Arthur were both bullheaded, and they'd always been bossy and opinionated, she said, but they had managed to enjoy one another's company. They played tennis together, and bridge, and the two families often threw joint parties and dinners. Then, as Maria put it, the money changed hands. "Tony acted like Arthur shouldn't make a business decision without talking to him, as if my husband didn't have years of experience in management."

One day, Tony learned that Arthur had taken a mutual friend and two potential clients to play golf. Tony was furious; he felt that Arthur should have invited him along "to keep an eye on things." The blowup between the two husbands reached a legendary level, and since that time their mutual rancor had maintained itself through "fantastic interpretations of each other's actions. They can read malice into the way a glass of orange juice is poured. Neither of them has behaved well," said Maria.

The next morning, I was surprised—and pleased—to find Cathy waiting in the departures area at the airport. "I wanted to say goodbye," she said shyly. I was moved to see that she had brought a small doll as a gift for my daughter.

As we waited for my flight to be called, I asked Cathy about the battle of the husbands. She essentially concurred with Maria's interpretation that both men were to blame. "They are both, in their way, extremely difficult men," she told me. Cathy believed that for Tony, at least, the battle was also about the relationship between the two sisters. Tony, himself an oldest brother, had always believed that in some way Cathy's loyalty to Maria was greater than her loyalty to him. His efforts to help Arthur were not simply benevolent; they were, as well, an attempt to seize control (or so it appeared to all the other players in this family mini-drama).

Was Tony right? Did Cathy feel more loyalty to Maria than to her husband?

This was a question she had clearly spent a good deal of time considering, and once again she was quite sure of her answer. "Tony has turned out to be a great deal like Maria was as a child," she told me. "He's cranky a lot of the time, and what I learned early is that the best way to deal with cranky people is to avoid situations that will get them upset." She laughed. "And to avoid them completely when the unavoidable happens, and they start going bonkers."

I nodded, curious to know where she was leading.

"Maria and I never get angry at each other. We get along. You could say that I'm easygoing and she overlooks a lot," she continued, checking to make sure I'd gotten the joke. I nodded, and smiled.

She kept looking at me, smiling in return. The pause continued for just a moment longer and then I realized that she was finished. Cathy Pantera Guerra had answered my question.

Maintaining Boundaries

Despite the many emotionally wrought, all-consuming sibling relationships of literature and myth, real-life brothers and sisters generally manage (most of the time!) to neutralize their feelings toward one another. The concept of deidentification, discussed in Chapter Two, is just one way in which siblings unconsciously labor to prevent jealous or angry feelings from spiraling out of control. Just as one learns to maintain appropriate boundaries with spouses, children, parents, friends, and co-workers, an individual erects defining walls with siblings, limiting each relationship to some personal set point of bearable intimacy. As sibling experts Stephen Bank and Michael Kahn acknowledge in *The Sibling Bond*, geographic separation is perhaps the most convenient, socially acceptable way to establish such a boundary: Moving halfway across the country is certainly one method for avoiding confrontation. "Such lack of contact reflects no lack of feeling," write Bank and Kahn, "but is, instead, an energetic neutralization of anger, guilt and competition."

Many of the brothers and sisters in the population that psychologists Bank and Kahn treated and studied initially described their relationships in neutral terms, unaware that they actually had reserves of emotion tied up in a sibling's sphere of influence. Other siblings "seemed so confused about their feelings that it was hard to know what they really were," write Bank and Kahn. And still others lapsed into stereotypical comments, or seemed comfortable only when speaking in the abstract about their sibling connections. These kinds of confused, diffuse descriptions may actually be defensive postures, speculate the two Connecticut psychologists, adopted in order to keep disturbing and rivalrous feelings in check. In other words, neutral feelings are fairly unlikely where a sibling is concerned: A sister who "has no feelings" about her brother may actually be creating a shroud of disinterest to protect herself from feelings of resentment and rage.

Geography and the denial of emotional content are just two ways in which adult siblings make distance from one another. There are other methods that people use to control the natural feelings of competition, envy, or resentment that are often the hallmarks of a shared physical, emotional, and intellectual inheritance. One defensive posture that brothers and sisters frequently adopt to avoid experiencing jealousy and rage is to devalue another sibling's worth. If the image of this bossy elder brother or this manipulative youngest girl can easily be torn apart by the skeptical eyes of an all-knowing sibling, well, then, who needs to worry about him or her? The former rival is vanquished, beneath contempt, simply not worth worrying about. Why bother to be upset about someone as pitiable as all that?

The alternative, note Bank and Kahn, is to idealize the sibling, to view him or her as all good, all benevolence and talent. "By idealizing a brother, one can avoid feeling and facing vengeful thoughts that might tarnish one's own cherished ideas of brotherly kindness." One is, not surprisingly, far more likely to idealize a sibling who seems more like oneself. Thus, an identical twin, particularly one with a strong sense of self-worth, would tend to hold positive opinions about the other with whom the womb was once shared.

Frequently, siblings come to accept one another because of the experience of their common childhood and shared parents. The tendency to minimize differences among adult brothers and sisters derives from the sense that solidarity is more valuable—and more virtuous—than maintaining a childishly accurate family ledger of perceived wins and losses.

And, upon a certain skeptical examination, even the negative aspects of sibling relationships seem to provide immense gratification.

By contrast *and* by what we have in common, our siblings continue to confirm our sense of who we are. The deidentification that defines two sisters such as Maria and Cathy so firmly in their specific roles also makes the world much safer and more controllable. For two people who grew up in a family in which safety and stability were so deeply yearned for, what a psychological gift this actually is.

Remember the tiny bedroom that Maria and Cathy shared in childhood? It was so small that the head of Cathy's bed was tucked underneath a night table each morning in order to get the bedroom door to open. It's no wonder that these two had to create such definitively separate childhoods; they literally slept with their heads together. In adulthood, just as their relationship again threatened to overwhelm their individual identities—when they lived only a few miles from each other, had mutual friends, threw parties together, and talked "thirty times a day"—their husbands (by fighting) provided them with the psychological equivalent of separate bedrooms.

As long as they play within the unstated rules of their family, Maria and Cathy can continue to provide each other with the friendship and support that is their tradition. What do they lose as a result? Both women lack the full pleasure in their marriages that might perhaps be theirs if they ever broke free of the unspoken Pantera dictum that men are not partners in friendship, just providers of economic support. Were they to attempt to elicit greater emotional connection to and from their husbands, they might perhaps be pleasantly surprised by what they would find. Other rewards and freedoms might have been theirs. Perhaps what the Panteras lack is a certain courage, a certain willingness to experiment outside the traditional tried and true. Nevertheless, the love and support they provide for one another is without a doubt to be envied.

CHAPTER SIX

Richard Patch

"I Had Two Wonderful Families"

At first glance, fifty-three-year-old Richard Patch has no place in a book on siblings: After all, he was the only fruit of the short-lived, largely acrimonious bond between his parents. Nevertheless, despite his only-child status, siblings—half sisters, in his case—have been remarkably important influences in his life.

We had spoken on the phone long enough for me to know that Richard Patch was married and had four children (two boys and two girls). He worked in marketing for a small retailing chain run by his father-in-law. Richard, by his own estimation, was a pretty average guy. He liked sports, didn't read very much, voted Democratic most of the time, although he'd voted for Ronald Reagan's second term. He loved his family and he lived quietly. He didn't have much to tell, he'd said, but I was welcome to come and interview him.

Now, as Richard opened his front door to me for the first time I was startled by his unexpected good looks. No note in his voice when we had spoken over the phone had prepared me for such a striking man. He appeared to be ten years younger than I knew him to be, strong-shouldered and lean like the experienced sailor he was, a good six feet tall, clean-shaven with blond hair that showed no sign of thinning. He was handsome, with well-arranged features and an aquiline nose that carried only a slight reddening, a mild hint of his true age—or perhaps, I instinctively speculated, of the effects of a certain amount of dissipation.

"Come in. We can sit in the living room," Richard said as he led me down three elongated steps from the white-tiled foyer. Two of the walls were almost completely glass, with a small white forehead of plastered wall butting out above. The wooden floor was bare and the few pieces of furniture were large; the spareness was surprising and beautiful. When I complimented Richard, he confessed immediately that it was his wife Christine's design. "I don't know anything about furniture, or decorating," he said. "The home is really her arena."

As soon as we sat down, I became aware of one other feature of such a sparse design: Our chairs, though the closest together in the room, were a good eight feet apart from each other. Furthermore, there was no coffee table upon which to place my tape recorder. I stood and placed the small black recorder on the arm of Richard's chair. As I turned to go back to my own seat, he spoke, as if our interview had already started. He said, "The most fundamental thing I have to tell you is that my parents weren't married."

Psychotherapists and salespeople alike frequently witness a certain phenomenon that, however, continued to surprise me no matter how often I experienced it during the writing of this book: the curious and predictable lag time between meeting a stranger and erecting a wall of social correctness. Richard Patch, like almost everyone I interviewed, made a basic personal revelation in that first sixty seconds of our acquaintance; then he closed up like a bivalve, holding on to the inner sanctum of his privacy with determination. I didn't pry with Richard Patch; it wasn't my place with him or anyone else I interviewed to force uncomfortable revelations. As a writer—not a therapist—I did not want to be responsible for bringing someone into a state of emotional distress that I wasn't trained to help him out of again. In all my interviewing, I tried to remain vigilant about this danger.

Nevertheless, eventually Richard began to reveal himself. In time, it seemed that he naturally arrived at a point at which he felt comfortable enough to acknowledge what I and several psychotherapists I'd consulted about him had already guessed—what he'd already, unknowingly told me.

For Richard, who had early witnessed just how terrible a relationship could be, commitment and loyalty were the foremost issues of life. Coming to terms with his own adult connections—his wife and children, his half sisters, his parents—was an arduous and nearly impossible task. He found it hard to trust others, and as a result he was intimate with very few people. In many ways, he had never known a family where it was safe for him to be, where the threat of loss did not loom and overshadow the possibility of friendship and pleasure.

"I can't talk about me or my sisters, I mean, there's no point in saying a word, unless I tell you that my parents never married," he blurted out in that original unguarded confession, "and if they *had* married, they would have divorced. They were such a horrible couple that even a five-year-old could tell how wrong they were, how bad for each other."

"I Was Unusually Lucky"

As a child, Richard had his first home in a dreary brownstone apartment that his mother, Grace, and father, Joe, filled with screaming battles, with meals quickly consumed in enraged silence, with raised voices and threats, slammed doors and, inevitably, the tread of footsteps heading down the front steps.

Fortunately—or so their son said—his parents split up shortly after his fifth birthday. Richard's father had long been involved with another woman, Rosalie; he left in order to be with her. Joe and Rosalie eventually married, and the new couple's bond was apparently a strong one, for they remained together until Joe's sudden death, twenty-five years later.

"My dad's leaving was not a climactic event," Richard recalled. "He was away a lot, and then he was back. I would feel good when he was there, and bad when he wasn't. Then it became very clear that he wasn't coming back."

Richard remained convinced that his own mother and father were simply a poor match, for both of his parents did prove in the end to be good partners to other people. They each married and made long-term commitments to another mate. Richard made his home with his mother, but did occasionally spend time with his father and Rosalie on weekends. "As a result, I was unusually lucky," he told me. "I had two wonderful families, and I went back and forth between them. My mother and Sam never had any kids of their own, so I was the only child for a long time. And then, after my father and Rosalie's girls came along, I had these wonderful little sisters."

"That must have been hard to get used to," I offered.

"Oh, no," Richard said immediately, as if in an instant he had grasped my suggestion, mulled it over, and summarily written out a rejection slip. "I never resented them, I adored them."

His expression was so ingenuous as he made this bald statement that I couldn't help shaking my head in disbelief. "No, really," Richard repeated. "They were wonderful." Those huge blue eyes continued to watch my reaction, unblinking.

Later, he casually mentioned that he hadn't spoken with his two half sisters for five years following their father's death, but even then, he averred that he'd never had any feelings of resentment or dislike. He had been ten years old at the time of his first sister's birth and eleven when the second was born, he said, and had had no reason to resent them. "I wasn't a baby anymore. I didn't need the things they needed. And I liked taking care of them," he told me. "I would go to my father's house, and baby-sit. I changed their diapers, I played games with them. They worshiped their big brother. They were so special."

Joe and Rosalie's little girls, Laura and Sara, were special, it's true, particularly because they provided young Richard with something he hadn't had before, a way to be needed and useful; they gave him a foothold in the center of things. By caring for his little sisters—by loving them rather than resenting them—he ensured himself an active, ongoing place in his father's new family.

The Positive Side of Rivalry

As mentioned earlier, the birth of a younger brother or sister is, in the words of British psychoanalyst Dr. Joseph H. Berke, "a peak unfair experience." However, Dr. Berke, author of *The Tyranny of Malice*, which focuses on the individual and societal impacts of envy, greed, and jealousy, points out that the greatest threat to survival is not rivalry *but the lack of it.* He observes that the worst possibility is "not the presence, but the absence of fraternal figures against whom one can measure and discover oneself." In fact, learning how to compete honestly is, in the long run, a form of vaccination, the essence of fair preparation for life.

Perhaps young Richard Patch had so mature a perspective at the age of ten that he was able to understand the advantages of these new siblings. If he had been someone else, with another attitude and sense of the world, however, think how unfair, even frightening, his sisters' arrival could have seemed: Combined with the loss of his original family structure (for whatever the turmoil therein, it was what young Richard knew, and thus his interest would have been in maintaining it) and the presence of the new spouses, who augmented his difficulties in securing either of his parents' attention, the "wonderful" little girls could easily have been the last straw, the factor that sent the boy spinning over the edge into resentful anger and depression.

Furthermore, the little girls' arrival could have been particularly difficult because, as the work of sibling researcher Judy Dunn, of the Institute of Psychiatry in London, has revealed, young children tend to become most angry and fearful about the potential loss of a father's attention. Young kids generally seem fairly confident that nothing can really come between them and their mothers, but endure more jealousy at the thought that Daddy's affections might be diverted onto another child. Thus, when Joe and Rosalie became the proud parents of two darling little girls, the potential threat to Joe's son must have been inordinately high.

However, as Richard pointed out to me, he *was* for many years the only child either set of adults had. In thinking about Richard Patch, therefore, it is best to consider him a hybrid plant, part only child and part half-sibling. A child like Richard, who reached the age of ten before being faced with the trauma of sibling rivalry, has already formed many life attitudes as an only child, according to psychiatrist Jacob Arlow who, in an even-handed *Psychoanalytic Quarterly* article, summarized the positive and negative aspects of being an only child. An older child may be far enough along, in developmental terms, that the new infant does not encroach upon his fundamental sense of self. By the time the competition actually arrives, Dr. Arlow noted, the child "is more mature and can deal with the altered circumstances in a presumably more adaptive fashion."

It is also true that some children, like Richard at the age of ten, seem able and eager to brush off difficulties in their life situations, to accommodate and adapt. They accept support and love as it is available, rather than focusing on what is denied them by circumstance. Obviously, these are children for whom, by nature, the glass of life is half-full. Dr. Berke describes such youngsters as having a high capacity for love and a low capacity to hate. He contrasts this type of child with those who "hoard hurts like squirrels garner nuts," seemingly indifferent to the forgive-and-forget sequences most typical of family (as well as playground and, much later, marital and work) life.

Richard's childhood pain *was* acute, but it was by no means simple sibling rivalry, as slowly became evident to me as I mulled over his life story. The greatest source of his pain was still difficult for him to acknowledge even a whole lifetime later: Apparently, when Richard's father, Joe, initially left, he had had no intention of maintaining any tie to Richard or his mother.

"This Isn't the Way Things Are Done"

Eventually, when Richard began to speak of this sensitive memory, he sketched in vivid terms a nearly fifty-year-old vision of his mother in the kitchen of their Greenwich Village apartment. The room was chilly, a gloomy reflection of the winter rain outside. His mother sat, sobbing and rocking, her arms tightly around her waist as if she were ill or freezing. She was wearing a thick, ugly cardigan sweater and her blond hair was caught back in a ponytail; he remembered noticing the careless angle of the hair clip when she suddenly lowered her forearms to the table and rested her head on them, just as he always did during naptime at his nursery school.

There were two men in the room, and he knew they were his father's friends. "I don't think I saw them again in that apartment," Richard told me. "But I know they told her they would talk to Dad, get him to help us with money. This one fellow said, 'This isn't the way things are done.' "

Richard looked at me, his charming smile twisted a little ruefully.

"I've never forgotten those words," he said. "I haven't always known exactly how things are done, but I've always tried to figure it out, to be a gentleman."

To be a gentleman.

Oddly enough, just before he'd said those words, we had returned from a trip to the kitchen to get two glasses of seltzer and lemon. As we walked by Richard's study, I had noticed the rows and rows of books that lined the walls. I remembered that he'd told me that he never had time to read, that he relaxed with physical activity, such as jogging and sailing. These volumes were in such perfect order—arranged by size and style, paperbacks separated from hardcovers, graduating heights neatly rising along each shelf—that I wondered if they'd ever been read. Some part of his image didn't work, something about the idea of Richard Patch as a gentleman made me suspicious, even uncomfortable. In Shakespeare's *Macbeth*, Duncan could not see the Thane of Cawdor's treason writ upon his face, for the Thane's true self was hidden under a cultivated veneer: "He was a gentleman, on whom I built an absolute trust." Here, too, it was as if a major sequence in a life story hovered beneath the surface, never revealed but occasionally—accidentally—betrayed by a false gesture like the seemingly untouched books, a tiny bubble of the truth gently rippling the perfection of a neat and pleasant life.

On this day, I was being introduced to the idea that Richard Patch did indeed have, while not a treasonous side, then certainly a tortured and unhappy one. As much as he appeared to skate skillfully on the surface of his life, below that surface lay a vast reserve of turbulent and painful life experience. He was more aware of it than he had initially appeared to be, and he would tell me much of it during the course of our conversations. Eventually, his half sisters, the only people in the world with whom he had previously shared his dark thoughts, would fill me in on certain details that their big brother hadn't been willing to share.

In fact, it wasn't until my next lengthy conversation with Richard that he felt comfortable enough to confess that his childhood had not been idyllic. This is how Richard allowed his memories to filter through, slowly and carefully, as if he were monitoring my responses at all times, always trying to see if it was safe to make the next revelation.

We had been sitting in my kitchen on a morning in early September, drinking coffee and talking about his sisters. Richard was wearing a gray and white striped shirt and khaki shorts: he'd driven over early, just after his morning jog, and was dressed for summer even though the day was turning cooler as the morning wore on. Just before he began to speak, he'd asked me to shut the front window. As I took my seat again, he said, "You know, maybe it's fairer to say that I had two half-happy homes. I mean, they were two happy homes that I wasn't really part of. My mother didn't have any children, she was happy alone with her husband. And my father had the girls."

He had been staring to my left, out the window I'd just closed, and now he turned to me and shrugged. "They were occupied with what they had. I was welcome but I wasn't sought after. My father always called me his son and heir, you know, that was how he would introduce me." His voice, during this whole long exposition, had been calm and reasonable, as if he understood completely and forgave all.

"And I was a teenager, I wasn't so much fun. I'm sure I wasn't a compelling interest all the time. I was somewhat of an intruder in each of the families."

Unbelievably, he was actually trying to justify his parents' lack of involvement with their son. "And you worked very hard to be welcome," I said. "I mean, you were a very positive figure, weren't you?"

"Absolutely," he said, straightening in his seat. His gaze drifted over to the window again. His tone grew quieter. "Which means I held back my own feelings. I wanted to do the right thing. I had the feeling of being an outsider, pressed against the window. I enjoyed them all tremendously, but you know, I always had the feeling that I could drift away and nobody was going to make an issue of it."

And in fact that was true. Richard told me that he had hitchhiked across the country by himself the year that he was fifteen. No one had tried to stop him from leaving, for his father saw the trip as an adventure and his mother and stepfather were in the process of moving to a new home. "The timing was good, she was so busy," Richard said of his mother, "and so it wasn't totally unpleasant for me to be . . ."

"Gone?" I said at last.

He shook his head, as if to organize his thoughts. "To disappear for a while. I'm reading things into her mind but I don't know . . ." He trailed off again, and then, although I'd said nothing, he made the following excuse for her: "I gave the appearance of being pretty confident."

"Were you?" I asked.

I'm not sure if he heard me or not. He was watching someone through the window, a neighbor working in her garden. The room was silent for a minute or more as he gazed at her, and I studied him.

"My father was powerful," he said, in one of those abrupt changes of subject that I believe were his method of coping with the soft spots in his hide. He would explain something up to a point that he could handle, then change the subject, often returning a long time later, without warning, to the troublesome question. At first, this habit gave our discussions a certain bewildering quality, but after a while I began to understand. He had to set the pace: As long as he led, made the decision to reveal, he would talk about himself fairly freely. "My father was dynamic," he repeated. "I've met some powerful people in my life but I would say he ranks right up there. He ran his business with personality and nerve. He was just a natural leader. When I went to work in his business, he just amazed me."

"So those were big shoes to fill," I said. "Was that hard?"

He was startled. "Who told you I took over the business?"

"That's not what—" I began, for I knew that he actually worked in his father-in-law's company, but he interrupted me, looking at his watch. "I have an appointment," he said. "I'd forgotten." And then he stood and, in a flurry of polite motion, was gone. I didn't know what I'd said, but I frankly didn't expect to see him again.

Lonely Onlies?

Only children occupy a unique place in our cultural consciousness, the source of envy and pity at one and the same time. What is the experience of those who don't have siblings and what does it demonstrate about those who do have them? For example, what role does a *lack* of brothers and sisters play in character formation and the development of feelings of self-worth?

This is an important question to consider, for in the last twenty years, family size has continued to decrease. Over the same two decades, there has been a decline of more than four million in the number of married couples with three or more children. There are approximately 1.7 million more families with two children than there were in 1970, and there are approximately 1.4 million more families with just one child. There are a number of factors contributing to the decline in family size: High rates of divorce in the first years of marriage obviously contribute to an increase in smaller families. Another element is the delaying of marriage and childbirth that is increasingly common among the professional classes: Fertility decreases with maternal age, so, in and of itself, this is likely to mean that more and more couples will raise just one child.

Historically, economic stress and periods of war have also had remarkable effects on the size of the average family in America. If we look at the time frame from the Great Depression to World War II, then through the rise of the counterculture in the 1960s to the surge of women into the work force, we can see how rates of childbearing have clearly shifted in response to societal flux. During the huge economic downturn of the 1930s, women began to have fewer and fewer children. Birth control was far less sophisticated at the time, but, certainly, fairly reliable contraception was available. In addition, societal depression contributes to individual distress, and there is nothing like stress and malaise for quelling sexual desire. During that time period, there was actually a 10 percent *increase* in the number of women who had just one child. This trend toward smaller families continued until the end of the Second World War. After the war, however, when soldiers returned home and America entered a self-satisfied heyday, the number of thirty-year-old women with only one child dropped by half, to only 15 percent of the population. The postwar economic boom was accompanied by the famed baby boom increase in family size; during the 1950s, an only child became much more of a rarity. Currently, however, it seems that raising a sole child is more and more common: Rates of birth per female have been falling fairly consistently since the mid-1960s. Despite the increasing prevalence of only children, however, societal opinions regarding the one-child family are far from charitable.

"The general opinion regarding only children is so negative," writes psychologist Toni Falbo of the University of Texas at Austin, who along with Dr. Denise F. Polit performed a substantial analysis of the existing research on the circumstances of only children, "that the most commonly cited reason for having a second child is *to prevent the first from becoming an only child.*" It is a construct of our culture to believe that only children are more self-centered and demanding, socially maladjusted, lonelier, and as a result, less happy.

Most of us believe that one learns cooperative skills from interacting with siblings. The thinking is that a child who tends to be successful—one who generally emerges with a measure of satisfaction from sister-brother contests—will have a powerful sense of personal right. In the workplace, in the marital partnership, and with friendships, such inner strength is a valuable resource. However, psychologist Falbo and others believe that, to the contrary, the absence of sibling rivalry actually frees only children to be more trusting, to develop into adulthood with the expectation that others will be helpful and nurturant. Since they grow up in a noncompetitive home situation, these children naturally learn to feel strong and are unthreatened by give-and-take with others.

In his own practice, psychiatrist and educator Dr. Jacob Arlow also posited that the developmental situation of only children was perhaps less scarring than we have been culturally trained to believe. "In fact, the widely prevalent notion that the only child is a special type of person who is neurotic, self-centered, unable to tolerate frustration, noncompetitive, demanding, and hypochondriacal," he comments, "may well arise from the envy and hostility felt by those individuals who are struggling with intense sibling rivalry."

Dr. Arlow also observed that in the psychoanalysis of only children, one of the most striking—and typical—features was that onlies weren't free of rivalrous feelings. Even before the children entered the "sibling surrogate" environment of school, they experienced guilt and fear in regard to sibling figures. Typical manifestations of this discomfort were shyness and avoidance of competition; but Arlow also frequently noted the converse behaviors of ingratiation and compensation. Thus, Arlow said, some only children were "very popular with their classmates because they are generous, share food, money. Others amuse their new substitute siblings by telling stories or making jokes. . . ."

In truth, only children have sibling issues just as brothers and sisters do; the difference is in the manner in which they experience these conflicts between rivalry and longing. First of all, they must cope with the ghost sibling, the vanquished rival(s) that they have annihilated. Each only child must, at some point, come to terms with the reason for his or her singleton status. Despite the fact that approximately 15 percent of children are singletons, being an only child feels unusual, and the youngster must develop an explanation of why he or she is an only, even to the extent of musing about what responsibility lies with him. Very early in life, whatever information is gleaned from the parents will be combined with fantasy in order to construct a workable, psychologically acceptable explanation. Later on, when the singleton begins to form serious love relationships, it is possible that competitive feelings will finally find a suitable arena for expression. Rivalries may be acted out with the spouse or lover because of the only child's unconscious identification with a mate as a sibling. This is analogous to the manner in which actual siblings act out childhood rivalries within their marriages, a matter we will touch on in further detail in the next chapter, which focuses on the relationship of Richard Patch's sisters, Laura and Sara.

No matter what one believes about the advantages or disadvantages of having brothers or sisters, it is of course true that in adulthood, only children—like left-handed people, blonds, or superb dancers—take their place in the human population and make their life contributions without notable functional differences from their siblinged peers. They turn up with a rich variety of character traits, observes Dr. Arlow, reflecting "the different ways in which certain problems of the only child are resolved in the course of development."

Not surprisingly, growing up is as complex for only children as it is for those with siblings. Only children are subject to the same unpredictable interplay of parental marital stability, gender, family expectations, and other factors. As psychologist Falbo comments, "Personality characteristics are developed through processes that are not a simple summation of family members." Rather than regarding only children as deprived, it is more useful to think of them as "enriched with experiences that promote a different course of development." Since, in the long run, the life paths of onlies and adults who were raised with siblings are likely to converge, Falbo believes, only-dom turns out to be merely a different path to maturity, with advantages and disadvantages of its own.

Furthermore, despite the widely held negative notions about the lot of only children, the supposed victims themselves—and their parents—dismiss the idea that their position is a disadvantaged one. The most important fact to keep in mind is that only children and children with siblings all *do* eventually grow up to have lives that are functionally similar. Thus, here's the rub: What can be learned from the study of only children is not that siblings are irrelevant, but, rather, that the issue of brothers and sisters has effective importance for development in our culture, *whether one has them or not.*

In other words, if one has no siblings, one finds them and creates them and dreams about them and constructs fantasies around them. And—ironically enough—if one does have them, one does precisely the same thing. Think back to Dr. Joseph Berke's observation that the greatest threat to a child's development "is not rivalry, but the lack of rivalry; not the presence but the absence of fraternal figures against whom one can measure and discover oneself." Even a child whose siblings are adopted may experience the thought of losing them to their original families as terrifying, as the psychoanalyst Stanley Rosner has observed. Luckily, it is human nature to find surrogate siblings everywhere.

If one's fantasies about siblings are actually somewhat more important than the objective realities of who they are and what they actually provide for us, is it possible in this culture to live one's adult life without actual contact—ignoring and discarding one's siblings—and have a complete and interesting life? The factual answer, of course, is yes. But the richer and more psychologically compelling answer is no.

Let me explain.

The Clash of Mini-cultures

I have a wise and psychologically aware friend who affectionately describes her own older sister as "pre-Freudian," or as completely uninfluenced by the popular emphasis on having a rich inner life, on the satisfaction of the individual, and on one's potential for personal development. This psychological innocent manages with relative ease to raise her two children, maintain her marriage and home, and enjoy her extended family and friends. When the first of Sally's kids was born, my friend Denise (who has no children of her own) immediately recognized that there had been a power shift in the overall family. Sally couldn't even understand the terms twenty-six-year-old Denise was using in explaining how impossible it had become to arrange a family get-together without kowtowing to the little boy's needs. "I can tell," Denise confided to me, "that Sally is using him to push our parents around, but she really can't see it. She doesn't have any idea what she's doing. She places his needs so inflexibly ahead of anyone else's that there's no room to negotiate."

Denise and Sally were, in fact, engaging in a clash of cultures. Denise was still primarily a member of her original family, and Sally was establishing her own new nuclear unit. Sally may not have understood the *why* of her own behavior in such terms, but nonetheless she knew what she had to do. She was compelled and motivated by what she saw other young mothers doing with their children, and also by what her own mother had done with her as a young child. From Denise's point of view, however—embarked as she was on establishing her autonomy and independence but not yet established in a new family of her own—Sally was changing the rules in a shocking and demanding way.

I raise this as an example not merely to describe one situation in early adulthood in which sibling relationships can be subjected to a great deal of strain, but also to demonstrate how, on even the most local level, our expectations of relationship are culture bound. Denise's mini-culture is still the young adult's culture, in which every family member has an equal right to negotiate—any individual can take the priority position on a particular topic, depending on his or her current needs. She finds Sally's demands unreasonable and inflexible.

Sally, on the other hand, has moved into a conventional maternal mini-culture (now further solidified by the birth of her second child), in which she is identifying more closely with her own mother and feeling freer to make more stringent demands because she is verbalizing on behalf of an infant and a toddler as well as her own self. From her perspective, she is acting unselfishly on the side of the helpless when she insists on meeting for dinner at an hour so inconvenient that Denise must leave work early in order to join her family.

Is this simply a reworking of childhood battles, leftover feelings of sibling rivalry again in play? Denise and Sally have a history of real closeness, and I believe that they will continue to be friends throughout their lives. They are not merely acting out rivalries, they are renegotiating roles as their lives evolve. I also suspect that part of the problem has to do with a clash of life phases.

These sisters are stuck on either side of a cultural chasm, each believing that the other is being difficult as part of a power struggle. In fact, Denise and Sally are not able or willing to acknowledge how their current life roles have changed them, altering what they need and want from their parents and each other. In a certain sense, neither sister can see who the other is.

If my friend Denise can eventually realize what Sally is going through, her own transition to parenthood will be better informed. And if Sally can remember to empathize with the strains and pressures of her sister's busy professional life, she may find her own eventual transition *out* of full-time motherhood a little easier. Most important, if they dismiss one another now because one does not understand what the other is focused upon, it doesn't bode well for their ability to tolerate change in other important relationships.

As we grow and change, our loved ones, including our brothers and sisters, help us to keep the life we knew and the life we know in balanced perspective. They matter on the positive side of the ledger and they matter on the negative as well. Yes, it is possible to live without coping with those difficult boon companions, our siblings. We can simply write them off. Doing so, however, devalues not just ourselves and them but also the rich environment we share.

The Devalued Relationship

The more we learn to appreciate our adult siblings, the better off we will be, but sometimes it's difficult, even unacceptable, to focus on these traditionally devalued relationships. We live in a culture that emphasizes the parent-child bond and the spousal bond to the relative exclusion of all others. Siblings in America, according to anthropologist Thomas S. Weisner of the University of California at Los Angeles, "are culturally expected to leave home and separate for life. Important decisions about economic and social life are expected to be made along with one's parents, spouse, friends, or work associates, but not primarily with one's siblings.

"The parent-child relationship and the couple bond," Professor Weisner goes on to say, "represent the cultural relationship ideals Euro-Americans strive for in life and are the ideals presented in myths and in the popular media."

In other cultures, however, sibling roles are imbued with a great deal more importance. In South Asian societies, for example, older siblings help to raise their younger brothers and sisters. They also participate in decisions about marital partners, provide financial resources, and often spend extended periods living in one another's households. This involvement and assistance extends to the children of one's brothers and sisters as well. The shared cultural understanding of the sibling bond is that it is active, ongoing, and mutually supportive.

The sibling connection is also strategically important: The economic and social life of an individual is culturally linked to the web of brother-sister ties. Whether or not each set of siblings successfully assists one another is a function of individual variations in personality and situation, but in the cultural aggregate, the sibling relationship is a significant lifelong bond in South Asia.

While in our society the sibling relationship is not "culturally elaborated," as Professor Weisner has observed, those individuals who do enjoy a safe, supportive, and trusting relationship with brothers and sisters count themselves as extremely advantaged.

Furthermore, we have discovered in the last two decades that there are advantages in moving away from certain Eurocentric cultural norms in the raising of children: The societal tendency now is to breast-feed children until they are much older than was the practice in the recent past, and we tend to carry infants and toddlers with us rather than confining them in playpens as was the practice only twenty-some years ago. However, we still consider it wrong and "unfair" (that word again) to require that older siblings take on responsibilities for care of junior family members, even though, as anthropologist Weisner notes, such regular duty is among the most common forms of child care in societies around the world (and in certain subcultures in the United States as well).

Such early child-care duty tends to be the first step into a lifelong involvement with siblings that ranges from input on marital decisions to shared housing and joint rearing of nephews and nieces. In those cultures where the sibling bond is considered to be a meaningful connection—not merely the tip of a hat on the way into a more personally fulfilling existence—brothers and sisters are deemed from the outset to have distinct emotional, physical, and psychological utility. Wouldn't there, in truth, be many calculable advantages if such were the case in our own culture as well?

Unfortunately, societies are extremely slow to change. For example, one of Professor Weisner's main areas of study for the past two decades has involved tracking a group of far from conventional parents—commune members, single parents who chose to have children without a partner, cohabitating parents, and other nontraditional family groupings—as they raised their children to adulthood. For all these notably unusual parents, one might have suspected that child rearing would involve equally notable alternative approaches. Surprisingly, however, Weisner and his colleagues found that the parents —although extreme by conventional standards in their predisposition to gender-neutral rearing techniques, refusal to use plastic toys, insistence on natural foods, interest in alternative medicines, flexibility in regard to sleeping arrangements, and prolonged breast-feeding—had remarkably normative stories. Weisner discovered that unconventional ideas were being implemented, but not on any dramatic scale: It was not simply that no families involved older siblings or other children in regular responsible child care, but also that "not a single parent used their sling or carrying device to carry their baby around six to ten hours a day," as Weisner observed, and, "very few conceived of breast-feeding past eighteen months . . . [although these practices] are widespread around the world."

In addition, despite the emphasis on co-equal child rearing, mothers were the primary caretakers for 95 percent of the infants Weisner studied. Parents who used herbal or homeopathic medical techniques for themselves still tended to have their children immunized and used traditional pediatricians; and all the parents placed conventional high values upon literacy and scholastic achievement. Such attitudes are normative, basic elements of the mainstream American cultural milieu. What Dr. Weisner's studies demonstrate, above all, is that though values have changed over the past quarter-century, behaviors have not altered as significantly as one might suspect, at least when evaluated on the broader scales of genuinely different cultures.

Nevertheless, the first steps have actually been taken on the journey toward cultural acceptance of what Professor Weisner and his colleagues refer to as "pronatural child rearing." This is not, however, the case in terms of cultural acceptance of the significance of siblings, despite a burgeoning appreciation of the family unit, in general. Perhaps the fact that so many different disciplines in the social sciences have been scrutinizing sibling relationships for the past twenty-some years is just the beginning. Change will not be rapid (it never is), but I suspect that eventually the lifelong interrelations of brothers and sisters will achieve a more significant, acceptable status within American culture.

Joe Patch's Castle

Until then, this relationship without rules will continue to be of great importance for many brothers and sisters; the sibling connection was of such significance to Richard Patch, for example, that he was eager to persevere with the interview process despite the emotions that assailed him during it. He had returned my call and agreed to the next meeting without a word about his abrupt departure from my kitchen. I mentioned, hesitantly, that I had thought he might not want to continue, and he said, "Oh, no, I'm really enjoying this." Then he laughed, adding, "How often do I get to sit around and talk about myself for hours on end?"

In any case, he was willing to have another meeting. Our next interview took place at his home. When I walked into the living room, I saw that Richard had a photo album ready to show me. I expected to see photographs of his mother and father, his sisters, and his wife and children, but to my surprise the pictures in this small book featured only one subject: a house. To learn more about that, one must backtrack to 1956 and visit a large building lot on Florida's Gulf Coast.

No member of the Patch family—for later I saw an identical reaction from each of Richard's sisters—could describe the house their
father designed and built without taking on a rapturous, dreamlike
expression, a nostalgic smile reminiscent of the manner in which one
recalls a first romance. The halo that surrounded the house was perhaps the glow of Joseph Patch himself, unless the photographs that
Richard showed me failed to do the place justice. No matter how I
studied them, all I could see was a workmanlike ranch house on a flat,
sparsely wooded parcel of land. Clearly, the water view was lovely, but
for his offspring the house itself seemed to have been imbued with
more: a certain quality of worship, a respectful reverence not for the
nondescript house but, rather, for its builder, Joe Patch.

"My father was a truly charismatic person," Richard told me,
the yellowing photographs held in one relaxed hand; his head was
supported by his other hand as he sat in one of several modern chairs
in his living room. "He was larger than life, a king in his castle.
He and Rosalie, they were like Scott Fitzgerald and Zelda, always
surrounded by people, always laughing, always the center of the
party. We all just wanted to be near them."

I realized, with a start, that Richard had returned without a blink
of discomfort to the topic that had sent him out of my door only a
few days previously. Now he began to describe his father's childhood
with sympathetic energy.

Joe Patch was a completely self-made man. He had found himself
on the streets of New York City at the age of twelve; his own father
had thrown him out in a fit of anger. He went to work in a shipyard
and then joined a construction crew. "My father was one of those
people who worked hard and didn't worry about the consequences,"
said Richard. "He had so much energy. Whatever he did, he did well."

In his teens and early twenties, Joe helped Richard's maternal
grandfather establish a chain of discount stores throughout several
eastern states. Although Joe was widely known to be an enthusiastic
womanizer, his employer, Grace's father, seemed to approve of the
relationship between the young couple, even to the extent of helping
his unwed daughter and her boyfriend out financially when Richard
was born. Richard's grandparents encouraged them to marry, apparently failing to realize that neither Grace nor Joe was happy with the
course their relationship was taking.

In the early 1940s, Joe was made a partner in the business, and his financial future was assured. Shortly thereafter, he abruptly sold back his partnership shares; no one in the family understood why until the day he walked out on Grace. But Joe didn't wait very long before beginning again, even carrying out a little uncalled-for revenge: He started his own store, made a success of it, and went on to develop a directly competitive chain. In one short decade, Joe Patch bought out the business of his former mentor.

As Richard recalled, "This was just around the time that the girls were born, I think, maybe a year or two later. And I remember how furious my mother was. Her whole life, she was in a state of rage about Joe and what he'd done to her family. They did so much for him, and how did he pay them back? He ruined my grandfather's life. And my mother—even though she went on to have a long and happy marriage with her second husband—she always grumbled about Joe. In some way, she felt he had destroyed her life also."

"Did he ruin your life, too?" I asked quietly.

"No. Absolutely not." Richard's voice was firm.

He leaned back, relaxed against the smooth sueded surface of the black chair. I saw a solid and well-cared-for man, a handsome fellow who managed to brush across the top of life without getting snagged by thorns or tangled vines. He had fallen into what appeared to be an honest reverie, eyes staring vacantly at a colorful Lichtenstein print above and to the right of me. I, on the other hand, felt transported to a vivid place of raw and angry memories, even though I had no sense of any emotional distress from him. It was as if he had described this humiliating event of watching as his father again betrayed his mother and her family, and he had given me his feelings without experiencing them himself. Oddly enough, I felt infuriated at Joe and unable to express it, as if Richard were the stranger to the situation, the person who would not understand.

"Do you want to stop for today?" I asked. Richard had taken me so carefully through his father's history that we'd been talking for nearly two hours; perhaps he was tired.

"No," said Richard, shifting around slightly in order to smile at me. His two hands were open, palms down, one upon each knee, as if he felt some inclination to stand up and come over to comfort me.

"Did it ever bother you?" I asked, cautiously returning to the original subject. "I mean, was it embarrassing or disturbing that your parents weren't married?"

"Honestly?" Richard asked.

"Of course," I said. I watched, amazed, as his sympathetic smile lost its verve, literally erasing itself and becoming nonchalant. If it were possible, he relaxed even deeper into his chair.

"It never bothered me at all," Richard said. He put his right hand up to his shirt pocket, although his glasses rested on the chair arm. Finding nothing, he leaned back again, that smile still holding his lips apart.

He was silent, and I decided not to ask another question, curious to know what he would say if I ceded control of the interview. We said nothing for a long time.

When Richard finally spoke, he said, "It was the house, you know, that bothered me. More than anything. When Dad died, I mean. I was married, I had kids, I worked for him, I did everything the way he wanted me to. And when he died, he left me nothing." He picked up the photographs again, turning one around so that I could see the small vacation house again. "When I was there, I really felt like I was part of the family. That house was all my happy memories as a kid. What did I ever do that he hated me so much?" This time, I could see that Richard was on the verge of giving in to tears. The house, finally, was something he could emote about.

"Tell me more about the house, about what you did there."

"Next time," Richard said, and he stood. Now, it was apparent, the interview was over.

Good Shoes or Bad?

Richard never really did return to the topic of the Florida summer house. And, in truth, the house was simply the most obvious manifestation of what Richard had suffered at his father's hands. As he told me, he'd believed he would inherit a share in it, but there was a great deal more. Once he began to speak about his father's cruelty to him, the stories just kept coming. In our next interview, I remember, he was literally leaning halfway across the kitchen table, speaking as fast as he could, stories about his father tumbling between us like toads jumping out of his mouth.

"It is of moment to a young man when entering life to decide whether he shall make hats or shoes," wrote the novelist Anthony Trollope, "but not of half the moment that will be that other decision, whether he shall make good shoes or bad." So it was for Richard Patch, in that the decision to enter into his father's business was not made, it simply happened. He had returned from his cross-country trip as a fifteen-year-old and gone directly to work in the company, without pausing to consider college or an alternative career. The decision to fail, however—to make, as it were, bad shoes—was a matter of character and fit, Richard now suspected. For he had yearned to connect with his father, to please him, in much the same way that he had yearned to please his father's customers. Deal making showcased his weakness for compromise. He lacked the avidity that marked his father, and it was clear that his father wished he were more persistent. "I was always trying to shrug off the sense that I disappointed him, that he thought I was lazy and should try harder. He'd say, 'Go out and find better deals,' and for him, it was as simple as that. But I was really a square peg in a round-hole business.

"He paid me less than anyone else that worked for him, by a huge amount," Richard told me. "And I had a wife and a bunch of little kids, and it was just impossible to make ends meet. So every month, he would ask me into his office, and make me show him my accounts. He would criticize everything. He'd say, 'You're spending too much on soda, next month, don't spend so much.' Then he would write me a check out of his personal account to cover any bills I couldn't make on my little weekly paycheck.

"I was a grown man. He treated me like I was a child. Sometimes I hated him, and sometimes I thought he was right," Richard admitted. "But since I knew I was going to inherit the business, I guess I thought it didn't matter if I paid my dues. In the long run, I would have the chance to prove myself."

"Your father does not come through as a very benevolent person," I ventured.

"My father was capable of doing a lot of good things. And occasionally he did some very bad things." Richard looked up at me, head tilted to the side, eyes eager to see that I was understanding him. "One of the problems, though, is my participation. Once I might have said that it was all his fault. But you know, I was a grown man, married, doing my work, and yet I was still going in to my father and not saying to him, 'Pop, screw you if you don't want to pay me the salary . . .'"

"That you deserved?" I said.

"Yeah. That was my part of it. The five-year-old in me was always there, thinking uh-oh, Daddy might walk out again."

"You could have gone to work somewhere else, perhaps?"

"Yes," he said, "but when he took me into the business, it was almost biblical, the son and father together once again."

I nodded. I really did understand how much he must have wanted to endure any difficulty thirty years previously, just to feel wanted and appreciated by his elusive, captivating father.

"Then I was in California for several weeks on business, and I got this call from my sister Laura. She was home from Smith, she said, and did I know that Daddy was dead? I said, what? I couldn't believe it, but he'd been hit by a drunk driver down in Florida, the guy's car hopped across a median, I think. And nobody ever called me, they never even thought. And by the time Laura called me, he was in the ground and buried."

"That's terrible. You must have been shattered."

"Yeah," Richard said. "I was."

"Then, when they read the will," he continued, brushing quickly over the fact of his father's death to get to the next significant fact, "I was cut out completely. Even though he'd said for years that I'd inherit the business, he left everything to Rosalie and the girls."

"Oh, my God," I groaned. "It just gets worse and worse. What did you do? Did you contest the will?"

"No, I didn't. In fact," he said ruefully, "I began to drink. I stopped speaking to anybody, my wife, my sisters, my kids, I just dropped out. At first, I tried to set up a store of my own with some money I'd begged from Rosalie, but I couldn't get it together. I couldn't be him. I was drunk all the time. My business died before I could get it off the ground. I drank like that for four years, all the time. I ended up in the drunk tank more often than I care to admit."

"The drunk tank?" I knew enough about alcoholism to know that it was an illness that could strike even the most unlikely looking people. I'd written articles in which I interviewed a number of "high-functioning" alcoholics, in fact, and so I was aware of the way in which some heavy drinkers simply blend into the population. I couldn't picture this well-dressed, well-spoken man in some tiny police cell, surrounded by visibly deteriorated drunks. And yet, as he described it, he must at some point have been a stereotypical "falling-down drunk."

"Yep." He shrugged one shoulder, a quirky gesture, implying that he, too, was aware of the odd contrast between that vision and the man before me.

"How did you feel while you were drinking?"

"I drank because it made me feel good, at first. And then, well, actually I had some good times all along the way. And that was compelling. Sometimes I thought well, gee, maybe I'll have a good time again. Toward the last part, in the last year, I would buy a bottle and sit in my car and drink. Then I'd go to a movie in the late afternoon and sleep there. I'd go home, drink, fall asleep on the couch."

"Were your kids aware of this?"

"You know," he said evenly, "I don't really talk with my kids about things like this. We're not big on talking. They were young, too, of course, but I guess they must have known, it was obvious. Then I lost this terrible job I had. I was a night watchman in a factory, and I got fired from this job I thought I was too good for, and that was the worst."

I nodded, encouraging him to continue. I could tell, just watching him, how much all this was costing to confess. It seemed clear, though, that some part of him wanted to go on talking. "I was drinking and drinking, for days, I think. And I passed out, and Christine, my wife, just panicked. So she took me to the hospital. I was there for several days. And on the last day, she came into my room very quietly and sweetly—if you met her, you'd know how gentle she can be—and she laid down the law." He ran one hand through his thick blond hair, shaking his head at the memory.

"She said she wouldn't stay unless I stopped, and I looked at her and saw that she meant it, that I would lose her and the kids the way I'd lost everything else. I went to Alcoholics Anonymous for about a year, and I haven't touched a drop since the first meeting. That was more than twenty years ago."

His face, across the table, seemed ashen and older all of a sudden, as if even now he were reexperiencing the panicked moment when he almost lost his wife and their children. "I'd *made* those kids, with her; they were part of me and I wasn't going to lose them. I wanted my family together. I couldn't sink as low as my father, be that cruel. My kids deserved better."

"So did you." I said the words quietly, but I think he heard me.

"You know, it's funny," he said then. "Practically nobody that I know now has ever seen me drunk. You have to admit it's hard to imagine. Isn't it?"

"Yes, it really is."

"But the other thing is, well, I stopped because of Christine but she had a hard time accepting the new me, a little. I mean, there was a reluctance to let go of some of the old ways."

"The patterns of—"

He broke in eagerly. "Of drinking, yeah. You don't have to take a drunk seriously, he's like a little boy. And that year that I stopped, well, Christine had the liquor cabinet filled to the brim. It was bulging with scotch and vodka and bourbon. She would say she needed it for entertaining, but we never had anyone in."

"Why do you think she did that?"

"She was angry at me for changing, I think. And also, I was fat while I was drinking, I weighed maybe fifty pounds more than I do now, and I was so out of shape. I was huge, huge. She was always the good-looking one and I was pretty ugly."

"There was only room for one looker?" I said, smiling.

"I guess so," he said. His grin was strained, perhaps from embarrassment or even anger; it wasn't easy to tell what he was feeling. "When I started to lose weight, she started cooking up a storm. I mean, I was getting enormous plates of food every night, a mound of scalloped potatoes spilling out. And I have a weakness for chocolate, and every night she would have some special dessert."

"Why was she doing it, do you think?"

"I've thought about this a great deal," Richard said. "I think she was afraid I was like my father, that I would leave her. So first she tried to test me, to see if I would go, and then she tried to keep me so unattractive that I couldn't leave."

"Would you have left?"

He shifted in his chair, uncrossing his left leg and lifting his right leg up and over his thigh. He leaned forward, and something about the gesture was reminiscent of the way a much heavier person might move. "I am sure that I could have found someone else and made a new life for myself," he said, enunciating carefully. "The marriage has not been perfect by any means. But I chose to stay. I would never do what my father did.

"I've never been a great success in business, like he was. Still, I've made a decent living and I've learned a great deal. Women have been good to me," Richard said. "Christine and my sisters, they've been the ones who stood by, who forgave and understood. There's a big difference there, though. I love Christine but I'm not like her. Our marriage is good for what it is, I know that, but we aren't intimate. We aren't soul mates. My sisters, though, when I got back in touch with each of them, I felt I had made a complete life for myself."

"How did you get back in contact?"

"Laura. She wrote me a letter and asked if we could have lunch. It was as simple as that. I don't know why, I was just ready to get back to them. I was healthy, I was holding down a decent job, I felt good, but I'll tell you, when Laura called? It was like a lifeline being thrown."

"They are very important to you, your sisters."

"They're how I know who I am," he said. He looked happy just at the thought of them, his blue eyes a little brighter, his posture just a bit more erect. "I can tell them anything. We understand each other, and I think without them my life would not be—" He stopped speaking abruptly. Then he laughed and looked up. "You'll see when you meet them," he said. "My two sisters are my best friends. We're each other's closest friends. We'd do anything for one another."

He looked at me earnestly, and said, "It'll sound strange, but here goes. You'll see when you meet them: My two sisters add up to the perfect woman."

I raised my eyebrows. I hadn't met them yet, but it seemed an awfully enthusiastic compliment. I felt a twinge of envy, suddenly wishing that I'd had a big brother of my own.

"Really," he said. "When they were little, they were these adoring little sweethearts. I just loved taking them places and doing things for them. Now they're just the most amazing people, they are outstanding."

He paused for a moment, then summed up with a flourish. "Yes," he said, and his tone was proud, "you put them together, and they are my ideal."

CHAPTER SEVEN

Laura and Sara Patch

"No Day Is Safe from News of You"

I'll never know whether I might have decided on my own that Laura and Sara Patch added up, as their brother said, to the perfect woman. Each of them was an intelligent, accomplished, and interesting person; nevertheless, I strongly suspect that they had attained the highest level of joint perfection, from Richard's point of view, partly because of the pure quality of their intense devotion to him.

While it soon became clear that none of Joe Patch's offspring lacked for involvement with the others, I learned to think of the relationships they enjoyed—and suffered—as sibling bonds of strikingly different calibers. This is perhaps best illustrated by a Sylvia Plath poem Laura Patch gave to me, one that she said was a perfect description of her deeply felt connection to her sister.

THE RIVALS

If the moon smiled, she would resemble you.
You leave the same impression
Of something beautiful, but annihilating.
Both of you are great light borrowers.
Her O-mouth grieves at the world; yours is unaffected,

And your first gift is making stone out of everything.
I wake to a mausoleum; you are here,
Ticking your fingers on the marble table, looking for cigarettes,
Spiteful as a woman, but not so nervous,
And dying to say something unanswerable.

The moon, too, abases her subjects,
But in the daytime she is ridiculous.
Your dissatisfactions, on the other hand,
Arrive through the mailslot with loving regularity,
White and blank, expansive as carbon monoxide.

No day is safe from news of you,
Walking about in Africa maybe, but thinking of me.

The wholehearted admiration Richard Patch had for his sister Sara
was apparently experienced somewhat differently by his sister Laura.
The two little pals whom Richard had described were now vibrant
women with unique personalities and a vitally ambivalent connection.
The Patch sisters still adored their big brother; they did not, however,
have the same safe unconditional regard for one another, by any
means.

Psychologists often use the concept of the triangulated relationship to describe the manner in which three individuals can develop a
comfortable and stable set of roles. A triangulated relationship occurs
when three people function more perfectly in concert than any two
of them do. For example, a father and mother and adolescent child
can grow into positions in which the child and mother have a stronger
connection and Dad, who prefers emotional distance, remains unen-
cumbered by his wife's need for affection. This triangle maintains a
marriage by meeting both mother's need for intimacy and father's
need to avoid it. In this case, the child can be the emotional victim,
for he or she may not become free to leave the family circle and
establish independence. Another version of this classic triangle may
allow the parents to avoid their distress about aging and evolving life
positions by focusing on the child's accomplishments. In different
triangulated situations, the adolescent may be seen as an angel or a
devil; it is the freezing of positions that is the critical element. The

convenient presence of a third wheel, the child, helps to bear all the negative weight of the parental connection.

Or, in another example of a stable triangular pattern of give-and-take, this time among three sisters, one woman may be the odd one out who is labeled "not a team player" or "not like the rest of us." The exclusion of this sister actually strengthens the bond between the other two women, providing the inner circle with a very clear view of the benefits of membership. They needn't look far to see how lonely the outer circle could be.

A related explanation for Sara and Laura's simultaneous feelings of affection and mistrustful rancor for each other very quickly became apparent. An incident that took place early on in my interviews with the family immediately pinpointed the nature of the conflict between forty-three-year-old Laura and her younger sister Sara.

I had called Laura to arrange a meeting. On the appointed morning, she telephoned and said that her brother Richard and his wife, Christine, had driven over to spend the day with Laura and her husband, Bill. "Would you mind very much if Richard came with me?" Laura asked, adding, "Otherwise, I'll have to cancel. I don't get that much time with Richard and I'd really hate to miss a chance to see him."

I thought quickly. I'd never done a first interview with an audience before, but I didn't want to miss the opportunity to meet with Laura during the two-week period that she was renting a vacation cottage in a town adjacent to mine. I felt that if I didn't make things easy for her, particularly since she was on vacation, she might lose interest in being interviewed altogether. "We can try it," I said. I was uncertain of what might happen, but I was willing to risk it because I was eager to find out more about the Patch family.

Richard and Laura arrived promptly. I noticed how lively he seemed, how easily they spoke in each other's presence about intimate marital secrets, their spouses and children, their professional successes and failures. We had a very long and productive meeting, and I was struck above all by their naturalness, the closeness between them. At one point, I said, "Tell me about Sara, does she envy your intimacy with each other?"

Without hesitation, Richard said, "Oh, no, I'm just as close to Sara."

"We're all close with one another," Laura said, and then she was silent, cocking her head and looking at me as if to assure me of her frankness. I realized that Laura and Richard shared this habit: When making a slightly questionable personal statement, each one would stare at me with tilted head and slightly opened mouth. As a distraction, it was initially successful. Whenever either of them made this gesture, I would marvel first at how bright and alert their gazes were, often focusing on the dubious comment only several seconds later.

Now I watched as Laura straightened and looked away. Her hand hesitated above a blueberry muffin on the platter between us; she was not a thin woman, and she seemed to be struggling with the desire to eat a second one and the self-control that helped her to manage her weight. Without looking at her brother or me, Laura broke off a good hunk of muffin and moved it onto her plate. Then she grinned up at her brother, uncomfortably, and shrugged. His expression was carefully unresponsive; still, I noticed that she never actually put another morsel in her mouth.

Laura and Richard were built along the same sturdy lines, but his elegant style heightened his looks while her carelessness about dress and hair did a great disservice to her natural attractiveness. Her stained gray sweatshirt made her seem plumper than she actually was, and her thick hair was only partly brushed, as if she had been distracted by something before taming the left side. It was obvious she really didn't care about her appearance, and that, in its own way, was charming. Nevertheless, it occurred to me that I would never mistake them for a married couple; their presentations were so at odds. Strangely enough, Laura must have been speculating along similar lines, for when Richard got up to use the bathroom a few minutes later, she immediately confided, "I think that Richard and I would have made a perfect couple, we complement each other so well. In a way, we're much more alike. I think we're closer in some ways than he is with Sara."

When Richard returned, she repeated the remark, as if she had gathered courage by trying the comments on me first. "I told her that you and I have a lot in common, that we're sort of perfect for each other, we have such complete understanding."

Richard nodded. Then he turned to me, and said again, "I'm close to both my sisters. They are both very different women but I'm equally close to each of them."

Laura kept smiling. I could see her pause a moment, stricken, then gather herself back together before continuing with the interview. She was, by profession, a lawyer; now she seemed to be regrouping for a change in courtroom strategy. I was regrouping also, for now I had my first inkling that although the sisters were united in their interests, they were hardly as close as their brother had earlier implied. I couldn't put my finger on the difficulty, but I felt sure that one existed.

Two days later, I telephoned Sara and spoke with her for the first time. When I told her my name, she burst into a flood of commentary. She told me, "You should have called me, you know, you shouldn't have met with them without me. Laura just wanted to have you think she was closer to Richard than I am, but it's not true. You should have called me and I would have driven down to be there with all of you."

"I'm sorry," I said, "but I certainly didn't plan for Richard to be present for the interview. It was all very last-minute. Nevertheless, I'm really sorry."

"I would have driven down," she insisted excitedly, as if she would have leaped into her car and made the four-hour trip to Laura's rented bungalow without any notice. "It isn't fair, you know. It isn't fair. She just wanted you to think he is closer to her."

Thus it was that during my phone call with Sara, I first became acutely conscious of how powerfully the competition between the sisters was focused on which of them was more loved by Richard, on which of them was the one he *really* preferred. It was almost as if the more he denied that he loved one sister better than the other, the more eagerly Laura and Sara vied for the coveted spot. They were a little like triathletes: At one phase in the competition, one was ahead and then, without warning, the other sister would close in and pass up to the leader's position.

Parallel Lives

"One amazing thing about my sisters," Richard had told me, "is the way their lives have gone in parallel. One gets married, the other does. One has an abortion, the other does. You get the picture. They've each married three times, had two abortions, been unable to conceive with their husbands, adopted two children apiece." He started to laugh as he continued. "Now Sara's just divorced her third husband, and I swear Laura's nervous, as if she and Bill are going to wake up one morning and find out that overnight they'd gotten divorced, too."

I mentioned this during my first meeting with Sara, and she, too, began to chuckle. "It's more than that, even," she said. "My first husband was a concert pianist, and Laura's first husband played tenor sax. And we both got divorced because our husbands were having affairs. Then we both immediately married men we'd known while we were married. Those marriages, mine lasted six months, hers lasted a year. Then the third time, we both married chemists, if you can believe it. I mean, how many chemists are there in the world? And even though we were bored to death, we stuck with those guys for years, adopted with them and everything. Our lives *do* seem to run in tandem. Now I've divorced Ed, and I'm living with someone else. No wonder Laura's nervous about her marriage."

"Do you think she'll divorce Bill?"

"Well, she should."

"Oh?"

Sara looked a little smug. "He's a lazy, negative bore. The only reason Laura stays with him is that she is frightened to be without a man."

"And you are not frightened of being alone?"

"No."

"That's odd," I said, "because from what you've told me, you've never worked, and you've never had to. You've never been without someone, a man, to support you."

Sara's smug expression wavered minutely. "Did Laura say that? She would say that."

"No," I said. "I'm just speculating from the history you've given to me."

"I inherited some money from my father, so did Laura, but she spent it all. She just doesn't consider the consequences of what she does, she moves too fast and doesn't think things through. I have managed my finances well," she responded. "I haven't been scared to be alone, though. Laura thinks if she leaves Bill she won't be able to survive. And the strangest thing is that Bill hasn't worked in years.

She supports him. She's the one who runs the household and takes care of their sons. But she thinks she couldn't make it alone. She already *is* alone. It's extremely strange."

"Was she always like that?"

"Oh, God," Sara said, casting her blue eyes upward and leaning back against her chair as if it would help her look back in time. "When we were younger, she was so confident, the most *energetic* person I'd ever known. She favored action over inaction every time, but she did some stupid things as a result. Maybe that's why she feels so stuck with Bill now."

"It Had to Be Laura"

Just a year before their father died, the two girls had gone to Europe, Sara told me. They were both about to start college (Sara had been jumped ahead a year when she was in the first grade and ever since then, the sisters had been in the same class in school), and this jaunt was a "farewell to childhood" gift from their parents.

"There were maybe twenty of us all together, all about the same age, and we stayed in a castle in Spain," Sara said. "We were supposed to be studying languages, and we were absolutely forbidden to go out unchaperoned or anything like that. But one night, Laura and I managed to get invited to a ball, given in this beautiful ballroom on another ancient estate. Somehow we had permission. It was the most romantic—" She stopped, and I saw that she was beginning to cry.

Sara Patch was one of those remarkable women who can cry and remain beautiful. The tears that welled up in her eyes only made her irises appear a deeper, truer blue. Her lightly tanned skin did not flush and mottle unattractively, nor did her nose begin to run. She could cry like an actress, and when she raised one long, slim hand to brush her dark blond hair back from her face, I realized that she was probably aware of it.

Sara was leaning back on a well-cushioned deck chair, and even though her posture was relaxed, I could actually *see* that she was remembering the music she had heard that night. One manicured finger slid and tapped on the armrest as if it were dancing some long-forgotten steps; the rest of her was stilled by the memories she was reliving. We were seated on the rough slate patio in front of Laura's little cottage and several hundred yards away, sailboats lazed back and forth before us on an unsheltered expanse of bay. The taut energy of the blue and orange sails and the scurrying of the little hulls was muted by their distance from our cozy duo of chaises, as if the boats were performing an elegant exhibition for our benefit. Sara continued her story.

"That was the night I met my first husband. I was sixteen years old, and I saw him across this huge room. I'd never seen such an attractive man," she said, speaking slowly as she tried to piece the memory into words. "And I decided to make my way to him, and as I did, he was coming to me. It was incredible.

"So then," she said, shrugging a little as her voice began to toughen and gain speed, "we saw each other every night. I would sneak out of Laura's and my bedroom and go to meet him. We spent every night together. And then one morning, I was sneaking back into the villa, up these incredible marble stairs, and I got caught by one of the program administrators. I was kicked out, and sent back home."

She looked at me, and I could read the anger in her expression clearly, even though her story was more than twenty years old. "Someone reported me, and it had to be Laura. She was angry, I know, because she didn't have a boyfriend and she felt abandoned by me. I hadn't realized it, you see, because my sister is such a gregarious person, she had no trouble making friends. Most of the time, she made friends for me, too, because I was so shy. But Michael was my friend; I found him.

"And she couldn't," continued Sara triumphantly, "break us up that easily. My life was Michael, and I was having a tremendous time.

"I always felt that she was associated with my getting kicked out, even though Michael and I always tried to include her in whatever we did. When we went to museums or concerts, we would ask her along. But she never said yes, so how could I know she was lonely? You see, even though she had more friends, I was more popular with men. And I think it made her angry," Sara repeated. "In any case, getting me kicked out, I don't know what she did exactly, but I know she reported me. It was a piece of viciousness I've never forgiven," Sara said, sitting up suddenly, her posture erect, eyes narrow, teeth bared.

"You aren't very much alike then, are you?" I asked.

"Oh, no. Laura leads an extremely tumultuous life, with tremendous ups and downs. I'm not like that at all. She's an extrovert and I'm an introvert."

"That's odd," I said, "because—"

"Of getting divorced, and having the abortions," Sara interrupted. "And ending up adopting children."

"Is it coincidental?"

"It can't be," Sara said. "The first time, when Michael and I broke up, I know I was influenced by her divorce. I had been trying to make the marriage work, even though it was falling apart. Michael was a passionate man who thrived on romance and women, and I was struggling to keep his focus on me. When her husband left her, I saw that the world wouldn't end if I left Michael, too."

It is human nature, I think, to be most comfortable when one can define people in either/or terms. If Sara had positioned herself as a victim, Laura must perforce be the victimizer, the bad guy in this sister-sister duo. In my next meeting with Laura, I couldn't resist asking her about the incident in Spain, watching carefully to see how she defended herself against the charge of "intentional cruelty to sibling." I was surprised when her face remained a complete blank; she genuinely did not recall the incident. "I thought we left together," she said. "I think the program was too strict, that's what I remember. We weren't having a great time, and we got permission from our parents to leave and travel to Italy together. Michael came with us, I know. I really liked him then. We didn't go straight home. I'm sure of it." Laura appeared at first to be completely puzzled by her sister's memories. As we talked on, however, she told me a story about their childhood which *she* felt would explain their relationship.

"Our Mother Wanted to Make It Up to Her"

"You know, our mother was a fraternal twin," Laura said. "And she and her sister were very different. Her sister had a terrible life. She was raped by their father; she got pregnant by someone else in her teens and had an illegal abortion. Then she became an alcoholic. She never married, and she died in her early forties. And I think my

mother always held herself back so that her sister Ellen wouldn't feel
so bad. Momma was very talented, very beautiful, but she never
accomplished anything. I was so much smarter than Sara, so much
more sociable. I think Momma wanted me to protect her the same
way."

"Her sister was molested? That's horrible," I said. I was surprised
as much by her matter-of-fact presentation as by what she was revealing. "Did your grandfather ever try anything with your mother? Did
your grandmother know this was going on?"

"My grandfather never laid a finger on my mother, that's all I
know," she said. "But—" and here an odd expression worked its
way onto her face, her lips became two thin lines that seemed to be
straining to prevent a smile from erupting. "Sara, he tried something
with Sara when she was five or six."

Sara remembered her grandfather coming into her bedroom during naptime on a warm summer afternoon. He lay down against her,
big belly to small one, and the next thing she knew, her cotton sun-
dress was damp and sticky. When she subsequently recounted the
story to me, she realized that she wasn't sure how she had known
that her grandfather had done something bad. But she was certain
that neither girl ever visited their grandparents again. Laura's memory
of the incident was equally sketchy, but similar in recalled details.

"As young as I was, I think I was told about it right away. But the
thing is," Laura told me, "that my grandmother had been my closest
friend in the family. Richard had my father and Sara had my mother,
but my grandmother was mine, the person who made me feel special
and loved. And I never really spent that much time with her after
that."

There was a long pause. Then Laura spoke softly, looking down
at the worn carpet in my office, "She used to tell everyone, 'Compared to Laura, Shirley Temple is a dog.' She just thought whatever I
did was great.

" 'Compared to Laura,' " she repeated dreamily, " 'Shirley Temple is a dog.' " She looked up at me. "She was great, wasn't she?"

"Yes," I said, trying not to break the mood. "She sounds wonderful."

Laura's tale provided a superb example of how one common
thread can weave through many siblings' histories. Family themes, as

we have earlier noted, tend to repeat themselves. Such repetitive elements may mutate over time, but clear parallels can often be drawn from generation to generation to generation.

Based on information provided by both sisters, and with the able guidance of several therapists whom I consulted, I grew to believe that Laura was right that their mother's insistence on Laura caring for Sara had to do with the mother's own need to atone for the unhappiness her twin sister Ellen had endured.

"You know, I never resented it, not for years, I just thought it was my job in life," Laura said. "Part of who I was. I was supposed to share my friends, my knowledge, my clothes. I was supposed to include her in everything, and I always did." She leaned forward excitedly when she said this, folding her torso to her thighs in her eagerness. Her gestures were often like this, expansive and apparently uncomfortable. She seemed to have no physical sense of herself, no consciousness of her corporeal being. It was almost as if, in some way, she had no sensation of being physically *anywhere*. "But Sara, if she made a friend, she would never share. Her clothes, her friends, nothing. It was as if I always was expected to include her, but she never had to think of me."

We were in my office, a second-floor retreat that was a far cry from the idyllic charms of Laura's waterfront cottage. It was a sticky, uncomfortable August day, and Laura's thick blond curls were plastered against her forehead and neck. She seemed tired, but for the first time she was really *talking*, not simply being polite and friendly. Up until this point, I thought, she'd been eager to paint her relationships as completely positive, even though hinting that her connection to Sara was complicated.

However, something had happened during the previous week: Sara forgot that she'd agreed to attend Laura's younger son's tenth birthday party, and she hadn't even bothered to apologize when Laura called her the next day.

"I don't care about the party," Laura said, "and it wasn't such a big deal for Bobby either. It was just the way she dismissed me, so typical, as if she is a better judge than me of what's important in my own family.

"My sister is incredibly selfish," she continued. "All our lives, I've goodheartedly shared everything with her: my secrets, my friends, my clothes. She wouldn't even introduce me to a friend of hers, though, or lend me a blouse. Everyone in our family always treated her like she was a hothouse flower, and me like I was a sturdy old dog, and I accepted it for so *many* years.

"Ever since I was a kid, our mother has always told me to be nice to her, to take care of her, acting like Sara was so injured and helpless. Like our mother wanted to make it up to her for what happened, and *I* was responsible for making things better."

Laura's voice was higher now, her words tumbling out quickly. "But she was mean to me, you know? And nobody ever put a stop to that meanness. My mother, she made me absorb it and absorb it, and that was really how her relationship was with her sister.

"You see, it was the main job of my childhood to protect Sara, to introduce her to my friends and always let her tag along," she said. "All my life, it's been a pleasure for me to be with her. I've *enjoyed* my sister, but I've never really understood her. And just recently, I've realized the truth," Laura said, leaning forward to confide in me, striped bateau top slipping uneasily off her shoulder. One hand propped her torso upright on the comfortable black chair, while with the other she plucked at her drooping sleeve. "I know the truth," she said firmly. "Sara doesn't like me. She doesn't wish me well. It's as simple as that."

Laura explained that her sister's behavior became completely comprehensible when considered as a result of malevolent intention. "At my fortieth birthday party, she got up and told everyone about how *she* had gone to my junior prom even though I hadn't been invited. What was the point of humiliating me like that, more than twenty years later? The point is, she wants me to feel bad."

"How about you? Is that what *you* want?"

Laura knew what I was asking. "What I want is for her to be happy. When we were little girls, our mother made her my responsibility, and I have never neglected that for an instant."

"But now," she continued, "I think it's fair that I be happy, too. I have to understand that I cannot expect friendship from her."

"You're Going to Kill Somebody"

Only a few weeks previously, Laura told me, she had gone to visit their mother for the weekend. "I'd had a cold, but I called in advance and she told me to come along. And when I got there, Sara had driven over for the day. We spent the entire time sitting in the living room, me sniffling, her bringing me tissues. She was really sweet."

The following week, Laura had tried to telephone her sister several times, but her calls were never returned. Then their mother told her that Sara had pneumonia and that she was angry at Laura for giving it to her. "So I kept calling, and finally she picks up the phone and she starts screaming at me, 'You gave me pneumonia, you had no right to expose me to your disease.'"

Laura's eyes were wide; she stared out the window behind me, intent upon the experience of remembering. "And I finally put it together. This woman, who I love, she sees me as toxic, she sees me as lethal—"

"A virus," I interrupted.

"A virus that would purposely hurt her," Laura said, nodding. "No one could live up to her standards."

"How," I asked, "does all this relate to your brother Richard?"

Laura began to laugh. "Bingo. It's all about Richard."

She launched forward immediately. Today she was not editing herself at all. "They weren't loving people, really, our parents. I mean, they were dramatic and intelligent and fascinating, but they weren't warm. Sara's still like that, helpless and dependent like my mother, but cold at the same time. Richard and I, we're both very physical people, very strong, very capable, but we need warmth and reassurance and attention."

"Sara seems perfectly able to care for herself," I commented. It was only one of several elements in her statement that seemed out of synch with my own impressions; for example, it also seemed odd that she saw Richard as competent, given his shaky record in business. Perhaps her need to see him as a perfect "other" stood in the way of her ability to see him as he actually was. Similarly, her need to see Sara as both cruelly powerful and helplessly weak did not apparently seem contradictory to her at all.

"I know that, and you know that," Laura responded angrily. "I had this dream once, not very long ago, just about the time I started realizing how much I have sacrificed for Sara. I was on stage, and it was like the Oscars or some other award I was winning for being the best at something, but I don't think it was acting. I was just the best and everyone was clapping, clapping furiously, and I looked down over the podium and there were these guys in white running down the aisles with a stretcher. And they wheeled my sister Sara up the aisle with a sheet over her face. She was dead."

"What did that mean to you?"

"Oh, that's simple. I could have answered that before I even opened my eyes from the dream." Laura was grinning that familiar smile, head cocked once again to the side. "In my family, if you come into flower, full creative flower, you're going to kill somebody."

"And what does holding back net you?"

"That's the problem. I'm not sure." Laura paused, looking down at her tanned knees. Then she said, "If I stay with Bill, you know, I'm breaking the pattern. If I break the pattern, what will happen to everybody else?"

I paused, unsure of how to answer. She did not continue, and so I made the decision to change the subject.

"Is Sara your mother's favorite, would you say that's true?" I asked.

"Maybe," Laura said. "I don't know. They're more alike, very calm and artistic. And even though I adored my grandmother, I was definitely my father's little girl. Richard and I are like my father. I'm outgoing and funny, I have lots of energy, I love excitement, I get things done. I'm exactly like them." Her blue eyes were frank and friendly once again.

The Patches were physically similar, blond and blue-eyed. The women were substantially shorter than their brother, both hovering just on the up side of five feet tall. Sara Patch seemed as well cared for and elegant as her brother, while now, as I studied Laura, the elder sister still gave the impression that she really couldn't be bothered about her looks. Her beige and white pullover was worn and wrinkled and her thick, curly hair barely brushed; the best word to describe her looks was "slapdash," as if she'd rushed to pull herself together, as if vanity was decidedly not her bailiwick. As if her connection to the world was not through the feminine at all: Her strengths were, as she so emphatically believed, more like her long-dead daddy's.

When I subsequently asked Sara which parent she was more like, she unhesitatingly named her mother. "Temperamentally, my mother and I are very similar," Sara said. "And in terms of our talents as well. We are both interested in music and literature. Laura never was, even though her first husband was a musician. She was more of a manager than a fellow traveler. It was no surprise when she became a lawyer.

"Oh, and also," Sara added, "my mother is the younger twin, and I am the younger of two girls as well. That meant a great deal in terms of understanding each other. We come from the same place."

"Were you always aware of that?" I asked. I was doubly curious because of a repetition in my own situation: My mother and I are both the third in a run of three girls, and I'd become aware in adulthood how important that re-creation of her childhood experience had been in enhancing our connection to one another. I wondered whether Sara's awareness of the parallels to her mother's original family had been part of her childhood worldview or a more recent development.

Sara hadn't been aware of the connection until her thirties, she said, "but the older I get, the more aware I am of the similarities in my mother's life and mine."

Split-Parent Identification

As described in the chapter on Justine and Edith Arkady, deidentification, the process of defending ourselves against rivalrous feelings toward a sibling, helps each of us to carve out pieces of the family world that belong to us and us alone. It is an unconscious mechanism by which a person becomes defined, for example, "If I'm artistic, she's scientific." Or "If I'm neat, he's sloppy." Or even "If I play baseball, he plays the saxophone," and "If I'm focused on career, she's focused on family."

Often the correlation is simply "If I'm like Mom, she's like Dad."

Even when logic flies in the face of certain unreconcilable facts, such a simplistic identification can continue to persist. Thus, Laura felt that her major family experience was a repetition of her mother's caretaking of a sister, and that her only experience of unconditional love had been with her grandmother, but she remained convinced that her primary psychological similarity was to her father. Laura and

Sara are not unique in this pairing off; such a connection to one parent is known as "split-parent identification," and it follows as a natural elaboration of the deidentification concept.

A significant body of experimental research and psychological theory supports the idea of deidentification, demonstrating that an individual comes to a sense of who he or she is by comparing oneself to others. We estimate the value of our accomplishments in relation to those achievements that other people have made. Getting a 92 on a test tells a student little about his progress unless he knows how other children have fared. Similarly, a salesperson who is offered a salary of twenty thousand a year will think highly of herself if she is told that starting pay is usually two thousand dollars less; she will be enraged when she learns, a year later, that the two other salespeople in her department have been given 10 percent raises while hers was only 6 percent.

Social comparison helps one to gauge progress, status, and accomplishment. I suspect that it is one major explanation for the popularity of biographies of famous people. Celebrities' life stories are so fascinating to read because one is curious to know *what* such persons did to become unique, *when* they knew that they were special, *how* they were driven, and *why.* We also want to know what they were forced to sacrifice in order to become so accomplished and well known. How, we wonder, is such a person like us and how are we different?

As explained by psychologist Frances Fuchs Schachter, Ph.D., who originally introduced the terms "deidentification" and "split-parent identification," in every competitive situation there must be winners and losers. With each comparison—over height, weight, hairstyle, self-confidence, athletic ability, or academic achievement— one party is shown to be superior to another. The resentment and envy that are the natural result of such inequities would continually jeopardize relationships, particularly the intimate and competitive bonds among siblings, were it not for the blessing of unconscious psychological processes that reduce rivalrous feelings. According to Dr. Schachter, "Disruptive feelings can be mitigated by making the other different from oneself so that he/she becomes noncomparable. In this way, painful comparison can be avoided."

If one defines oneself as being unlike a sibling, this keeps feelings of rivalry under control. Deidentification actually diminishes any potential damage to the relationship, in that siblings are apt to like one another better, notes Schachter, adding, "It can also diminish the costs to the siblings in that their self-esteem is less likely to be threatened."

Schachter has speculated that a boy's early Oedipal conflict is resolved in a related manner. The little boy who longs to conquer his father and marry his mother instead becomes more closely identified with his father. *Rather than competing with father* for the love of mother, the young boy becomes more like his father. One more case of *if you can't beat 'em, join 'em.* However, for brothers and sisters, "joining" or becoming more alike would only mean increasing competition. Competition leads to conflict, and then to anger and uncontrollable passions. Luckily, deidentification quells and prevents such raging emotional impulses. This is the reason that Schachter also calls deidentification "the Cain Complex," the process of becoming *less* like one's sibling in order to avoid the murderous feelings Cain had for Abel. If fury can be controlled, family harmony is maintained.

Support for this hypothesis comes from a series of studies done at Columbia University and Barnard College during the 1970s and 1980s. Researchers found that when there are more than two siblings, it is the first two who define themselves as least alike. These are, of course, the two siblings who are in direct, unmediated competition with each other for parental attention. Later-born children do not have the need or opportunity to divide up characteristics so neatly, because the deidentification effects are diluted by the time they trickle down to them. Younger siblings don't deidentify so much because they don't have to; the more intense battle for primacy with the parents has already been fought and the spoils divided.

Also, the sense of deidentification in regard to personality characteristics—"She's extroverted, I'm introverted"; "He's tense, I'm relaxed"—is more pronounced with siblings of the same sex. Two sisters are *much* more likely to define themselves as markedly different, even though instinct tells us that a sister's and a brother's natures would actually be less alike. In other words, the more similar siblings are, the more unalike they must teach themselves to be.

Furthermore, when two siblings deidentify, each one tends to pick one parent with whom to become aligned. Like Laura and Sara, siblings who see themselves as an unmatched set will each select one parent with whom to identify—heaven forbid it's the same one!

These findings are particularly interesting because psychoanalytic theory has traditionally concentrated on the notion that boys identify with their fathers and girls with their mothers. The concept of split-parent identification has, however, been confirmed by findings that demonstrate that each member of a pair of same-sex siblings is far more likely to identify with a different parent. Dr. Schachter speculates that the effects of split-parent identification are more dramatic with the first two children in a family, and that personality development in subsequent children may be more dependent on identification with the same-sex parent. As happens in deidentification, the first two siblings in a family are those most able to identify with a specific parent, and most needful of that connection. Later children are able to connect to elder siblings, as well as to parents, because they have a wider available field for identification.

It is important to note that in family groupings where the desire for a child of a particular gender has been an overwhelming issue, the identification patterns are less predictable. For example, a mother who has desperately attempted to produce a son may, when she produces him after having had two girls, actually identify with the little boy more closely than with either of her daughters. That heightened connection will likely be mutual, so that the mother-son relationship will be the primary parent-child bond, against which the elder sisters measure their own maternal experiences.

Within each particular family, of course, many factors can disturb the clean information that researchers provide. Obviously, a half brother like Richard Patch, old enough to play a quasi-parental role, can serve as a source of identification; so also can a grandmother, as she did for Laura. Laura partly identified with her father, and her brother, and her grandmother, and even her mother, but overall she viewed herself as the masculine sister, Daddy's Girl. She continued to take a traditional masculine role, for she was the primary breadwinner not simply in her present situation, but in all three of her marriages. Furthermore, in the competitive situation with Sara, it later became clear that Laura saw herself as Richard's soul mate while her sister saw herself as the physical embodiment of Richard's preferred woman.

Ultimately, one can speculate that Richard seemed to have diverted his sisters from their original split-parent identification in order to make a viable spot for himself in the family; as a result, his sisters were two grown women still bickering over who was loved more completely by him. The Patches' parents appear to have played a minimal role in supplying them with love and affection, and when the two girls turned to Richard, he found in them a gratifying source of devotion. In a sense, all he had to do was to maintain his sisters' disequilibrium, keeping each of them sure that he was holding back from anointing *her alone* as the queen of his dreams; then, both women provided him with the admiration and affection he craved.

Overall, as Dr. Schachter reports, some consistent pattern of deidentification and split-parent identification can clearly be articulated in most families, playing "a significant role in personality development." The pattern is unique to the particular family, but it exists. The most important thing to understand is that identification with the parent of the same sex is not a given in a particular child's development.

Furthermore, these selections and identifications do not appear to take place in a vacuum. The divvying up of the children occurs at two levels at once, and both children and parents play their part in selecting one another. "Each parent can have one child who seems consistently to prefer him or her when (parental) competition arises, who seems to attest to the superiority of his or her approach by consistently adopting it," suggests Schachter, thereby maintaining the benefits and minimizing the costs "of the competition and comparison between parents that comes with rearing children." By extension of the argument, in fact, one might easily argue that the parents, in playing out their own childhood-based competitive feelings *with each other,* are demonstrating the remnants of early sibling deidentifications of their own!

A Common Language

What happens when the deidentifying, the making of difference, becomes so extreme that two siblings don't have common ground any longer? This probably happens more frequently than we realize, for one notable sibling conflict in adult life centers around the differential memories one has of one's childhood experiences. The explanation for this brings us right back to the notion that siblings from the same original families are often as different from one another in terms of personality as they are from members of the population at large.

The formula, for all who are looking for a simple answer, is this: There is no formula. Some siblings have a great deal in common and know it; some have a great deal in common and aren't aware of it. Some like this situation and some don't. Some are very different, and quite comfortable with their uniqueness; others yearn for symbiotic connection and resent differences.

Moreover, out of any set of two children—different because they are created that way and tend to become even more so as a result of life experiences—one may be a better fit in his or her family than the other. The difference may be microscopic, hardly worthy of attention, or it may be obvious and noticeable. An anxious child may fit well into a group where anxiety is normal and tolerable to the other family members. An active child will feel like an outcast in a family of couch potatoes. But the couch potatoes may be disturbed as well, finding the athletic child disturbingly aggressive, disapproving, or disruptive.

In every family, the sense of reality is tilted and personalized to that grouping's experiences. Such an intrafamily sense of perception can become extremely skewed: One therapist with whom I often spoke during the course of this project told me of a young patient of hers who was depressed and, as a result, had a very dull and dreary manner of presenting herself. In her family, however, where *everyone* was extremely depressed, she was seen as the family comic, the light and cheerful entertainer. It was only in the world outside her original family that this young woman found people responding to her as if she were blue. This was so disconcerting that eventually she ended up in therapy.

"The impact of individual differences on a family system is often dramatic," suggests psychologist Elizabeth Stone, Ph.D. "It isn't an issue of maliciousness, or neglect. The people involved aren't bad people: It's just that the question of their fit with one another has been radically undervalued." In other words, these family members have believed that—simply because they *are* family—there should be

a certain level of ease in their ability to understand and respond to
one another.

However, the truth of the matter is that quite often family members communicate using lexicons that are entirely at odds: They believe they are using the same language to say certain things, but
specific words have entirely different meanings to different people.

This is something we take entirely for granted when dealing with
strangers: We naturally proffer meanings in early conversations with
someone we think we'll like, proving by our willingness to reveal our
understanding of things that we are seeking common ground, that
our intent is basically friendly and open. And yet, with family members, we assume that because of our shared background, the language
we use to describe feelings and history will be nearly identical. With
siblings in particular we believe our shared experiences should be
almost identical: After all, *we grew up together.*

The truth is that, in childhood as in adulthood, we know our
sisters and brothers completely, *and* not at all. This contradiction is
at the root of any sibling relationship. Siblings understand each other
with what psychologist Stone (who happens to be my own sister
Betsy) calls "an impossible combination of certain knowledge and
absolute prejudice." We believe that we know each other because of
our shared experiences as children, even though we may have completely unique interpretations of those events and their meanings.
(Witness Laura's and Sara's differing recollections of Sara's European
romance.) Furthermore, as adults, we often neglect to take into account the changes wrought by our evolving life circumstances. While
there are occasions when we are uniquely equipped to see into a
sibling's core self, more frequently we are far off base, pompously
drawing conclusions about a person who exists largely in our fantasies, frozen in time at the point where we left the family in search of
our own independence.

Frankly, to return to the by-now familiar refrain, no matter how
much one wishes to believe the opposite, each person grows up in a
family by himself. No single person experiences life precisely as another one does. Experiences and memories can be shared, to be sure,
but it should never be assumed that one is sharing the same sense of
an event as another's. Human beings are so unique that recollections
of family life, of shared difficulties and mutual affection, may be

based on entirely unrelated memories. Completely different stories arouse emotions in different siblings.

Keeping in mind that perceptions are unique to each individual can make life a whole lot easier—in the family and in the world at large.

"A Constant Crude Awakening"

A relationship with a brother or sister is, in general, somewhat less safe than that with a parent. Each sibling, unlike most parents, is primarily *self-interested.* Thus, from the first, sibling relationships are more dangerous and challenging. As Eleanor Bossard and James Boll acknowledged in their 1956 book *The Large Family System,* "Relationships between siblings permit little or no dissembling."

They wrote: "Life among siblings is like living in the nude, psychologically speaking. Siblings serve as a constant crude awakening." Even though Bossard and Boll were writing about siblings in childhood, to some extent siblings continue to interact with one another in such a frank manner. Whatever the frequency of such "crude awakenings" among siblings in the adult population at large, certainly Laura and Sara Patch were continuing to live in a state of psychological "nudity" with one another.

At one point, Sara complained to me, "You know, when we were children, I did anything she wanted. If she wanted to see a particular movie or visit such-and-such a person, I just trotted along after her, the perfect companion." On this occasion, I had traveled to Sara's lakefront home in the Berkshire mountains of Massachusetts. We were conducting the interview reclining in deck chairs out on the neatly trimmed lawn. Sara hadn't wanted to drive out to Laura's again, for she was very busy helping to start a new string quartet that planned to base itself in this community near Tanglewood. She didn't play the flute anymore, even casually, but she remained actively engaged in the musical world. As we talked, I gazed out at two water-skiers who buzzed in huge arcs, back and forth before us. As the skiers circled one another and the perimeter of the lake, the sound of the boat engines ebbed and grew, so that every few minutes it became hard to hear Sara's exact words. Nevertheless, her meaning was very clear:

She felt that, twenty years earlier, Laura had resented losing control
of her little sister's social circle, that she didn't want Sara to have
friends of her own.

"Now Laura will tell you that she had to take care of me. That my
mother made her feel responsible about me, socially, because I was
the little sister, the shy one."

I was quiet, waiting for her to continue.

Sara, like her sister, began each story speaking in slow, measured
tones and then revved up, gear by gear, until by the end of the tale
her words were racing to get out. In one sense, interviewing each
sister was disturbing: Similarities of speech, a certain twisted gesture
of the hand that began in the air and then brushed the thigh, even
specific stories would recur from sister to sister, underscoring their
deep emotional connection, yet always at odds with the ambivalence
they continued to acknowledge.

Sara moved into high gear. She said, "I had guilt too, you know, I
had to take care of her and hold back because I was more popular
with boys. I was prettier and so I had to feel bad that boys didn't
want her as much as they did me. I had to feel responsible, too."

Then Sara said something that brought the conversation back to
square one—if not to the original source of their conflict, certainly
to the lifelong manifestation of it. "You know, when Laura came and
had her interview with Richard there, that's the same thing, her not
holding back the way I would. But she won't get anything out of it.
He wouldn't be attracted to her, not in a sexual way. Physically I am
more Richard's type, more the kind of woman my brother admires."

I sat in my deck chair, speechless.

"There Has Always Been Strong Attraction"

"Nothing ever happened between us, understand that," Laura told
me, when next we met, "but there has always been a strong attraction.
I know he's my brother but, remember, he's only my half brother.
Our mothers are different. I am drawn to him, I acknowledge it. I'm
sure Sara is, too, in her way. And I know he is attracted to us. To
me."

"How?" I asked, not completely sure that I wanted the answer.

"There was an occasion in my early twenties. He'd been drinking, that was when he was just beginning to drink a great deal. He was gorgeous, you know, and he was rubbing my back, and it was just sort of . . ."

"Sexual?"

"Sexual."

"What happened?"

"Nothing. Nothing at all," and in her voice I could discern the tiniest trace of something that I tend to believe was regret.

Later, on the phone, I asked Richard if he was attracted to his sisters. His answer was immediate. "Yes," he said. "Absolutely. You know, when they were adorable little girls, I never realized that they were competing for me. But later, after our father died and we went through the period of not speaking, Laura told me she didn't want to be involved in competition for me anymore. And I made some comment to Sara, laughing about it a little, and I was shocked when she agreed that they'd been fighting over me as children."

He paused, and I said, "H'm-h'm," to encourage him, unsure of where he was leading.

"But now," he continued, "for the first time, I saw them as women, beautiful adult women, and we talked about everything, even our sex lives. It was erotic, you know, it became somewhat sexy . . ."

He trailed off for a moment, and then he said, "Oh, yes, and Laura, once she sent me a letter that said she found me sexy. Her words were, um, 'Older brothers can be sexually interesting,' but I never responded. I never wrote back about it. We never talked about it."

"Do you know why?" I asked.

"You know, total honesty has been the deal between us, ever since we got back in touch. I remember I said something to Christine once, and she could tell I'd talked to my sisters about our sex life. And she said, 'Well, that's not really something that brothers and sisters usually talk about,' and I thought, 'Wow, it seems okay to me.' So, in some way our interest in one another is expressed by *talking* about sex, you know? It's on the periphery, but it's there."

It wasn't exactly the answer to the question I'd asked, but it was an answer, all the same.

Siblings and Sexual Development

The topic of sibling incest is an incredibly loaded and complicated one. Interpretations of sibling vulnerability and potential psychological damage, as well as estimates of its prevalence, vary widely. Certainly, any two siblings growing up in the same household must at some point cope with an awareness of each other's sexuality. Longing is in some sense inevitable, for just as children must wrestle with sexual yearnings and impulses toward their parents, so must a sibling cope with the erotic pull—or lack of it—to a sibling. In most cases, this happens on an emotional level well below consciousness. When it occurs more consciously, the range of action can run from fantasies and quickly dismissed reveries, to a small boy peeping in on his adolescent sister as she dresses, to mutually desired sibling incest, or even actual rape.

One way to think about siblings and sexuality is to understand that much of the exploratory interaction between sisters and brothers in the early years is just that: exploration. From the earliest game of Doctor to the sex play that often occurs around the period before the development of secondary sexual characteristics (such as breasts, facial and pubic hair, and the like), most curiosity about sex is oddly unerotic. The hormones are not yet raging. Thus, the little boy who peeks in on his sister in the bathroom is mainly curious—about how and why the hair grew "down there," or the strange way her breasts have been changing. The two brothers who have peeing competitions are learning and exploring as well, as are the two sisters who play Romeo and Juliet or pretend that one is the pirate and the other the princess who has been kidnapped. Even when a young brother and sister practice kissing, curiosity tends to be more paramount than sexuality. Such an interest in physical or romantic play with a sibling tends to be of short duration, lasting for a period of weeks. A combination of detective work, romantic fantasy, and speculation about the unknown, such games are a kind of playacting about adulthood, part of the trying on of different aspects of the self that marks much of childhood. The siblings are learning about themselves and their desires, but mostly they are practicing for the time when sexual drives will become fervent, and emotional and sexual fulfillment will be sought outside the family.

Of course, sexual play with a brother or sister is benign *only* to the extent that the interest is truly mutual. If one sibling is being overpowered or pressured to join in exploration with the other—whether to please a beloved older brother or sister, or out of fear—the situation takes on aggressive overtones and can no longer be considered innocent or acceptable.

An important argument in the discussion of siblings and sexual longing is made by psychiatrists Marianne Kris and Samuel Ritvo in a 1983 article in *The Psychoanalytic Study of the Child.* Typically, psychoanalytic thinking has placed erotic longing among siblings in the category of Oedipal displacement. Many analysts believe that in childhood, siblings only experience a certain attraction to one another because it is psychologically more acceptable than yearning for erotic contact with the even more forbidden parent of the opposite sex. This, argue Kris and Ritvo, discounts the very real fact that a sibling —closer in age and physical condition, emotional maturity, and inter-ests—may simply be more appealing as an object upon which to transfer one's yearnings of impossible love. In an individual situation, the sibling may, for any number of psychological, emotional, or fam-ily historical reasons, become the figure that triggers the erotic charge. While perhaps less loaded in Oedipal terms, the sibling—like a rock idol or movie star—may be more glamorous in terms of actual at-traction.

According to Kris and Ritvo, "... the sibling relationship is al-ways a factor in the choice of a marital partner because it involves overcoming the incest barrier against the peer generation which de-rives from the sibling relationship and thus ultimately from the Oedi-pal incest barrier." In other words, one has to leap across the sibling fence before finding it possible to long for a peer in an erotic fashion. All of this happens on the subconscious level, nonetheless, and so awareness of such a mental leap is most likely minimal.

In normal development, however, any erotic attachment to a sib-ling quickly transmutes into a kind of admiration for the sibling's qualities. Thus, a boy will find his sister beautiful or wish he were as tall as his older brother. He won't necessarily yearn for, or envy, the sibling on any conscious level, but he will have incorporated aspects of his admired and envied siblings into his own sense of what traits are attractive and desirable in a loved one.

By mid-adolescence, any erotic connection may also be completely repressed, or expressed as anger, or experienced as a compelling need for distance. Later on, a dislike of a sibling's spouse may in fact be rooted in jealousy at sharing a loved one's affection. Or, more rarely, the remnant of early childhood fantasizing may actually be expressed in adolescence or adulthood as frank sexual yearning.

Brother-sister incest (including sexual behavior among adopted or half- and step-siblings) comprises about 20 percent of the total estimated cases of sexual involvement inside the family. The sexualizing of a sibling relationship, suggest Stephen Bank and Michael Kahn in *The Sibling Bond,* may actually serve as a form of nurturance in situations of extreme emotional neglect by the parents. In such a circumstance, a brother and sister, or sister and sister, or brother and brother may become sexually active in a kind of benevolent desire to provide one another with a sense of security and love. Such so-called "nurturant incest" is perhaps the least erotic of sexual relationships, more lifesaving than exciting.

In the vast majority of situations, however, as Bank and Kahn conclude, the effect of incest between siblings is far from nurturant. Even when two siblings believe that mutual agreement lies at the basis of their sexual engagement, issues of power, domination, and manipulation must be taken into account. An inability to form intimate ties and a lack of trust in others may be the long-term result for both partners.

The sexual drive, or libido, is an unconscious element of a person's nature. Very early on in life, certain basic situations become stimulating to an individual child and at some level, those same triggers are at the basis of what the child finds emotionally stimulating for his entire life. A measure of aggression exists in all of us, to be sure, and, as psychiatrist Charles Brenner has written, "even the most callous act of intentional cruelty . . . still has some unconscious sexual meaning to its author and provides him with a degree of unconscious sexual gratification." Aggression is the boon companion of sexuality. Thus, a child whose erotic self developed in a violent and aggressive atmosphere may be coping with violent and aggressive urges throughout his life.

Abusive sexuality can have a lifelong devastating effect for both the victim *and* for the perpetrator. Two brothers whom I interviewed during the course of this study, the only children of a violent and drug-addicted father, very early became involved in a sort of master-slave relationship. The elder boy, who himself had often been severely beaten by the father, would force his then ten-year-old brother to perform fellatio, often slapping and punching him in order to ensure submission. Fifteen years later, the elder boy, now thirty, was still striving to atone for his childhood violence. For years he showered his brother with gifts of marijuana and other drugs, as if he could numb him into forgetting. More recently, he had converted to Catholicism, and one of his often-stated goals is to bring his brother into the Church with him. "He doesn't understand that I know what he's been through. If he would let me in, I could help," he told me sadly. By his own account, this man, who had had incredible mathematical skills as a child, was working as a night watchman, living alone, locked in a prison of self-hatred and repentance. He could not move ahead with his own life until he had his younger brother's forgiveness.

The younger brother, however, had been in and out of drug facilities since his midteens, and now struggled to quell his own violent urges by drinking and smoking pot. "When I'm out of it," he told me quite plainly, "that's the only time I feel calm." True, both men were victims of their father's cruelty and failure to be an adequate parent, but both were also very conscious of the elder brother's hurtful role in his younger brother's life. Abusive sexual dominance of a sibling is far from nurturant for either participant.

Erotic Longing

When a certain amount of disturbance in the family has perhaps gone unacknowledged, attraction to a sibling can remain a lifelong struggle. In the case of the Patch sisters, each of them had initially married men who, like their half brother Richard, had manifest difficulty in impulse control. While Richard's struggle was with alcoholism, Laura's and Sara's first spouses each had trouble remaining faithful. Men like Richard were extremely appealing, and not just in the present generation. Impulse control had been a problem for Laura and Sara's grandfather as well, for he had molested his own daughter and attempted to molest his granddaughter. This was a family in which, on at least two occasions, sexual boundaries *had* been crossed when a man from a more senior generation made sexual overtures to a younger blood relative. In the case of Richard, Laura, and Sara, however, where the incest taboos were most assuredly less profound— not simply because the Patches were of the same generation, but also because they shared only one parent, Joe—their sexual behavior was apparently under control. The sexual longing, on the other hand, was evident.

This issue of siblings and erotic longing is quite primal to the relationship. Thus, once again we must scrutinize early childhood and siblings' first awareness of one another. As has been explained in earlier chapters, the birth of a sibling stimulates sexual curiosity. Freud said that trying to figure out how a sibling has been created is at the root of human intellectual growth. Our brothers and sisters enter our consciousness bathed in a halo of incomprehensible eroticism and, perhaps forever, remain tinged with a mild glow of Eros. The intensity of sexual exploration and fantasy about a sibling is very likely exacerbated by differences in gender. Our unconscious mental processes, however, subvert that longing into other emotions; the particular mixture of jealousy and admiration that one sibling has for another has been worked out over a lifetime—and, frankly, is only one aspect of a complex relationship that continues to evolve throughout life.

One basic tenet of Freudian thinking that is often ignored is the idea that *most* emotional functioning is unconscious. Sexuality, or the erotic drive that propels one to action, is, nevertheless, present in every individual from the earliest phases of life. Lest the reader shrug shoulders and say, "This is ridiculous," let me counter this skepticism by saying that any parent can observe an example of the uninhibited and innocent eroticism of very young children. The desire to marry Mommy or Daddy, or to play Doctor, or to be kissed on the belly button until weak with laughter, can all be viewed as aspects of a sexual self. As a child grows older, the habits of repression settle in and the ability to recall that uninhibited toddler self vanishes. Nevertheless, it is surely possible that elements of those exciting moments in early life are at the root of situations that still remain charged for us when we are fully grown.

Most of us will never know exactly why we have become who we have become or, more precisely, why our natures have developed as they have. Understanding what makes each of us anxious, or happy, or excited, may forever remain a mystery. Nevertheless, that element of curiosity—the part of you that was motivated to read this book—has its roots in questioning about where babies come from, and why, and how. And it is in that first moment of questioning also that the seeds of lifelong sibling rivalry can be planted.

In Chapter 2, I discussed the way in which a child is able to make sense of otherwise incomprehensible, frightening, or overstimulating information, based upon his or her current sophistication regarding the world of human relationships. Again, this activity does not take place at a conscious level; it is an unconscious process each individual uses to *allow* information to come to the conscious surface in a comprehensible and emotionally bearable manner. At every phase of development, as an individual child's intelligence and ability expand, he or she processes the world in an increasingly complex manner. The child's ability to cope with the conflicting emotions surrounding a sibling's birth will be affected by his or her developmental phase, which affects the level of sophistication at which the child can "organize" the experience of the new sibling's birth.

If the newborn is of the opposite sex, the elder child's envy of the sibling may become tinged with envy of that opposite gender. Watching the parents fuss and coo over the baby can stimulate the thought that they prefer the baby's gender; that, for example, a little girl was being awaited all the time that the elder child felt himself supreme. The child's *unconscious* internal organization of self will be affected by this extreme feeling of envy, and it may become part of his or her view of the opposite sex. The question of whether this particular event becomes a life theme for the young child greatly depends on his personality, his parents' response to his inevitable anxiety, and his age and emotional development at the time.

The important thing to remember is that kids *have* developmental crises; they must, for nobody could or should grow to adulthood without experiencing glee and sadness, and developing the resilience to handle both. Otherwise, adult life would be unbearable. It would actually be impossible to avoid some level of trauma, because even in the most perfectly cosseted existence that one can fantasize about, the youngster would inevitably become distressed by an ear infection, or a misunderstanding with a peer, or a huge, barking dog. The birth of a sibling is just one predictable moment of difficulty; others include potty training, a divorce or death, the beginning of schooling, and any other watershed moment with emotion-laden potential.

This fundamental fact—that a certain amount of hardship helps to breed resilience—is often ignored in popular psychological writing, as if a childhood without stress were a viable possibility. The implication is that our failure to have a perfect experience is always someone else's fault, without taking into account the fact that our natures predispose us to experience events and actions as if they were meant personally. The father whose children remember him as unavailable may have been working at three jobs to support his family during the Depression; a younger woman who thinks her sister had no time for her once she left home may not understand how difficult the elder sister found her first year at college, and how ashamed she felt to confess her unhappiness to her admiring younger sister. Individuals, in most cases, act based on their own perceptions of the world to protect themselves and their loved ones. Since each has a different set of perceptions, understanding even a close relative's actions may be more difficult than one might suspect.

Nevertheless, some families *do* negotiate the rocky shores of development better than others. Every adult was once a child in a family, in most instances with a sibling or two or three. And, most people *do* manage to grow up, separate from their original families, and create independent lives of their own. Sometimes they may yearn to be back in the safety of the childhood home, to be sure, but they are securely planted in the world of independent adult life.

Separation and Individuation

The issue for the Patches, all three of them—and for the family overall, in the previous generation at least—seems to have been the issue of separation and individuation, or so the majority of the psychologists with whom I spoke about the family speculated. Sexuality for the Patches, several experts suggested, is more of a metaphor for extreme closeness, a longing for a complete union of souls.

Each of the Patches felt that they knew one another so well that they could understand what the others were thinking. Moreover, each one of the Patches actually seemed to *experience* the others as part of him or herself. The emotional linking of twins in the previous generation had now become a new sort of symbiotic prison: As the old joke goes, if Laura stubbed her toe, Sara said ouch. When Laura felt she was struggling against forces that compelled her to divorce her husband, she was experiencing herself as an element in a larger being that comprised Richard, Sara, and herself. Her will, alone and in combination with her husband's, was not enough to keep her apart from the siren call of her siblings. In merging with them, she found the only love she considered to be unconditional.

Unfortunately, there was a rider on this sibling contract that none of the Patches wanted to read: Be a part of us, or be unloved. This was a threesome that was most alive, and most exhilarated, when they were together. Spouses, children, parents, and friends had their place and time, but these three were the only ones who made one another feel whole.

By returning to the Sylvia Plath poem with which this chapter began, one can get a feel for the fundamental relationship among these two women and their brother. The last line of "The Rivals" reads: "No day is safe from news of you,/walking about in Africa maybe, but thinking of me." This was a relationship in which each person felt sure that he or she was the central obsession of the other ones. Just enough doubt existed to keep the connection at its most stimulating.

At this point, the Patches seem wrapped up so tightly with one another that it might be downright impossible for any one to separate. At the same time, they also seemed to exhibit an absence of empathy—a lack of acceptance—that was a surprising companion to such enmeshment. Not one of them ever said to me, "Well, my brother or sister has had a complicated or difficult life"; rather, each endeavored to convince me that his or her life had been the hardest. Though they sat together in the boat of their relationship, everyone was paddling toward a different shore without concern for the others. All that furious paddling churned up lots of water and gave off the appearance of great activity, but kept everyone floating in the same, familiar place.

To some extent, I suspect that each of the Patches exists largely as a distorting mirror for the others: If Laura looks in the mirror, she sees herself as Snow White and her sister as the Wicked Queen; when Sara looks in the mirror, she sees the virtuous victim who has suffered at her sister's hands. And the Handsome Prince, well, I feel sorriest for him. Whom does he see? Is it the loved elder brother or the disdained only son? Quite possibly, he views both those people on different occasions; sadly, he doesn't seem able to see an adult man with a wife, a family, and a life that are his alone.

■

CHAPTER EIGHT

Ginger Farr

"If I See a Therapist, Am I Sick, Too?"

■

"Let's begin with your parents," I said. "Tell me about your parents, what they're like, what you do with them, is that okay? Why don't we start with your mother?"

I couldn't tell if Bobby Farr was capable of understanding me. I'd been too wary about asking for specifics about his mental abilities, and now I was paying the price. In my ignorance—and also my eagerness to connect with him—I couldn't stop repeating myself. "Tell me a little about your mother, can you do that? Is that okay?" I asked again as we seated ourselves in the attractive central room that served as the hub of the three wings of his residential care facility.

Bobby responded at once. "Are you sure?" he asked.

I didn't know what he meant. I looked for assistance to his sister Ginger, who sat on a folding chair to my right. Her voice matter-of-fact, she said, "He wants to know if that is the question you want him to answer, if you've made up your mind."

"Yeah," said Bobby softly.

"He's a little jumpy," Ginger said.

"Are you?" I asked. I was about to tell him that I was on edge, too.

"Well, I don't know you," Bobby said. His words had been

■

slurred and indistinguishable when we'd first met in his room ten minutes earlier, but now I was beginning to follow the speed and awkward rhythm of his inflections. "I can be scared until I know you. After I know you, then it's okay."

There was a pause as I tried to figure out the most empathetic and reassuring thing to say. Before I could speak, however, Bobby continued. "Now I'm not scared anymore," he said conclusively. "Now I know you. We're friends."

Ginger shrugged, a kind of fatalistic "you see?" gesture. "He's okay," she said. "He's fine."

Forty-year-old Bobby Farr was the eldest child in his family. Whether physicians were unwilling or unable to inform his parents that their son had been born mentally disabled is unclear; certainly, a firm diagnosis of what was then called "trainable mental retardation" wasn't made until much later. (Note: In discussing Bobby, the Farrs continue to use the terminology in currency during his childhood, and, where they are quoted, such terminology will be used. The current term for Bobby's condition falls under the general heading of developmental disability; a more specific diagnosis of his condition would be "mentally disabled.")

The Farrs' next two children, first a boy and then a girl, each died only hours after birth. Although each pregnancy had apparently been normal, neither infant lived long enough to leave the hospital. In each case, an excess of amniotic fluid led doctors to believe that the fetus had muscular dystrophy and was unable to breathe properly *in utero*.

Five years after Bobby's birth, his sister Ginger was born. Now she was thirty-five, a healthy, intelligent woman with a strong back and shoulders and a mop of copper curls. She worked as a special-education teacher in the public school system, lived alone in a cheery apartment, and seemed somehow to be mature beyond her years: accepting, matter-of-fact, and sturdy. I imagined that she was superb with her students, for she was honest and refreshingly direct, brooking no nonsense.

While Ginger's manner was frank and brisk, her brother's was all charm. Despite his disability, he was skilled in social interaction, actively responsive to conversational cues, eager to please, and sensitive to nuance.

Nevertheless, Bobby's conversation was difficult to comprehend. His words were mumbled low, and his speech was rapid. I would catch a particular emphasis in his voice, and if I could "get" what that word was, I could generally grasp his general intent. Still, it was like trying to communicate across a language barrier; one never knew where the holes in his comprehension lay, so it wasn't easy to predict if a particular question would confuse him or, alternatively, be patronizing.

I can't say that I truly got to know Bobby, for my prior experience with persons who have developmental disabilities had been minimal, and thus I spent most of our interview time feeling my way on how to connect with him. I was able, however, to come to a certain basic understanding of the facts of Bobby Farr's existence, to learn that he was an immensely likable, intelligent child of three and a half encased in the body of a forty-year-old man.

He was at least five feet eleven, and he weighed, he told me proudly, 165 pounds. He had brown hair, I could see, because wisps of it extended beneath the edges of the white bicycle helmet he wore to protect himself from the frequent falls he took as his muscles slowly deteriorated from muscular dystrophy contracted in his early twenties. His nose was long and elegant, his cheekbones prominent, and his eyes deep-set and endearingly open. He was clean-shaven and his color was healthy.

Bobby's stomach protruded over the waistline of his pants as he slumped in his padded chair. The seat had an especially high vinyl pillow to give him the extra height he needed if he chose to try standing up solo (with his newly fitted leg braces, he couldn't bend his knees, and so he was having to relearn this skill). Overall, it was some quality of absence—although barely definable—that gave away Bobby Farr's disability. His jaw was flaccid, even the muscles in his cheeks seemed off duty, as if much of his appearance were governed by gravity. His eyes continually rolled back to rest inside his head, so that I spent most of our conversation looking at the whites of his eyes.

Ginger later told me that the extent of Bobby's condition had finally been confirmed when he was about two years old. His parents had seen that he wasn't developing normally; they used to call him "Little O" because his mouth was always open. More important, he wasn't yet walking, a developmental task most children master long before the age of two. "Now they realized that he didn't have the muscular coordination to close the left side of his mouth. He couldn't smile because his facial muscles couldn't pull."

"He can't smile? That must be hard for him. And you," I added, as an afterthought.

"Oh, no, he has his own expression that we understand as a smile. When you know someone and live with them, you see—" She broke off for a moment, and then she said abruptly, "Nobody ever said that he was retarded, not for years. My parents brought him to all kinds of doctors, and the most anyone would say was 'well, he won't be college material.'" Her tone had been sarcastic and harsh, but now she began to speak more gently. "He did enter kindergarten, a regular class, but he just couldn't keep up. He could play and listen to songs, but he couldn't write, he couldn't skip. He didn't have the coordination."

She had told me over the phone that she and Bobby looked alike, but as I looked at them next to one another, I had found this hard to see. Ginger's features were tightly controlled; she was as consciously on duty as he was open and unguarded.

Bobby was one of three men and six women who lived on this particular wing of the building. The residents were all what is called "high functioning," even though they had developmental disabilities. Most of them rode a bus to work each day in a special factory, where they packed dishes into boxes. The jobs provided them with self-esteem and active social involvements; they had other friends there and garnered rewards for years of service. Each of the residents earned his or her own salary, which the residence staff banked until the resident identified an item—a magazine, a video, an article of clothing, a gift for a family member—upon which to spend it.

"Bobby's wing is a great one," said Sherry Gannon, the wing's senior administrator. Sherry, Ginger, and I talked while waiting for Bobby to join us for another interview. "These guys run the entire building. They help me file paperwork, they plan parties, they even go to visit the more severely disabled residents on the other two wings. They are useful and important members of this residence. We call Bobby our social director; he practically runs the place. He knows exactly what time each of the staff members is supposed to be here. If one of us is a minute late, he'll be out at the door with his watch. He helps the cook make salads, and set the table. He's very special."

Ginger agreed. "Even though these guys look kind of funky, I mean, to you, they are very high functioning, very intelligent."

"They're unbelievable," said Sherry. "They really get along well. I mean, they argue among themselves, but we are never asked to interfere. Most of them have been together for five years, they have strong relationships."

"Bobby Is Very Smart"

Sherry explained how Bobby continually struggled back and forth between the independence he desired—being able to go to a movie with Gary, his best friend and roommate, for example, or to go on a date with a female resident—and his declining muscular strength. The new set of leg braces he sported had automatic locks on the knees, so that if he fell, his knees would not bend backward and injure him. Although Bobby understood the reason for the new braces and appreciated in theory that he might be able to walk more and use his wheelchair less, he had been sulky about the locking mechanism and disinclined to practice using it.

"So I asked him what he might want to work toward, you know, what kind of reward? He could earn the reward by learning to work with the braces. So, he said he wanted to go out to dinner with me," Sherry explained, her cheerful grin widening as she told the story. "And then he told me where he wanted to go, to Huddleston's because that's a place his sister likes and then he told me that I have to have shrimp because Ginger always orders shrimp."

Sherry was listing off Bobby's requests on her fingers good-naturedly. "Then he said he wanted to order for me, and then he said he wanted me to wear this red dress because it's his favorite, and then, well, what happened was that he was being an angel whenever I was in the building, but—" She paused dramatically. "Whenever I was busy, or in a meeting, or in the mornings before I got here, he was just awful. He would sulk, he wouldn't help us get him up out of bed. He would refuse to take his bath."

"Now Bobby's heavy, if he's being a dead weight, we can't get him to stand up," Sherry continued.

"Couldn't you just . . ." I motioned with my arms.

Sherry blinked twice, quickly. "Oh, no, we don't ever use force with them. We negotiate and reward. We would never want to do anything forceful or overwhelming."

"So today," she continued, "was the day we were supposed to go to dinner, but he really hadn't kept up his end of the deal. Now we're aiming for three days from today. We're going to try breaking it down into three-day increments. If he tries really hard for the next few days, then we go to dinner . . . still, here I am in my red dress, all the same!" She chuckled.

Ginger, who had been standing next to me and nodding in vigorous understanding all through the telling of this story, chuckled with her. "I know what that's like. He can be so moody," she said. "But the funny thing is, that restaurant? We've only been there once, maybe two years ago. You can never tell what sticks in his head. Did he tell you he wanted a glass of wine?"

"Yeah," Sherry said. "I know you guys have a glass of wine with him, I know he likes it, but I can't do that, I'm working. So I'll have to tell him I'm taking medicine or something, that I can't drink, so could he please not have one either."

Sherry turned to me and said "It's hard with Bobby. Most of the clients here can be rewarded with a quarter, or a magazine, or something simple. But he doesn't want things like that, so rewards for him are more complicated."

Ginger jumped in, saying, "You see, he's very smart. He is an amazing manipulator. So talking about his mental age can be very deceptive. Academically, he's a three-and-a-half-year-old, but socially he's incredibly sophisticated."

Sherry's nod of agreement was enthusiastic.

Thunder interrupted us, ominous and loud. Ginger and Sherry looked at one another knowingly. "Is he coming yet?" said Ginger, who had been standing with her back to the wing. "Bobby, he's not great about thunder and lightning, although he's a good deal better than he was," she explained to me.

"I don't see Bobby yet," said Sherry, peering down the hall. "I'm surprised. He's got a sixth sense for thunder, sometimes he'll be down here before it even starts raining, and, lo and behold, the thunder will come."

"Oh, tell me about it," Ginger said, her tone both world weary and somewhat proud. "I remember when we were kids, Bobby used to hate thunder so much he would sleep with a flashlight in his room. That used to get me because his room was right across from mine, and I never liked to sleep with a light on. He'd start blubbering at two in the morning. I wasn't too compassionate, I was maybe fifteen and he was twenty. I'd be yelling across the hall, WHAT'S THE MATTER! I wouldn't get up and go to him, but he got over his fear. He used to go crazy when it thunders; now he just wants to be around people. It's much better."

Where were your parents when he was sobbing in his room? I wanted to ask, but didn't. I imagined, having already met at length with Ginger, that she would jump down my throat for even raising the question. She believed, and had vehemently stated so, that responsibility for Bobby was to be shared among her parents and herself, and that ducking that obligation would be unthinkable. She hadn't allowed herself, ever, even to consider this a difficult or disturbing burden. It was, she stated matter-of-factly, just the way things were. In subsequent conversations, however, I began to realize that she was deeply involved in a struggle to quell an anger that existed despite her wish to deny it, a persistent resentment about the sacrifices she had seemingly made so easily. As much as she wanted to take her difficulties for granted, she was in a crisis, and some of those angry feelings were beginning to seep through. I didn't learn this, however, for several more days, for it was not until I began to understand the transmission patterns of muscular dystrophy that I knew just why Ginger Farr was hitting the limit of what she could handle. On this occasion, I simply suppressed the question and chuckled along with the two other women.

"Sometimes," Sherry added, for my benefit, "you have to help them get over what they're feeling, rather than give in to it. Bobby's a very emotional person, and that makes his life complicated."

"Yeah," I said, "there was one point during the interview where I suddenly realized that he was trying to make me feel sorry for him."

"Boy, did you get his number quick!"

Ginger and Sherry were laughing in unison. I was struck by the notion that, for Ginger, sisterhood might best be found among these women who, like herself, understood what someone like me, with healthy siblings, might never fully comprehend.

"Well, it was mostly because of the way you clamped down on it when he was starting to talk about how much he missed you now that he lived here," I admitted. "You asked him, how come you never call me, and he said he was too tired and unhappy. When you told him that he was never too tired to call his girlfriends, he laughed. That's how I knew that he was trying to put me on."

"You know, he was at home until he was thirty-five years old. When he used to fall down, he would lie there and cry," Ginger said, solidly enunciating each word. "My mother has muscular dystrophy too, so she was sick herself, and she couldn't pick him up. Before Dad retired and I moved out, if he fell, I was the only one around to pick him up. But I couldn't pick him up alone, he was too heavy. So I would just get tough, and say, 'What are you going to do, lie there? You have to help me get you up.'" Her voice grew louder as she spoke; I was hearing the domineering tone she'd used to overcome his sense of helplessness as well as her own. "People would be shocked at the way I talked to him, but that's their problem. If you say 'oh, poor baby' to him, he'll play it for all it's worth. If you let him know he can't get away with stuff, he'll be happier and so will you."

"I Only Knew My Family"

"So what was it like to grow up in a house with him?" I asked, about twenty minutes later. We were standing outside, in the parking lot of Bobby's building. Even though the rain had stopped, the humidity remained high; the scent of lilac seemed to inundate the heavy, still air. I noticed that the grounds were carefully landscaped, all flat, grassy, accessible surfaces, with only a few grand clumps of lilac and laurel bushes set far back from the wide paths.

"Well, for me, it was very normal," she said simply. Through the picture window behind her, I could see the odd lineup of wheelchair, high chair, and regular chair at the dining room table; it was dinnertime and, now that Bobby had joined his housemates, each seat was filled. As in other situations, each of the nine residents manifested different difficulties here, from needing to be strapped into a special seat to needing to be spoon-fed; only one of the residents, a woman who appeared to be in her mid-twenties, was eating without any apparent assistance. "For me, I knew nothing else, I only knew my family," Ginger continued. "It was a very loving, happy family. Bobby had his activities, and I had mine. I went to religious instruction; he went to religious instruction for the handicapped. I went to Girl Scouts; he went to Boy Scouts with a handicapped troop. He went to dances, and I would be a chaperone. He went to a special summer camp. I volunteered there for many years."

"It occurs to me that you had two choices, sort of," I ventured. "One would be that you could have said, 'this kid is ruining my life,' and the other would be that you would say, 'this kid is making my life richer,' and that seems to be the choice you made."

"Well, as a kid I didn't make any choice," Ginger said. She began looking in her white shoulder bag for her car keys. "I was a kid and it was the way I was raised. He was just . . . We were just kids, and we were brother and sister. We fought like cats and dogs."

"How? When?"

She paused in her search, rolling her eyes heavenward at the memory. "Constantly. He's real bullheaded, stubborn, and so am I. Even if one of us was wrong, we'd stick to it, fight to the death."

"Physically, I mean, rolling around on the floor, tackling one another?"

"Oh, no, verbally, never physically," she said. "He never would have been able to fight well physically. But verbally, oh, God. When Bobby was young, my parents paid for two or three years of speech therapy to get him to talk, and unfortunately the therapist did a good job. He never shuts up."

"I get the feeling that you like him a lot. You do, don't you?" I asked. She rezipped her purse and began to sort through the huge ring of keys.

"Oh, he's great. He's a really funny character. If he was normal, he would have been the Casanova of Seneca County. I've always thought so. Now, I have to run, I'm really late. I have a committee meeting tonight," she said and, smiling apologetically, she slipped into her car. She had backed halfway out of her parking space before I'd even raised my hand to wave good-bye.

Coping with a Sibling's Disability

The issues that define—as well as blur—relationships among adult siblings can be magnified an unknowable number of times by the developmental disability or mental illness of a sibling. Some adults— because of conditions no parent could have predicted—need supervision, financial management, and simple loving care for the whole of their lives. While even a half-century ago the parent of a child with Down's syndrome would have expected to outlive the disabled youngster, medical advances have been such that this is no longer necessarily the case. Bobby Farr's parents were seventy and seventy-one at the time I interviewed him; although his father and mother might live many more years, there was still a strong possibility that Bobby would spend twenty to forty years of his life without his parents' support. Who would care for him then?

According to Donald Meyer, founder and director of the Sibling Support Project based at the Children's Hospital and Medical Center in Seattle, Washington, most of the forty-three million people with disabilities in the United States have siblings. As parents age, the burden of responsibility for managing the disabled sibling's care often shifts to a brother or sister. And yet, these well siblings' needs are very different from those of a parent: They are often focused on the new families they've created and there may be difficulties in integrating and assimilating the disabled sibling's needs into their new lives.

In Margaret Moorman's beautiful memoir of taking on the care of her sister, *My Sister's Keeper,* she describes how she went to a self-help group for families of the mentally ill and was the only sibling at the meeting. "When my turn came to speak, all I could say was that my mother was getting old, that I didn't do much to help, and that I dreaded the day the responsibility for my sister's care would fall to me," she writes. "The parents looked at me blankly. No one spoke. It was as if I were talking about *their* deaths, expressing reluctance to care for *their* sick children. Faced with their stares, I felt ashamed to be so free. . . . I left the meeting with a desperate sense that there was no one to talk to—indeed, that I didn't deserve help."

Moorman described the process of coming to terms with her responsibility to care for her sister—who suffers from a mixed diagnosis of schizophrenia and manic-depressive illness—after their mother's death, as well as the intense and ambivalent love she felt for her. She makes explicit that a large aspect of the well sibling's burden is the fear of somehow being secretly tainted with the potential for illness oneself. Those fears are often unspoken, because the well sibling may feel afraid of facing them, or think that it is selfish to voice such concerns, even though they loom over every other aspect of life. For example, once Moorman learned that she had only a slightly increased risk of transmitting schizophrenia and manic depression to her own offspring, she felt "every pore in my body open up. I felt as if I were Jacob, after a long, long fight, finally blessed by the angel." Margaret Moorman subsequently gave birth to a healthy daughter, and made peace with her sisterly responsibilities; although she didn't pretend that she would never again resent her obligation, she had clearly come to terms with it.

People with special health and developmental requirements represent a widely varying population: The specific needs of a person with schizophrenia may be very different from those of one with a chronic and debilitating physical illness or a developmental disability. Even more important, within each of these populations, the range of severity is wide. So, of course, is the basic temperament that the person with special needs brings to the mix, and the basic temperament of the well sibling, also. A violent and aggressive sibling will be harder to care for than a passive and gentle one, in most cases, but each situation reflects a completely different circumstance.

Certain generalizations about persons with special needs are possible to make, because issues of psychological and emotional adjustment for the family as a whole are believed to be fairly consistent across a variety of conditions. A series of studies appears to demonstrate that the severity of the disability is a more important factor than the nature of the actual disease or handicap. In general, the worse the disability, the more difficult the adjustment for the healthy sibling. Also, the smaller the family, the more pressure there is on an individual sibling; in a larger family, responsibility for the brother or sister with special needs may be diffused throughout the entire sibling network. Although the eldest well sister often becomes earmarked to bear the greatest burden, as at least one study has found, the opportunity for shared caretaking gives each individual child more chances to establish an independent life and maintain positive, supportive relations with the sibling with special needs. Furthermore, parental expectations for a well child may place him under too much pressure if he is the only one; with several well siblings of a brother or sister with special needs, the potential for healthy psychological adjustment is thought to be better (provided the family has enough financial resources to support each member with some measure of comfort).

This matter of family size is one area in which a sibling network with all healthy siblings may be uniquely different from a network in which one sister or brother has a developmental disability or a chronic emotional or physical illness. If Ginger's other two siblings had lived and been healthy, she might have had an easier time out in the real world and might have felt psychologically freer to pay more attention to her own needs and had less of a sense of obligation to weigh her down. In a "regular" family, on the other hand, having more siblings may lead to negative effects: a dissipation of financial resources, parental attention that is diluted too greatly, and elder siblings who are asked to perform more arduous parenting duties.

The Biggest Worry for Well Siblings

For Ginger, and for many sisters and brothers in similar situations, the issue of Bobby's eventual care was of paramount concern. As parents age, the fact that a sibling with special needs may never be able to live independently will always raise questions about eventual long-term care. Healthy siblings need to wrestle with issues of responsibility and guardianship; they also must consider whether their spouses and children will be able to accommodate the needier sibling. Since the happiness of the sibling with the disabling condition is also a factor, someone like Ginger Farr can find herself juggling competing needs and making extraordinarily difficult decisions.

Care of the person with disabilities can become one of the most important aspects of a well sibling's life. Ginger knew well that she would supervise Bobby's care when her parents died, but she didn't have any plan for what would occur if something happened to her. Who would care for Bobby then? For Ginger, the consideration *who will care for me?* took second place; she didn't resent that, she said, for it was a fact of life. But even if she chose to ignore the possibility of some freak accident or incident making her unable to care for her brother, she also (obviously) had increased concerns about her own genetic vulnerabilities as well as the risks of passing on an illness to a child or grandchild. At the time that I met with Ginger, this was a matter of extreme concern to her, for she was aware that new tests made it possible for her to learn if she, like her mother and brother, might suffer from myotonic muscular dystrophy.

This particular form of muscular dystrophy exhibits its first visible indications between the ages of twenty and forty. (Bobby's had probably begun in his mid-twenties, although there was some confusion on the precise timing because certain symptoms of myotonia strongly resemble the developmental disabilities with which he was born.) The first symptoms of myotonia, according to information provided by the Muscular Dystrophy Association, include stiffness in the feet and hands, especially following a chill, and difficulty relaxing one's grip. Frequent tripping and falling is another sign, as is facial weakness, such as the drooping eyelids and jaw that one could see with forty-year-old Bobby Farr. This weakening of the muscles spreads steadily, until walking becomes difficult.

"Do I Want to Know?"

Unlike certain other forms of muscular dystrophy, the myotonic variety is an equal opportunity caller with no gender preference. It is also a very slowly progressing disease, which may not impede daily living for years after its onset. According to the Muscular Dystrophy Association, myotonia—or, as it is also called, Steinert's disease—is one of the four most common forms of muscular dystrophy. It is distinct from the others because of a spasming of the muscles that occurs after exertion. As her parents aged, the question whether Ginger Farr should find out if she had myotonia was looming large. "If it weren't for Bobby, I certainly wouldn't want to know," she admitted one afternoon as we sat on the pretty Oriental rug in her living room, sipping hazelnut coffee, and watching her two cats chase each other across the couch and down the room past us. "But it doesn't seem right not to know," Ginger said, "if it means that I can begin planning for him now." She put her cup down on the floor, next to an Edwardian wing chair, drew her blue-jeaned legs up to her chest, and wrapped her arms around them. She ran one hand through her pretty curls, and then looked down at her sneakers. She shook her head harshly, just once, and I realized that she was trying to prevent tears from welling.

At last she said, "This isn't like me." She looked up for a moment, and then back at her feet again. "I never cry."

I patted her sneaker.

"No, really. I never cry," she said. "It's just been a really hard time for me." She was silent, struggling to get her tears under control.

At last, I said, "Tell me about your mother's muscular dystrophy. When did she get it?"

She sniffed and sat up straighter. "Adulthood. We didn't have a clue until she was in her forties. But she was born with it, like my brother."

"Because she had it?"

"Yeah. It's genetically transmitted," she said reluctantly.

"So there is a real danger for you," I said. "That must be frightening."

"Right now it seems a little more frightening than usual," Ginger said, her shoulders slumping again.

"Why?"

"Well, I went for a fact-finding session with a genetic counselor, and I know I have to make some decisions. I have to decide if I want to know or not." She looked right into my eyes, reminding me a little of a child who is confessing to wrongdoing or an untruth. "It's a blood test," she said.

"Do you want to know?"

In an instant, her expression was wiped as blank as it could be, a true vision of inscrutability. "I don't know," she said quietly. "I haven't made the decision. I mean, if I'm ever in a position to have children, I need to know, of course."

"How do you feel, given, you know ..." I was stumbling, for Ginger had been unusually unrevealing about her personal life and the history of her love relationships. While she had spoken openly and easily about her family, her relatives, her schooling, even her friends, she hadn't yet said a word about the place of romance in her life.

"Well, I'm not seeing anybody, so I have no immediate need to know," she said. I had the uncomfortable sense that she was a little embarrassed, and it surprised me, for she had spoken without apparent discomfort about such family details as cleaning her brother's bottom and clothes after an accidental bowel movement. I had labeled her too simply as a person of great self-confidence and independence, a woman who knew how to take care of herself alone and preferred to do so. When she had shown me pictures of her family, she'd proudly told me stories about a series of female relatives, for three generations back on her maternal side, who had remained single their whole lives. We were at that time seated on the rug in her living room, between two comfortable chairs, surrounded by family photographs going back to the previous century. Each framed picture had been carefully removed from a protective bag for me to view it; each was neatly labeled with the year it had been taken, the subject's name, and her relationship to Ginger. I'd heard stories about a woman who raised her children on her own in the mid-nineteenth century, about a career woman at the turn of the century, even about an aunt who'd headed out west in the late 1920s and didn't return until the 1950s. I'd just assumed that Ginger Farr felt a great connection to these relatives because she, also, for her own reasons, was choosing not to go the conventional route.

"I have no immediate need to know," she repeated, and then, without warning, her voice grew louder and harder. She began to speak in a staccato tone. "What I'm thinking, really, is what the hell am I going to do if I end up in a wheelchair and I'm single the rest of my life? I don't have brothers or sisters to help me. And Mom and Dad will be gone."

"I'm confident with my intellect," she said abruptly. "I'm not confident . . . well, let's put it this way. I want to be married, I want kids. I don't have it. So that whole social aspect I have no self-confidence about. I mean, once, about five years ago, I was seeing this guy, and he was just a user. He took such advantage of me. He was a self-centered user, and he was out for what he was going to get. I was low down on his list of priorities. It wasn't good."

"You are in a very hard position, it seems," I said. She had so much to offer another person, and yet all her gifts would have to come with a huge price tag. She was confronting a nearly insurmountable difficulty, that if she were actually ill, she might have nobody to

care for her. And how could she find someone when she felt so
tainted by her situation? The load of responsibility waiting to fall
from her onto a partner was a heavy one.

"It is hard. It is," Ginger said sadly, shaking her head and looking
down at her knees, which she had drawn up even tighter to her chest.
She shifted. She rested her chin against her knees so that her jaw
jutted out strongly. If I had seen her tilted chin and jaw, at that
moment and out of context, without noticing how they were supported by her legs, I'd have thought she was feeling angry; it seemed
clear, however, that she was feeling overwhelmed by helplessness, by
a wish for something, someone, to lean on.

Eventually, Ginger said, "This is a crisis, in the sense that I could
know stuff I couldn't have known before. This test is new." She
straightened her legs out before her on the pale rug, as if by guarding
them vigilantly she could will them to stay healthy. Eventually, she
said, "I guess, you know . . . I guess, well, that it's better to be informed than surprised, but it sucks, it really sucks. And somehow the
timing couldn't be worse."

"Why?"

"It's as if all this bad stuff is coming together, all at the wrong
time. My mother is getting worse, all my friends have gotten married,
I'm just lonely. And then to think I'm going to find out if I have this,
well, it's really a curse, I just don't know how much more I can
handle." She bit her lip and looked over to her right, at the window
over the couch, where only the shaded front of the house across the
street was visible.

After a while, she started to speak again, although she continued
to stare out the window. "You know, I've always been a doer," she
said. "I don't get down, I don't let myself. I just keep busy. Maybe
that's not a good way to be, maybe I'm avoiding something, but
that's what I do. I take classes, I run dances for folks with special
needs, I even call Bingo for them. I have a master's degree in reading
education, you know, and a post-master's in school administration.
I'm thinking about starting another master's this summer. I'm great
at going to school; I'm a really good student. It keeps my mind
occupied, it keeps me busy . . ."

She shook her head again, hard, as if to dispel some tenacious
thought. "Once I even took a job in a department store, just to have

something to do on the weekends. I was assigned to ladies' lingerie, and it was a gas. I had the greatest time, and I made some really terrific friends. We used to do stuff all the time, the five of us. We went to exercise classes together, we went out together, it was a lot of fun. But then, one after another, they all started to get married, to have families." I noticed her voice was growing harsh again, the way it had when she described her fears about being alone, or how she had handled Bobby's fear of the thunder.

"Now, I don't see why things had to change," she continued. "I mean, if I was married and sitting around on a Tuesday night watching a video with my husband, why couldn't I call up my friend Ginger and say, come over, watch a movie with us? But nobody does anymore. It seems like I have to do the work. I'm always the one who has to bend over and be flexible, who has to do all the pursuing and make all the effort. And it hurts."

She looked over at me, her hazel eyes boring straight into mine, and she asked, "What is it about me? I'm always the one who's doing and arranging and being a pal, but *who* is ever there for me? I'm a very giving person, very, very giving. Almost too much. I definitely repress the feelings. I know I do. I know I do. I know I do. I'm in a real . . . I'm lost. I'm blue. I'm in a slump. I'm lost. That's what it is."

Ginger's voice trailed off. After a moment, she said, quietly, "I'm sorry."

"You're not grappling with fake things. You know. You're not making up problems, you have a really scary and difficult decision in front of you," I said.

"Do You Think I Need a Therapist?"

Ginger shrugged and shook her head, tossing her curly hair back and forth, as if she could joggle the idea and make it go away. "People say that I come across as a very controlled, very confident person. But I always think my emotions are right out there on the table, even though I guess they really aren't. I perceive myself as being an open book, but—" She stopped and studied me for a moment.

"Let me ask you something," she said. The briskness was reasserting itself.

I nodded. "Sure."

"I have a lot of baggage. I know that. My friend said to me, the other day, she said, with everything you're going through, have you ever thought of talking to an impartial person? You know, a counselor?"

"Have you?"

She ignored my question, for the moment. "So we were on the phone, and I said, gee, I thought I was coping with everything. Am I that screwed up? And I was so taken aback that I just listened, and I didn't say anything. Finally, when I could think about it, I realized she was worried about me, she wasn't saying I was crazy. She just thought maybe a counselor or someone might help me put it all together, you know?"

"What do *you* think of that?"

"Maybe, maybe," she said dismissively. Then she looked up again, out the window. "What do you think? I mean, I don't know you, but do *you* think I need a therapist? Do you think it would help?" She turned, drawing her legs up to her chest again. Her chin returned to its resting place on her knees. She gazed at me as if I had the key to the universe.

I swallowed.

"I may be the wrong person to ask," I began cautiously. "I think therapy might mean something different to me than it does to you. I mean, to me, it's a very normal thing to do, very helpful, a healthy way to sort out feelings in a more objective setting. But I get the sense that it is more loaded for you, that going to a therapist means something terrible is going on."

She nodded. "To me, people only go to therapy when they're having a midlife crisis, or they have a tragedy to deal with. I mean, I know I have problems, but I'm healthy, I have a good job, nothing bad has happened to me. I just feel unhappy."

It was my turn to stare, in shock. "Don't you know that many people would say you have had a very hard lot in life, growing up with so much responsibility, with so much illness?"

She shook her head, no.

I said, "Do you know that your brother was only the second or third person I've ever met in my life with developmental disabilities? And the other ones were children. People in the unaffected population really don't have any idea what kind of life someone like you has led, or what your family has been through. It may seem normal to you, but it's not normal to someone like me."

"People are clueless," Ginger said bluntly. "When it comes to this, I find it unbelievable how ignorant people are. I think I know more folks who are mentally retarded than I know people who aren't. It's just amazing to me how people don't try to understand these folks, like when my friends bitch and moan about little things, I think, who could possibly get upset over something like that."

She was sitting straight up now, proud and sure of her ground, but my first thought was how much easier her life might be if she would only cut herself a little slack, a little space to "bitch and moan" like all those clueless friends. Just because her brother's lot—and her mother's—were so much harder than hers, didn't mean that Ginger didn't have the right to air a complaint here and there, about the "little things."

"When you were growing up," I asked, "did you ever resent him?"

She laughed, as if I had made an outrageous joke, but her answer was surprisingly specific, considering the vagueness of my question. "I got enough attention, believe me. I wasn't given the short end of the stick or anything. In my family, this was the way it was. No bitching, no moaning, let's just do what needs to be done. I never questioned it, those were the rules."

I nodded.

"They were good rules," she said. "They were the only fair rules."

I nodded again.

"He had chores, you know. He fed the dog, he took out the garbage. He had difficulties in the sense that he might mess himself because of his poor muscular control. I mean, there were certain things that I grew up with that were embarrassing, but they didn't make me angry. I am very open about my brother and his disabilities. The braces, whatever, it's a fact of life. It's no big deal that I have to help him get dressed, and pull up his pants, and lift him off the toilet." Her tone was defiant; oddly enough, the best way to describe it would actually have been that word she'd just claimed did not apply: angry.

"That's just the way it is," I said.

"Cleaning shit off the floor, that's no big deal. You clean it up, and throw it out. You know what I mean? Otherwise you're not dealing with him. You have to live with it, with him. That's not to say he didn't annoy me," she continued. "I mean, he has habits that really irritate me. He scrapes his teeth on his fork when he eats. I know he can't help it, but it drives me crazy."

"I guess that would bother me too," I said, smiling.

She stared at me, still a little angrily. "This is the way our family coped," Ginger said. "Of course, we had to make accommodations, but this is the way he is. Other families hide it, ship the kids away, put them away. . . . When it's not necessary. To me, that's—" She paused, searching for the word. "Bad," she said. "That's bad."

Back in the early nineteen-fifties, when Bobby Farr was born, the scientific community believed that it was critical to remove persons with disabilities from the family, since they might otherwise "infect" the entire circle with the burden of their care. According to Donald Meyer, "The family was assumed to be dysfunctional, experiencing chronic sorrow and pervasive guilt. Positive traits, such as optimism, were frequently interpreted as a sign of denial, not a sign of strength. Families, of course, knew better."

Thus, when the Farrs decided to keep their son at home with them, they were going against the prevailing psychological thinking at the time. On the other hand, they saw no other way in which to treat a member of their family. If they thought about it at all, they would have asserted that they were strong enough to handle whatever stress Bobby added to their lives, and that they knew he would more than make up for added difficulty with the pleasure he brought them. Recent research also supports the Farrs' belief, for it is now assumed that developmental outcomes are best for those persons with disabilities who remain at home at least through childhood. They had proven to be right in their son's case, certainly, for Bobby had become an extremely well-adjusted person, the "social director" of his residence hall.

Furthermore, despite the fact that Ginger herself was struggling with serious and unpleasant life issues, she was a strong and competent human being. She suspected that this could be attributed to the general tenor of acceptance of difference and individuality in her family. In the bad times, the Farrs had learned to use a great deal of humor to cope with the difficulties inherent in coping with Bobby. "What it is, you know," she said, "is that you're walking a borderline between laughing and crying. And the laughing, that makes it okay."

The Invulnerable Sibling

As a sibling—and, particularly, a sister—in her position, Ginger Farr's difficulties were not unusual; nor were the strengths and competencies she had acquired through her experiences within her family circle. Ginger and Bobby's was a flipped hierarchical relationship, in which she was predominantly the powerful one and he predominantly the weaker. Despite the fact that she was the younger sibling, she was certainly more able to be in charge. While, in a healthy family, the children's relationship would have become more egalitarian over time, in the Farr family, the hierarchy had become more entrenched as the children reached adulthood.

The brothers and sisters of a person with developmental disabilities or mental illness seem, in general, to be inclined to identify themselves as different from the unwell sibling. As sibling experts Stephen Bank and Michael Kahn put it, they "arm themselves with evidence that they are very, very different from their defective siblings, and point out to friends, family, but especially to themselves, that they are not vulnerable."

Being "hypercompetent," which Ginger Farr clearly was, was thus a typical reaction to a sibling who himself is clearly not so. As Bank and Kahn concluded in *The Sibling Bond,* having a disturbed or ill sibling is a double-edged sword. On the one hand, the well sibling *knows* that he or she is the healthy, superior one. And yet, on the other hand, being defined as healthy often means one receives less attention. It can also lead to having trouble facing one's own problems, because difficulties are the province of the other brother or sister. Having a developmentally disabled or ill sibling can also mean that one is frequently embarrassed or uncomfortable, as Ginger had acknowledged.

Another theme that runs through the research literature is the notion of loyalty, of the screening that the healthy sibling performs when selecting friends and lovers because "Love me, love my family," has taken on an entirely more loaded meaning. In Ginger's case, tolerance for Bobby's condition had been one huge element in screening her friends all along; now, with the threat of her own possible illness, she was concerned that she might be *over*screening her friends, demanding too much, putting them through "tests" of loyalty that were out of proportion to the relationships she had forged with them. She was beginning to wonder if, in her desperation to feel that she could make an alternative support network for herself, she was pressuring her pals too much and driving them away.

As a whole, well siblings like Ginger may be more compassionate and mature than the general run of so-called normal people. Psychologist Milton Seligman, Ph.D., chair of the counseling psychology program at the University of Pittsburgh and an esteemed contributor to the study of the relatives of the developmentally disabled, points out that while the difficulties such siblings face is often noted, well brothers and sisters may benefit in many ways from having a sibling with special needs. Siblings who have been "actively involved in the management of their handicapped family member tend to be well adjusted," he observes, adding, "It may be that the critical variable is how the parents interact with their handicapped and non-handicapped offspring, for example, by providing ample time and by communicating their love and concern to *all* of their children."

Professional Helpers

Researchers have observed that well siblings of a person with special needs are often very accepting of differences in other people. They have a greater empathy—the ability to see life from the perspectives of others—that is particularly notable during the adolescent years when self-involvement and conformity reign supreme. These teenagers may describe themselves the way Ginger did, as the kind of person who always helped out the weird kid in the class or the new kid in school. Ginger had a heightened understanding of what it felt like to be different and a more adult concept of what is truly important in life.

Interestingly enough, such well siblings frequently find themselves working in the helping professions, the social services, psychology, education, or medicine. According to Donald Meyer, "They are extremely comfortable with disabilities and appreciate the diversity of the human condition. Because they value their siblings' abilities, they are able to serve as passionate advocates for others like them."

That, of course, must have been an element in Ginger's motivation to enter the field of special education. One study found that twice as many college students with disabled brothers and sisters selected majors in the helping professions (special education, counseling, or social work). Ginger herself remembers that, when she went to her high school guidance department for college counseling and was asked what her favorite activities were, all her extracurricular enterprises centered around helping others. She had been a candy striper in addition to all her work with the developmentally disabled population, but she truly didn't like the more medical aspects of that role, and so she naturally veered toward special education.

When Ginger graduated from college, the job market was extremely tight, and she was lucky to get a position in a small Pennsylvania community. She found herself unable to make a life there; she wanted more than anything to return to upstate New York and to be near her family and friends. Three months into the school year, she received a job offer from the school she'd attended as an elementary school student. She accepted immediately and was back home in two weeks. She had worked in this school system, and lived in her present apartment, ever since her return. In one of our last conversations, I asked her how physically tied she felt to the area now, fifteen years later.

"Oh, I would move if I met someone and wanted to marry him," she said. "But, frankly, he would have to have a lot of money, because my mother is physically tied to this area and so is Bobby. I would have to be able to travel back and forth as much as I wanted. They're both getting worse every year, in terms of health, and neither of them will ever uproot. I would do it, I mean, I would absolutely do it, if I met the right guy. But it would be very, very difficult."

On that occasion, as I made my way down the stairs, I suddenly remembered a question I had been meaning to ask her, one that I'd put to each one of the siblings I interviewed. She was standing in the door, watching me leave, and when I turned, her face lit up just the tiniest bit, as if she wouldn't mind continuing our talk. "If there were a book, just about you," I asked, "what would its title be?"

"Oh, God," Ginger said, "I don't know." She put her head to the doorjamb, and closed her eyes for a moment. "Oh, I guess, I know, the Ever-Ready, that's me. That would be the title, *The Ever-Ready Battery*. I just keep plugging away, and I don't quit, even though part of me—" She gave a dismissive shrug of the shoulders, followed by a cheery smile. It wasn't merely that she was preventing me from hearing the end of that statement, I suspect; Ginger herself wanted to avoid the thought.

"I Think I Hit Rock Bottom"

Several days later, I called Ginger and gave her the telephone numbers of several therapists of whom I think very highly. She dutifully took down the names, but she was short with me, and I had the uncomfortable feeling that she was slightly offended.

Ginger and I did not make arrangements to meet again, although we spoke on the phone shortly thereafter. I had to call her, because I realized that I had never gotten a consent form signed for her brother Bobby. Legally, he had been unable to authorize the interview, but Ginger had cleared it with their parents, who were his guardians. Now I had to contact Mr. and Mrs. Farr myself for their formal permission.

I called Ginger several times over the period of a week to ask for her parents' phone number, but I kept missing her. Finally, I left a message on her answering machine and asked her to call me back. When she did, it was immediately apparent that her spirits had lifted. Her voice was happy and excited; even over the phone, I could tell that she was smiling. She immediately provided me with her parents' telephone number and address, and then I asked her, "How are you doing?"

"I have news for you," Ginger said. "I went into therapy, I think it saved my life. I had really hit rock bottom, the worst down I've ever had in my entire life, and I feel so much better now. I went from ten feet under to ten feet high, that's how I feel! I needed it, it's so amazing what's coming out."

"Oh, that's wonderful."

"Yeah, it really is," she said, her voice practically bubbling down the wire. "The thing is, you know, I've always thought therapy is idiotic, why would I want to go back and bitch and moan about my childhood? My idea was that if I wanted to fix my problems now, in the present, then I should be thinking about the present. Why go back and get obsessed with what's already happened?"

"Well, it's important because—" I began.

"I know, I know," Ginger interrupted impatiently. "Now I understand. If I think about what's happened to me in the past, and what I learned when I was very young, I can begin to change what I do with people now, what I do that doesn't work. I just didn't understand before."

"I'm so glad," I said. "I'm so glad to hear about this."

"Oh, it's wonderful," she agreed excitedly. "It's great, it's so great, to talk about Bobby, and my mother's illness, and wanting to get married, and all that's gone right and wrong for me. I'm getting some perspective, and the funny thing is, I feel like a kid again, isn't that funny?"

In the moment of silence that followed her question, I wondered if Ginger Farr had *ever* felt like a kid before. She had been strong, and serious, and responsible, the picture of health. Now she was feeling her oats a little bit, and I suspected that there was nothing better for her to feel. "That's terrific," I told her. "I'm really glad for you."

"I feel like a teenager, all giddy! Thanks for giving me those names," she said.

"Oh, you're welcome," I answered, feeling extremely pleased. "You're very welcome."

Many months later, I called Ginger Farr to clarify several questions relating to her brother's medical condition. As soon as I identified myself, she chuckled and said, "I have good news!"

"What?"

"I don't have it! I don't have muscular dystrophy!"

"That's great," I said. "When did you find out? When did you decide to do the test?"

"Last fall," she answered. "I was talking to my cousin, and she said to me, 'Ginger, you might live *your* life very differently if you knew you had it, or that you didn't.' After that I just knew I had to know. So I called and made the appointment."

"What did they do?"

Her voice sounded rapid and girlish, even more chipper than it had been at our last conversation. "First I had a physical, you know, where they test your reflexes and all. They drew blood, and took a family history. Then they did a test called an electromyogram. They inserted needles into my muscles to see how they responded, if there were changes in my muscle activity. And on December twenty-ninth, the doctor called to say everything was negative, thank God."

"You must feel wonderful!"

Here Ginger's voice slowed and began to sound somewhat puzzled. "It's been two months, I know, since I heard, but the reality still hasn't set in. I mean, it was a total relief, the most wonderful way to start the New Year, and I got all choked up when she told me."

She paused, and then said, "I was misty-eyed for about thirty seconds, but then, I don't know . . . I guess it just hasn't hit home yet . . . I don't know why. Maybe I should see that therapist again."

"You stopped?"

"Yeah," she said. "It just didn't make much sense after a while. I mean, it's not in my head, what my life is. It's real. I thought it wasn't practical."

There was a longer silence, and then Ginger said, "I mean, in one sense, knowing I'm okay changes everything, and in another, well . . ." Her voice trailed off again, but her meaning seemed fairly clear. While Ginger now knew that she'd be alive to care for her brother in his declining years, that picture wasn't necessarily such an attractive one. In truth, she hadn't even begun to grapple with the other large problem that dogged her. She hadn't yet learned how to take even a smidgen of life's pleasures for herself; she hadn't yet allowed herself to imagine what might possibly bring happiness to Ginger Farr.

CHAPTER NINE

Rebecca, David, and Miriam Shulman

Acceptance Is the Key

▬▬▬▬

Rebecca Shulman's tale began in Cologne, Germany, in November 1938, when the two-year-old's life was suddenly altered—and probably saved—by the defiance of someone whom she never met, a Polish Jew named Herschl Grynszpan, who was living with relatives in France. Seventeen-year-old Grynszpan had left Poland, as had his sister because, as historian Howard M. Sachar has written, "economic depression and government-sponsored discrimination had reduced at least a third of Poland's 3.2 million Jews to the narrowest margin of survival. Pogroms were becoming common occurrences."

In October 1938, some twenty thousand Polish Jews who—like Grynszpan's sister—had emigrated to Germany, were expelled from their new country. They soon found out that the Poles would not allow them to return to their old land. Sachar writes, "When the Poles denied them entrance, they were reduced to subsistence in open fields along the border zone." Young Grynszpan, in Paris, learned that his sister was one of those caught in no-man's-land, and he conceived of a plan to draw international attention to the plight of the Jews in Eastern Europe. He bluffed his way into the German embassy on the pretext that he had a package to deliver. Once inside

▬▬▬▬

the office of a lower-level Nazi official named vom Rath, he shot the man; vom Rath died two days later.

Adolf Hitler's reaction to vom Rath's death was to suggest that his storm troopers be allowed a "fling." The result was the violent night of November 9, 1938, which became known as "Kristallnacht." Shards of shattered glass windows lined streets all over Germany and Austria; the storm troopers' riot ended only after the wholesale destruction of Jewish businesses, homes, and synagogues. Following Kristallnacht, some twenty thousand Jews were sent to concentration camps, writes Paul Johnson in the best-seller *A History of the Jews*, because they were deemed responsible for bringing the trouble onto themselves. Adding insult to grievous injury, German courts subsequently fined the Jewish people a billion marks (about $400 million) for the violence inflicted upon them.

Rebecca's parents, Anna and Peter Shulman, had certainly been aware before that November night that it would be wise to leave Germany. Most of their extended families had already departed: Anna's sisters had been in America for several years, and Peter's father was in Kenya, where he had gone more than a decade previously, several years before Hitler's rise to power. (The question of why he had left was a great unanswered mystery, one that seemed to mystify the Shulmans even two generations later. Had he started a new family? Did they have other aunts and uncles and cousins? No one ever knew.) Peter's mother, on the other hand, remained in her native town of Breslau despite the Nazi threat; she and her eldest daughter had no interest in leaving. They simply couldn't believe that trading a known situation for the unknown was a wise decision. Both Peter's mother and his sister would later die in the concentration camps.

In fact, during the year before Kristallnacht, Anna and Peter had applied for visas to enter Palestine. Immigration policies all over the world—including the United States—were restrictive and difficult. By November 1938, the Shulmans had yet to hear if they would be allowed to enter Palestine. After Kristallnacht, however, they knew they could no longer wait. Now thirty-two-year-old Anna and thirty-seven-year-old Peter swiftly arranged to leave the country in which they had been born. They made it to Holland with their little girl and the clothes on their backs. The Shulmans were secreted for several days by a Dutch Catholic family. Eventually, they were able to travel to England, and then, finally, they took passage on a boat for America.

"You must have been so frightened," I said to their daughter Rebecca, expecting her to nod in agreement. Now in her late fifties, she was a well-dressed, neatly coiffed blond with impeccable posture and a lively presence. As she opened her mouth to speak, however, her younger brother David leaned forward and said, "No. I think they were more angry than frightened. I mean, they expected that they would be admitted to the United States because they were educated, they were in good health, and they already had relatives here who could serve as sponsors. But I'm sure they were angry at what had happened."

"How do you know that? Did they talk about it much with you?" David was born in 1940, in Chicago; he and their younger sister, Miriam, were first-generation Americans.

"No," he said. He shrugged his shoulders. "I assume it, because that's the way they were. It is symptomatic of what we all got, all of us in our family. Something happens and you could say, gee, that's the worst thing that could ever happen in anyone's life. But that doesn't stop you. The world doesn't stop, it just keeps going forward. And you always figure tomorrow could be a whole lot better. And in general, it is. Or the day after, it's better."

Rebecca nodded. "Or if not, then the day after," she said, with a warm, even-toothed smile.

"But wasn't it difficult to leave Germany? Did they lose everything? Didn't they have to buy their way out?"

"It was problematic," Rebecca said simply. Later, I learned from Howard Sachar's fascinating survey of the Jewish people in America that although the Nazis did little to prevent Jews from leaving Germany in the mid-1930s, the situation had grown quite difficult long before the Shulmans attempted to leave. By early 1938, Jews had to buy their way out of the country by sacrificing 90 percent of their money, property, and household goods. In June 1938, Jews were no longer allowed to take anything, Sachar wrote, and thus they left penniless, no matter what their financial situation had previously been. This certainly added to the already formidable difficulties in finding a country to go to, because the refugees no longer had anything but skills to bring with them.

Luckily, Peter Shulman had been a successful salesman in Germany, and when he arrived in America, he hooked up fairly quickly with a clothing manufacturer. "Illinois was his territory, and Indiana," David said. "So he was out on the road all week visiting store after store. He drove into every tiny town on the map."

"Every town off the map, too," interjected his sister. "He did not miss a fellow who sold suits out of his basement. He did not miss a one."

"He was a hard worker?"

"He traveled two thousand miles a week. Do you know how much driving that is?" asked David. "He enjoyed his work, he really did. He was always busy, always doing."

"Did you miss him during the week?"

"It's funny, you know, even though he was gone, he was definitely the one in charge. I remember when we got punished, my mother would say, 'Just wait until your father gets home.' It could be Monday, and you didn't walk our sister Miriam to school, and then all week long it would hang over your head that on Friday afternoon, you would get it."

"Not that he hit us," Rebecca said quickly. "But he would mete out the punishment, that's for sure. And waiting for it was worse than getting it."

"What do you remember most about your early years?"

David answered, "My earliest recollections are of a great deal of snuggling and closeness. There was a lot of tenderness and emotional support and stroking. From both my parents."

"Yes," said Rebecca, nodding, her expression gentle and somewhat dreamy.

David broke the mood. "And we were very active, we did lots of athletic stuff, we swam. We had a little bitty cottage right on Lake Michigan, we would go out west to a dude ranch and go horseback riding. We had fun together."

"Was Miriam born by this time? What is your first memory of her?" I asked, little knowing that, with this question, I was opening the family's only real can of worms.

Miriam's Birth

When David was five and Rebecca nine, Anna gave birth to her third child, Miriam. The older siblings were told that Anna had been given anesthesia by gas in the delivery room. The medical staff then left the room and so no one saw when she started coughing and then threw up. Apparently, Anna inhaled some of her own vomit, which caused an infection in her lungs. She developed tuberculosis.

Anna went directly from the hospital to a sanatorium to rest and recover from her illness. She remained there for quite a long time, perhaps even two years, according to her elder children.

When the baby Miriam, and a newly hired housekeeper, came home, the only family members left to greet her were her dismayed siblings. Not only was their father, Peter, gone during the week, as usual, but now Anna was gone all the time. They were only able to visit their mother on the weekends when their father came home. Even in the private conversations I subsequently had with each of the Shulman siblings, nobody seemed to connect this family crisis to any sense of abandonment or note it consciously as the beginning of the end of their early paradise. Both David and Rebecca felt sure that they were already on the way out the door, developmentally. In this initial telling of the story, David said, "I had my bicycle by then, I turned six years old right after she was born, and, whoosh, I was on my way."

"So you didn't resent Miriam?"

David chuckled, as did Rebecca. "We don't think of things in those terms, in my family," he said. "I think she was little and uninteresting, but I didn't dislike her. Did you?" he asked, turning to his elder sister.

"No, of course not," said Rebecca. "I remember that I had a great deal of responsibility, taking care of her, and it wasn't my idea of the best time, because I wasn't focused on home at that point. I turned ten the year she was born. I was involved in clubs and sports and all. By the time I was twelve or thirteen, I took up cheerleading—"

"She was homecoming queen," David interrupted smiling proudly first at her and then at me. Then he shrugged his shoulders and returned to the topic of his younger sister. "I was too old, Miriam was just an infant, and I was six years old. I was out a lot, I had my best friend, Kenny, across the street. I wasn't interested. So I didn't see her as an intruder in that way. I did dislike the housekeeper, though. She cooked foods that none of us wanted to eat."

"We just accepted that this was the way it was now. Somewhere early along we were taught to accept things," Rebecca said, supporting what her brother had just said.

"Like your mother disappearing for two years?" I'm sure that I sounded incredulous, but she nodded as if I had asked a reasonable question.

"Yes, I mean, because by example my parents never, ever, made a big deal of the fact that they had to uproot themselves from their home and come here. They didn't get stuck in the past; they kept looking forward. And we learned that from them." David was the one who said this, jumping in as if to protect his sister from my doubting query. She sat serenely at his side, nodding.

"So what happened when your mother came home?"

"Oh, God," Rebecca said. "By then, Daddy was sick. He developed a brain tumor within a year after she came back. I don't know exactly how it happened, but when they tried to take it out, something was botched. He was basically a vegetable after that, for many years."

"He lived until I was in college, so for nine years he was like that," added David.

"And your mother took care of him?"

"Yeah, he was at home for most of that time," he said. "Then it got to be too much for her, and she had him put in a nursing home. He died less than a year later. She hated to be around sick people after that."

"Who can blame her?" Rebecca said softly.

Rebecca's Boyfriend

I leaned forward, watching as the two of them looked affectionately at each other. By this time, I had come to enjoy defining the different ways that sets of siblings expressed their attachment; watching David and Rebecca together, I reflected that they really seemed to like each other. I wondered how intimate a friendship they had, whether they talked about life issues and romances. I asked, "How often do you speak on the telephone? Or see each other?"

"My sisters and me, these aren't high-maintenance relationships," David said. "It's just that whenever we're together, we keep going. We don't need to weed, or prune, we just go on from where we left off."

"How often, then?"

Rebecca shrugged, looking over at her younger brother. He was perched on a stool at the edge of his breakfast bar; her wicker stool was on the same side, against the wall, and she leaned back comfortably, one foot hooked on the chair rung and the other leg relaxed and lanky. "Once a month?" she said tentatively, and he shrugged in return.

"We don't talk that often," he said. "But much more than we used to."

"Why is that?"

"Well, maybe we're a little more dependent on one another than we used to be. We have more contact and more reasons for talking, about my mother's health, about our lives, because the families we made are gone. Rebecca's kids have families of their own now, and there's her divorce, too. And mine, of course. We've got more time."

I nodded. I'd already learned that Rebecca had been divorced for three years, and David for fifteen. Even though David no longer lived in the Midwest, he'd handled Rebecca's divorce from her husband, Gene, as well as the legal questions arising from the recent dissolution of the interior design firm Gene and Rebecca had founded almost forty years previously. Rebecca was working in an office doing secretarial work; "not my favorite thing to do," she confided, but her financial situation was a little precarious.

"You know," David said, struck by a thought for the first time, and then he paused, as if to formulate his revelation into words. Even when he was thinking deeply, as now, fifty-four-year-old David Shulman had a certain childlike quality. He was built on a small but athletic scale, and he had yet to develop the softer definition of a middle-aged man. His curly dark hair had only the slightest trace of gray, and his clothes—a polo shirt, shorts, and boat shoes—fit well enough to show that he had always maintained himself. As I studied him, he sat up a little straighter, propping both elbows on the counter. The white-tiled surface was uneven, and he shifted position once and then again, before continuing to speak. "This is my family right now," he said. "My mother and my two sisters and their families. That's what it is."

"Is it enough for you?"

"No. No. It's not enough. I mean, ultimately, you have to make your own family. That's the inner circle. Then the family you came from, that makes the periphery. You know, it's like another layer around you, a halo effect."

"Is that true for you as well?" I turned to Rebecca.

David said, "Her life is difficult right now."

In Rebecca's face, I could see no trace of distress at the way her brother kept jumping in to speak for her. I waited, hoping she would say something, but she remained silent, an enigmatic expression on her face. I let the pause stretch out for a long, uncomfortable moment. Rebecca remained still. Eventually, David shifted, recrossed his legs, and continued.

"I mean, life is a journey," he said. "You go on paths that diverge and ones that come back together. You can drive around all you want, but you never really get lost. You will come back out someplace recognizable. And I think that's probably what's happening to us, to me and Rebecca and Miriam."

"So Miriam is as involved as the two of you?"

"Oh, yes, absolutely. We've been taking vacations together, once a year at least, for the past decade, since Rebecca's two sons left home."

Rebecca leaned forward, the neck of her yellow silk shirt slipping open to show an expanse of reddish-brown, slightly crinkled skin. "Miriam and her husband have just one son, a twelve-year-old, and so it's easy to travel with them. And David's girlfriends, well, when they come along, that's great."

"But Rebecca never brings her boyfriend along," David said, his voice a little too jolly. Up until now, he had been maintaining her privacy, rendering her somewhat inaccessible to me, but here he was exposing a vulnerable flank to whatever arrow I cared to shoot.

Rebecca shook her head from side to side. "He's not really, I wouldn't—"

"She thinks he wouldn't fit in."

"Why not?" I asked.

Rebecca's blush spread across her cheeks and onto that visible patch on her neck and breastbone. She ran two manicured fingers through her tidy hairdo. "He just wouldn't. He's a good person, but he isn't like my family."

David said, in a mock whisper, "He's a younger man." He lifted his eyebrows, pretending to be shocked.

"He isn't educated, he isn't the sort of man one thinks of marrying," Rebecca said, "although I do enjoy his company."

"I hope so," David said, and then he turned to me. "They've been together for years, it's the same as being married."

"Do you like him?" I asked.

David said, "I don't know, I haven't really met him."

"Do you want to?"

"Well, yes, Danny's part of her life, and she's my sister. Ultimately, if he's not abusive, if she won't end up supporting him, then I want to know him."

"What happens when you go to her house?"

Rebecca laughed, and in a moment David joined her. Then he said, "He disappears. Like vapor."

When they finished chuckling, he said, "He may feel totally uncomfortable with us, too, you know. He may think he has nothing to say, that he's there under not very ideal circumstances, with no real standing in the family."

Rebecca didn't answer; did she know what Danny felt?

"Is he a gangster? What is it that's so different about him?" I was only half-joking, because clearly everyone was in agreement that Danny was totally unacceptable as a partner for Rebecca. I couldn't imagine what could be so wrong with him when at the same time he had been right enough for the relationship to have begun before her marriage ended, and to have lasted already for four years.

Danny's flaws were not to be revealed, at least not to me, and perhaps there really were none other than his relative youth. Rebecca mumbled something incomprehensible about his being "too young, just a nice fellow," and then David made a crack about the sexual prowess of a younger man. Rebecca's tanned neck again became mottled with embarrassment. Without a pause and, in fact, without exchanging a glance, both Shulmans immediately began talking about Miriam's son's upcoming birthday party, at which the entire family would convene on the following day. When we ended our interview, only a few minutes later, the questionable nature of Danny's acceptability remained in need of an explanation.

I did, however, learn something else.

As I began to pack up my tape recorder and notebooks, David left the room to check in with his office. I had already learned that Rebecca had been married straight out of high school to a wonderful man, that they'd had two beautiful sons together and jointly operated an extremely successful interior design firm, one that was nationally recognized. I also knew that, despite their divorce, Rebecca's ex-husband had planned to fly up to the family's Lake Michigan cottage to join in the upcoming birthday weekend, but that at the last minute he'd been unable to attend. I asked Rebecca how her marriage had ended.

She glanced back to the stool that David had vacated a moment before, and then she began to cry, her face crumpling as if it had been crushed. "David knows, it's no secret," she managed to say, "but I hate to talk about it. Gene, that's my husband, has AIDS. His condition is terrible. I'd be surprised if he lives to the end of the year."

I lowered myself onto the chair next to her.

"The kids were told, they know. We said it was a blood transfusion, but the truth is, he's bisexual, I didn't know then but I guess he always was . . ." She was sobbing without compunction now, unable to continue. I put one hand on her knee and waited as her crying began to abate. I wanted to say something, but I had no idea what words would help. And so we sat there, quietly, until David returned from his study.

David seemed to know immediately what we had been talking about. I saw how sympathetically he helped his sister from her chair and understood that he'd been trying all through our interview to save her from making this revelation. He hadn't been jumping to answer for her because he was being the smartest boy in the class; he'd been offering himself as a shield to protect his big sister.

As he hugged Rebecca, David looked over her shoulder at me and shrugged with a mixture of pride and discomfort. "My big sister," he said, as if that would explain everything. And, for David, comfort and support were precisely what a younger brother offered to an elder sister. It was a given, a rule of his world.

Birth-Order Disorder

I'm the kind of person who doesn't walk under ladders. When I spill salt, I always throw a few grains over my left shoulder. I'm superstitious for one reason, and one reason alone: I like the idea that if a person follows the rules, everything will work out well. The question is, and I'm sure this comes as no surprise, what *are* the rules?

I *wanted* to believe in the rules of birth order, to know that youngest children are the most accommodating, middle children the most aggressive, eldest the most achieving. If these roles were rules of the world, common to all, why then, life would certainly be simpler and more harmonious. Think about it: If you know what position it is your job to play, and I know which position is mine, we can each take our place without posturing or disagreeing. When roles are fixed, there is so much less to fight about. That's why children's fights usually take place at the beginning of play. They are bickering because they can't agree on what game to play, or who will play which part. When they know what rules they're playing by, and the game is safely under way—even when one person wins and the other loses—the likelihood of battle is less because the positions have been staked out.

In just such a way, Democrats and Republicans take their corners. Being a Leo means something different from being an Aquarius, if one believes in astrology. And if one believes in birth-order effects as straight, simple, and defining, one's role as firstborn, middle-born, or later-born is set early in life.

Until one goes out into the world, that is, and finds that some adult middle children are shy and some eldest children get passed over at promotion time.

I was struck one day by the depth of belief each of us holds about birth order, based on what we learned in our own families of origin. I was having lunch with three other women. We were each in our early thirties; two of us had been youngest children, one an eldest child, and one a middle child. The other woman who, like me, had been a youngest child, felt sure that youngest children were the most self-confident, most achievement-oriented, most ambitious. She was a rising executive; her elder sister was a housewife with a young son who, even in her working days, had evinced little interest in a career. The elder sister had worked because she wanted money and liked the companionship of her workmates. She was conservative and easygoing, a natural compromiser. My tablemate, on the other hand, was the complete opposite, someone who thrived on competition and accomplishment, a self-described workaholic.

As she finished speaking, I saw that the woman who had been a middle child was staring in astonishment. "*Middle* children are the most ambitious," she said. "They have the most to prove."

"Oldest children identify with their fathers," asserted the fourth woman, herself an eldest. "They're the most achieving."

They turned to me, knowing that I had been immersing myself in the existing sibling research for the past few years. What, they wanted to know, was the truth of the matter? Who, indeed, was right about her birth-order role? Which woman was scientifically proven to be the most ambitious?

I had to laugh. Each of the three had aggressively defended her position. It mattered to them to know whether they had the statistically proven right to be as achievement oriented as they were. I pointed out that clearly, even in this microworld of one lunch table at a busy restaurant, no two people seemed to share an identical view of birth-order effects. What each woman had learned in her family of origin about her birth position was what she believed to be true.

In 1970, two psychologists named Brian Sutton-Smith and Ben Rosenberg published *The Sibling*, an impressively large and important reevaluation of the research up to that time on sibling status effects—in particular the variables of gender, birth order, and age-spacing and how they relate to family power, academic achievement, and personality measures such as conformity and aggression. More than twenty years later, Professor Emeritus Sutton-Smith, of the University of Pennsylvania's Graduate School of Education, discussed his findings with me during the course of an extensive interview. "What do we actually know about birth order?" I asked him, once we were ensconced in the pleasant disarray of his book-lined study.

"Surprisingly little," he replied immediately. He then went on to explain his belief that most birth-order research is, inadvertently, research into other factors, such as parental age and maturity, social class, family size, or even, he suggested, the sibling position of the writer or researcher in question.

What did he mean?

Well, oddly enough, the preeminent researchers who continue to find that eldest children are the most achieving often seem to be (drum roll, please) eldest children themselves. And those who find later-borns are the most ambitious, struggling in response to feelings of inferiority, often seem to be (surprise!) later-borns. One of the most interesting birth-order speculations is the notion that marriages between people from complementary sibling positions (for example, youngest daughter marries oldest son) are the most successful. Unfortunately, there's little empirical backing for this notion, satisfying as it is. In fact, one study of business executives found *no* relationship at all between choice of marital partner and birth order.

In many ways, the most compelling of the birth-order contributions continues to be Irving Harris's 1964 book, *The Promised Seed.* Harris's approach was to group together famous men into firstborn and later-born categories and then try to piece together how their personality styles differed. Following is a list (compiled by Sutton-Smith and Rosenberg from Harris's work) of famous firstborn and later-born sons. As you read it, try to come up with a clear sense of the differences among these accomplished men. In the first column, profession is listed; in the second column, first-born famous men; and in the third column, later-born famous men.

PSYCHOLOGISTS	Sigmund Freud	Alfred Adler
	Carl Jung	Otto Rank
PHILOSOPHERS	William James	Francis Bacon
	Immanuel Kant	David Hume
	Friedrich Nietzsche	John Dewey
SOCIAL PHILOSOPHERS	Karl Marx	Jean-Jacques Rousseau
	Friedrich Engels	Niccolo Machiavelli

SOCIAL PHILOSOPHERS (cont'd)	Martin Luther King	Mahatma Gandhi
		Thomas Hobbes
		Vladimir Lenin
		François Voltaire
MATHEMATICIANS	Blaise Pascal	René Descartes
	Isaac Newton	
	Albert Einstein	
LITERARY	William Shakespeare	Fyodor Dostoyevsky
	George Bernard Shaw	Albert Camus
	Thomas Carlyle	Leo Tolstoy
	Oswald Spengler	D. H. Lawrence
		Henry James
		Theodore Dreiser
MILITARY	Ulysses S. Grant	Robert E. Lee
	George Patton	Napoleon Bonaparte
	John Pershing	Otto Bismarck
	George Washington	Erwin Rommel
MUSICIANS	Ludwig van Beethoven	Richard Wagner
POETS	John Milton	William Wordsworth
	Alexander Pope	Edgar Allan Poe
	Johann Schiller	Samuel Coleridge
	Percy Shelley	
	Dante Alighieri	
POLITICIANS	Theodore Roosevelt	Andrew Jackson
	Harry Truman	Cesare Borgia
	Julius Caesar	Cardinal Richelieu
	Winston Churchill	Oliver Cromwell
	Frederick the Great	Leon Trotsky
	Alexander the Great	John Kennedy
	Benito Mussolini	Nikita Khrushchev
	Adolf Hitler	

After Harris drew up his lists, he began to speculate about what they showed. Here are some of the notions that Harris came up with to differentiate among the styles of these firstborn and later-born historical figures. For example, firstborns, he claimed, are romantic; later-borns are realistic. This means that D. H. Lawrence, Dreiser and Tolstoy, Wordsworth, Poe, and Coleridge should be thought of as realists. (Now, I wouldn't put the outlook of the man who wrote *Women in Love* and *Lady Chatterley's Lover* in the same category as that of the man who wrote *The Tell-Tale Heart,* or that of the fellow who wrote *Sister Carrie* and *An American Tragedy,* but that is what Harris tries to do.)

Firstborns are depressive; later-borns are cheerful: Yes, that's right, cheerful, just like later-borns Dostoyevsky and Hobbes. (It's difficult to imagine which work takes a more upbeat approach to human nature: *Crime and Punishment,* in which a young student coldbloodedly commits a murder just to prove that he is a superior being who can do so, or *Leviathan,* in which Hobbes argues that the "life of man" is "solitary, poor, nasty, brutish, and short," and a "war of every man against every man.") In addition, speculates Harris, firstborns are stable and humanistic (that list includes both Hitler and Mussolini); later-borns, on the other hand, are histrionic or propagandistic.

Birth-order proponents on the whole tend to struggle and twist available information in order to make meaningful categories. Thus, one birth-order researcher writes about Sigmund Freud as an eldest son to back up his arguments; another neatly smuggles Freud into the later-born category, arguing that Freud's brotherlike relationship to his much older nephew Julius made him a psychological younger brother. It doesn't take a genius to realize that both these arguments are true—and false. Relationships just aren't clean-cut.

In *The Promised Seed,* Harris does acknowledge that the philosopher George Santayana was a later-born to his mother, a firstborn to his father, and that both these effects were mediated by his close connection to his elder half sister. Nevertheless, Harris fails to see that this weakening of a particular case applies not just in the specific, but in general. The point is that *nobody's* claim to a birth-order effect can be judged without considering all the possible influences of the specific situation.

Frankly, even if Harris's divisions of birth orders and character styles were vaguely provable, it would be hard to buy many of his generalizations. Happily, there is hardly any scientific backing for his claims. According to Sutton-Smith and Rosenberg's analysis, the best evidence Harris produced for any of his claims was that eldest-born political leaders are more likely to go to war. Here is the evidence he presented: Of thirty-five presidents of the United States at the time he wrote, seven of the twenty who were firstborns led the country into war (Madison, Polk, Lincoln, Wilson, Roosevelt, Truman, and Johnson). By contrast, McKinley was the only later-born son who did. It's hard to know what this small sample teaches us about birth-order traits in general, particularly in light of the fact that since Lyndon Johnson's time (and even if one dismisses second-born Richard Nixon's role in escalating the Vietnam War), the only two presidents to bring the country into battle have been second child Ronald Reagan, with the invasion of Grenada in 1983, and second child George Bush, who first invaded Panama in 1989 and then embarked the country on the Persian Gulf War in 1990–1991. All of a sudden, even those numbers don't look so impressive.

Ever since 1928, when later-born Alfred Adler first postulated in the journal *Children* that different personality characteristics were identifiable for first, second, and third-born children, enormous amounts of research time and dollars have been spent trying to prove precisely what those traits might be. The birth-order fad rears its head every few years or so, when one expert or another pulls together the ultimate data, "proving" that later-borns are more innovative, or firstborns more extroverted, or whatever.

One of my particular favorites was a 1970 study that found that nearly 90 percent of a group of striptease artists were firstborns. Now, in and of itself, this statistic might give one pause. But wait. The majority of the sample were between the ages of twenty and thirty. Thus, most of the women were born between 1940 and 1950, during part of the fabled baby boom era. Not surprisingly, given the war years, the baby that began a family's particular boom was often the first child that that family had. Nineteen forty-six, 1947, and 1948 were the peak years for starting families: 40 percent, 43 percent, and 39 percent, respectively, of all births in those years were firstborns. There were, it seems, probably more firstborns in *every* profession in the late 1960s and early 1970s because so many families had been started two decades before. It wasn't that strippers were likely to be firstborns, necessarily, but rather, that firstborns were overrepresented everywhere!

Furthermore, in several studies of scientific achievement done around the same time, firstborns were found to be overrepresented among the highly accomplished, but then, upon further examination, they were also found to be predominant among the less talented. There were, again, just *more* of them.

Moreover, as Sutton-Smith and other experts have argued over the years, once social class is factored into the birth-order mix, the picture becomes even murkier. Family size is known to be inversely related to the higher educational levels that tend to be precursors of higher accomplishment. To clarify: The larger the family, the fewer the resources there generally are for each individual child. Smaller family size is a hallmark of the middle class, as is higher educational attainment.

To continue this line of thinking about the importance of social class, in one huge study it was concluded that firstborns and lastborns were the most likely to go to college. Middle children were far less likely to do so. However, when the sample was controlled for family size, it seemed that in the college-bound families, there weren't as many middle children! No real differences in college attendance were found among different birth-order positions once the sample was controlled for this feature. What was really found was that middle-class families were likely to be smaller and middle-class children were more likely to go to college. Social class of origin was the predictive factor, not birth order.

What, then, do we actually know about birth order? There is a notable tendency for an eldest child to be more dominant and powerful in the family structure, at least in the early years, although there certainly are circumstances in which that tendency does not hold true. For example, in immigrant families, a younger child often becomes the leader simply because he or she learns to speak the tongue of the new country in school and can best solve problems and negotiate across the language barrier. We know that an eldest child may have greater resources and attention devoted to him before other siblings are born—and that this attention may be an advantage or, conversely, a disadvantage, depending on the individual circumstances. The eldest takes a psychological body blow when his or her first sibling is born, and yet some eldest children perceive that birth as an almost unmitigated positive. And, obviously, successive children in the family must be somewhat shaken, too, when they cede the role of youngest to a newcomer. Every time a new member enters a family, roles are renegotiated and people win and lose. The manner in which a sibling is affected by a new family member has a great deal to do with who each person is, and what the family is like. Some eldest children end up caring for their siblings; others end up forging paths for the siblings to follow. And still others are treated with equality, although they yearn to be thought of as the responsible eldest.

Once again, how a person copes with the triumphs and vicissitudes of life is largely up to that particular person. One's life course is not written on one's birth certificate. Life is not an assembly line, but a flexible interplay of intention, opportunity, and circumstance.

Does birth order, then, play a role in how one thinks and behaves? Of course. Being followed or succeeded by a sibling—as well as being the same age position or gender as a parent's loved or hated sibling— has a particular effect on a particular person. Who you are, who your sibling is, what your family is like, what life and circumstance do with you and to you, as well as what went on in your culture during your formative years—all these factors mediate a clear definition of what particular types are born in what particular position. Wouldn't a wealthy eldest brother in a society where laws of primogeniture ensured that he would inherit all his family's estates be affected in a distinctly different way from a serf's eldest boy who was sent out to be apprenticed at the age of eight? Wouldn't an eldest daughter in both those families have had entirely different experiences as well, particularly if her next eldest sibling was a brother?

In one family's circle, birth order can matter a great deal. In any simple time or place, it can have implications for one's entire life. These are local effects, not global ones. In the world at large, establishing ironclad rules for what those effects are becomes somewhat farfetched. As a result, much of what passes as absolute knowledge of birth order and personality type can be summed up neatly: It's plain and simple bunk.

"Family Members Love You in a Different Way"

Although the Shulmans were all to be together at the birthday party, I did not follow Rebecca and David when they flew to Michigan. I never did have the opportunity to see all three siblings in interaction with one another, although I was assured by all three that the well-informed and congenial relationship Rebecca and David had with each other was fairly analogous to the one each of them enjoyed with Miriam. I had a quick cup of coffee with Rebecca the morning of her departure, and—always slightly suspicious of the ability of a three-sided structure to be easily equilateral—I wondered aloud if her friendship with David was particularly important under her present circumstances.

For one thing that Rebecca and David had in common, most clearly, was that their life situations had the potential to bring them closer at this point in time. David lived alone, with no spouse, no lover, and no children. He had been married for fifteen years and divorced for fifteen; a few months earlier, a serious five-year relationship with another lawyer in his firm had ended. He worked hard, had some good friends (mostly married) with whom he played tennis, went to the movies, and had dinner parties. His life was full and yet, he felt that it was not complete without a partner. Just turned fifty-four, he believed it likely that he might still raise a family of his own. The mother of those children would, he knew, be willing to accept his sisters as an active part of his life, for that would be a given aspect of loving him.

Rebecca, on the other hand, with children grown and departed, a dying ex-husband, and a lover she wasn't willing to marry, felt that the fullest phase of her family life was behind her. She had turned to her siblings for safe, supportive companionship, something she admitted she'd had little need for previously. From earliest childhood, she recalled, she'd always been focused on her own life.

"When my brother and sister were younger, well, I had much less to do with them," she said. "David and I more or less ignored each other as little ones. Some of that was because he was a boy and I was a girl. And some of that was the four years between us. I was always very responsible; we would go swimming together and I would look to make sure he wasn't drowning. Not that I really watched him, but I *did* check on him."

When Rebecca married at seventeen, "We lived with Gene's dad and I took care of the books, and the house, and the cooking. Then I started having kids so quickly, two young ones by the time I was nineteen, I mean, when would I have had the time to be hanging around with my brother and sister?"

She seemed to be apologizing, speaking more and more quickly as she explained how distant the relationships had been back then. "I really wasn't that close to them," she said, "although I always loved them and wanted the best for them. I had my family to raise and a husband that took a lot of time, and a business. In those days, we didn't talk long distance too much, just birthdays and New Year's, and that was it. But about ten years ago, when I first learned"— Rebecca paused, her mouth twisted awkwardly, part grimace, part rueful smile, and then she continued—"about Gene, you know, that he was bisexual . . ."

I nodded.

"We always had a great time in bed, all along, even after I knew. I had no complaints there," she said, "but I started to get lonely about going out in the evenings. I wanted someone to go dancing with, and he wasn't around. It was lonely." She must have understood what question I wanted to ask, for she blurted out the answer quickly. "This was before AIDS, you know, nobody knew about it back then and well, I got tested as soon as we knew that Gene had the infection. I was fine. But I began to see I had to make my own life, and I started to go out, that's when I met Danny.

"I was very happy then," she confided. "Gene was my best friend, and Danny was a great lover, and the kids were doing well, and the business was hopping. But then Gene started to resent Danny, and he wanted me to break up with him. And I couldn't, I loved them both. So that's another reason we got divorced.

"Well, around the same time, David and Miriam and I just started making an effort to get together, two or three times a year. The first thing that happened was that Miriam called and invited me to go with her family to this house they'd rented in southern Spain, and I went. It was wonderful. And that's when I realized how important they were. There's something about family . . ."

She trailed off again, hesitantly. Rebecca continually wavered between two personae, one confident and expansive, the other shy and unsure. Oddly enough, her brother David seemed always poised, and her sister Miriam, I soon learned, was always reserved. On this one trait, at least, Rebecca straddled the extremes of her siblings.

"Yes, there's something about family," I said, half-teasing. "But what is it?"

The Shulmans were the first—perhaps the only—siblings whom I interviewed who seemed to have a satisfactory answer to this thorny question. This is what Rebecca said: "When things go wrong, a friend always wants you to be happy in the moment, you know? In that interaction, right then. She might not think through the consequences, she just wants to change the mood, help you feel better. That's because she loves you. But family members love you in a different way. They look after you, they have a little different perspective. They want you to be happy long term, they consider the long picture, they're honest."

I nodded my head, yes, I understood.

"They might say something that hurts now, knowing it will be better later. And you keep your dignity. It's private if you say something within the family. It's still private."

"You mean like Gene's illness?"

"Yes," she answered, "and maybe I should be ashamed of myself for wanting to be quiet about it, but I think he deserves his privacy. So that's why I asked David to handle the divorce for me, and to make up my will and Gene's. I didn't want anyone else to know."

She hadn't even told Miriam, trusting that David would perform the painful task of letting her know. I was surprised, when I met later with Miriam, that the younger sister felt no apparent resentment about the fact that she had not been in the "inner loop."

"I'm the Methodical One"

I had gone to visit Miriam in the office of the small engineering firm she had founded with a former professor nearly a quarter-century earlier. She had been unable to free an afternoon to meet at any other location because a major contract was coming due and she, as the partner in charge of business affairs, needed to monitor the negotiations at all times. After so many years, Miriam's firm was no longer an upstart but one of the old guard, and they were feeling the competition nipping at their heels for the first time. "I just can't leave," she'd apologized before expertly describing how to find her office complex in this Boston suburb.

If I'd been put in a room with them and asked to decide whether the Shulmans were siblings, I suspect I would have doubted that they were even distantly related. Rebecca was lanky and blond, well dressed and well preserved; David was short and muscular with black curly hair just barely streaked with gray; both were dramatic physical presences. Now before me sat tiny, blue-jeaned, forty-eight-year-old Miriam. Her light brown hair tumbled casually down her back; she wore glasses and no makeup. She couldn't have been an inch over five feet tall, and when she was seated at her desk, only her head and shoulders were visible. She almost disappeared.

"You aren't very like your siblings," I blurted out.

She responded almost as if she were unaware of the marked physical dissimilarity. There was a measured pause, and then, in a tone which made her answer appear to be previously prepared, she said, "I'm much more methodical, I know. I'm the only organized one. My brother and sister are impulsive, ruled by their hearts."

Rebecca was all conversation, bemusingly so, and I frequently had to bring her back on track and then cajole her through a certain amount of embarrassed consciousness of her chatter. David was a charmer by nature; he seemed constantly to monitor his effect on his partner in conversation, and he would change topics, slow down or speed up, almost as if he could read everyone else's mind. With Miriam, I was in the presence of yet a third phenomenon: Her reserve was single-minded and purposeful. Each of the Shulmans managed to maintain a certain amount of control of our interviews, I mused: When we'd met alone, Rebecca sped up the conversation, chattering away in order to avoid discussing her distress about Gene in detail; David's style was to slink over the topic of his failed marriage by making jokes about himself; and now, here was Miriam, who I imagined would simply say, "I don't want to talk about it" if I asked a question that she found too personal.

They were so different from one another that I wondered if it was this dissimilarity that allowed them to be friends. I asked Miriam what she thought of my idea. We had been speaking for less than half an hour at this point, but she thought a moment and then answered me with what I came to learn was characteristic frankness. Miriam Shulman was a woman who was comfortable enough with herself to speak consistently from the heart.

"I certainly agree that we're each so different that even if I were to ask my brother or sister for advice, I don't think it would be appropriate," she began. "It would reflect their life and experiences and values, which are different from mine. And not that mine are better, or worse. They're just different."

Her hands were folded neatly on the desk. She was so petite that I could see the little girl she must have been; the perfect student sitting calmly, drinking in all the information her teachers could impart. She had been such an outstanding scholar that, as a sixteen-year-old, she was offered a full ride through a prestigious Boston woman's college: tuition, room, board, and books. It was while auditing a class at M.I.T. that she'd met her husband, who also became an engineer. They had lived together since graduate school, been married for eighteen years, and had a twelve-year-old son.

"I like my siblings as people," she continued. "And they are my family, so I will always try to be with them when I can. I like to do as much with them as I can."

"Do you like them as friends?" I asked.

She paused, looking down at the three neat piles of papers, stacked evenly in front of her. She shifted the center pile, aligning it even more perfectly. When she looked up again, she said, "I think my friends are more like I am."

"That's very interesting," I said, letting my voice trail off so that she might continue.

"I mean, I chose my friends. These are my siblings. I didn't go out into the world and pick them."

"But you still choose to be involved with them. It's as if something happens with them that doesn't happen with your friends, and vice versa. I'm kind of curious to know what the difference is."

She stared at me as if I were an oddity, as if a person who didn't understand the difference was missing the key to life. "It's something our mother instilled in us, that family is family," she said. "You don't turn your back on them. You always accept them, wherever they are, whatever they do."

Miriam drew an analogy to her quarter-century of living with one husband and working with one business partner, explaining that she had learned early to maintain her commitments, to ride out the rough spots with people. She was well aware that she had given up certain fantasies along the way, that she had toned down some of her expectations of others, but she was sure that this was the real secret to longevity in relationships, and she was positive that such longevity was the real secret to contentment.

"We let each other be who we are, and we always have," she explained. "I would think very long and hard before I spoke to my sister about Danny, or before I said anything about Gene's illness."

"Well, then, what do you talk about with her?"

"I don't know," she said, a little peevishly. "Cooking, or whatever, plans for when we are going to get together. I just don't tread where she hasn't asked me to go. I would have to ask myself what I'm trying to accomplish by barging in where she hasn't asked me to interfere." I felt great admiration for the way in which she had decided to hold back and respect the boundary her elder sister had laid down.

"I would like to say something to her," Miriam continued, "and I would like to say good-bye to Gene, but I want to be careful not to . . ."

There was a long silence.

"Does she know that you know, about Gene?" I asked.

"I'm sure she does," said Miriam. "We are very, very close and very, very open with one another. And the fact that she has chosen to let me know in a roundabout way about this crisis in her life, well, that is something I have to understand and respect. And accept."

"It's as simple as that," I said quietly.

"Oh, yes," said Miriam, her tone equally hushed and low. "It really is."

The Long View

One measure of sibling closeness in later life is thought, oddly enough, to be predicted by social class. In the Shulman family, two of the three siblings had crossed over from lower to upper middle class; they had advanced degrees and licenses, went to Europe regularly, owned homes and cars that reflected their status. David and Miriam were no longer simply the direct descendants of a traveling salesman and his wife: they were upwardly mobile professionals. Rebecca's life, on the other hand, seemed to be proceeding on a downward curve: she had moved from her childhood home into a life of glamour and success, but in the past few years, she'd barely been able to scrape by. Once, in fact, she'd been forced to ask for help to make the payment on her condominium apartment.

According to the sibling research of medical sociologist Deborah Gold of Duke University, the higher one's educational level and social standing, the less likely one is to be intimately involved with siblings in later life. Her speculation is that higher achievers tend to have wider contact networks and have less need to rely on siblings for help, since they can ask unrelated individuals for the same assistance a sister or brother might be expected to provide. Now, in the Shulman family—and in many other families, of course, and for myriad reasons—siblings who began life at adjacent starting gates certainly had not ended up with the same standing and level of accomplishment. Perhaps it was not a coincidence that Rebecca, whose abrupt skid from comfort to struggle was a source of concern for everyone, became the sibling who engineered closer contact between brother and sisters.

The average sibling connection does tend to reprise in later life. There is a certain predictable cycle to the sibling relationship that begins with the close proximity of childhood and involves cooperation and competition for space and parental attention, as well as role modeling and assistance in identity establishment. In adolescence, siblings can play even more significant parts as positive and negative role models, both as experts to observe and mentors to question about confusions. A supportive sibling can also bolster one's self-confidence; a denigrating or teasing one can have a truly destructive effect on self-esteem.

In early adulthood, however, the sibling relationship often retreats in importance, evoking—and providing—little or no emotional connection. The young adult is busy firming up his or her own sense of identity, and the original family often seems unable to accept or understand the progress of these struggles. Typically, peer friendships serve an important function during this time as sources of emotional bolstering in the process of separation and individuation. Paradoxically, this is the phase of life when intimate friends are described as "like a sister to me" or "as close as a brother"—even though the actual siblings themselves are held at the most emotional distance that they will be throughout their entire lives!

Life continues on, and the young adult's primary area of concentration becomes establishing an adult identity, which can include building a career, making a home, finding a mate, and, often, establishing a family. It is not unusual, during this nest-building phase, for siblings to see one another only on holidays, to maintain contact through rare visits and telephone calls. Some siblings keep up with one another's progress only through indirect reports from parents or from another sibling. It is rare, in fact, for siblings to lose touch completely at any point in life. Generally, even if they fail to stay in direct contact, they still know where each one is, and each has a general sense of the progress of the other's life.

Disruptions of this "typical" cycle occur all the time and in all directions: For example, a brother may divorce and become eager to have contact with his elder sister; a parent dies and a brother and sister make a greater effort to stay in touch (or, conversely, find that they have no common ground upon which to meet); a sister becomes ill, or her spouse or child does. There are obviously all sorts of permutations of the cycle, from the most harmonious to the most hostile, the most tragic to the most fantastic. Nevertheless, the typical relational pattern of any two siblings, according to developmental psychologist Victor Cicirelli of Purdue University, the leading researcher on sibling relationships in old age, "is one of continuous decline throughout the life course, with a resurgence later on in life." Often this first recontact comes in response to problematic circumstances or events, as was true in the case of the Shulmans. Rebecca's disintegrating marital situation motivated her to reach out toward her brother and sister; in this case, all that was needed was one warm overture from one sibling for a fruitful and friendly connection to begin again.

One interesting feature of sibling attachment that Professor Cicirelli's work has identified is that while middle-aged and older siblings tend to find their relationships extremely intimate and satisfying, they still are not likely to ask each other for advice on important decisions.

Presumably, like Miriam Shulman, most adult sisters and brothers (nearly 75 percent of Dr. Cicirelli's sample) find themselves enough unlike their siblings in terms of experience and values that asking for advice (or giving it) seems inappropriate. Perhaps, satisfaction in the sibling relationship ultimately comes from realizing that, unlike a parent-child connection, this is a blood tie where functionality is not critical. Genuine affection may be the most important variable.

If one accepts that the sibling connection is not about re-creating or in some way "fixing" the childhood family, nor about having one's unmet early demands finally acknowledged, nor about deciding who the parents actually preferred, the potential for mutual enjoyment remains. In fact, the more limited interaction that adulthood allows can be enough to decrease any ongoing feelings of sibling rivalry. As one's life evolves, it seems as if the relevance of childhood issues really does decrease of its own accord. Maturity means having spent enough time musing about the experiences of childhood that they can be integrated into the present definition of the self and laid to rest. Then we can put away some of the losses of childhood and accept that the present is now of greater significance. In reconnecting with an aging sister or brother—or even in making a connection for the first time—one can be as gratified as the craggy old farmer who accidentally discovered gold on his back forty.

A sibling can become a source of surprising, genuine pleasure.

Each of the Shulmans had come to know such genuine pleasure and to understand how little sacrifice was inherent to their friendship. Respecting one another's ability to fend for him- or herself also meant that they interacted without infringing upon each other's private life. David Shulman maintained a law practice, having ridden the ups and downs that come with establishing a solo business; he had dated widely in the fifteen years since his divorce; and he had traveled around the world—with friends and alone. He owned a home near his sister Miriam and a rustic cottage in the country, two cars, and a vast collection of musical recordings. He loved to ride horses and he hated to swim, loved to play tennis and was bored by jogging. He was attractive and charming and accomplished; he felt his life to be, basically, satisfying.

"My secret is so easy, in a way. I just endure and get beyond," he said to me, during an interview some weeks later. "I'm not the smartest, or the best-looking, or the fastest, or the funniest guy around, but I can outlast anybody. So when the other guy says, 'This is too difficult,' or he gets tired, I'm the one who is still there. I don't ever give up."

"Whom do you talk to when you get depressed?" I asked, moving down the list of questions I'd prepared for the interview. We were sitting outside on the deck of his weekend cottage, in two ancient wire chairs that looked as if they'd seen more than their share of bad weather. Again he was wearing shorts, although the morning air had chilly overtones of fall. He sat with his arms crossed over his chest, the second and third fingers of his right hand tapping rhythmically on the small bulge of his bicep. "Would you talk with Miriam, or Rebecca, or neither?"

"I don't think I ever say I'm down to anybody," he said, his tone meditative.

"Even if you are?"

He slipped his left hand out from where it had nestled under his arm, and began to tap with that set of fingers as well. "If I am unhappy, ever, I'm never consciously aware that I am, because there's always so much to do."

"Meaning what?"

"Well, let's say one day I woke up thinking I'm feeling a little down today. Maybe I would passively think that I'm feeling down, but I don't think it would take me more than thirty-five seconds to think about all the things I need to do, which would make me feel —" He stopped, almost as if he were confused by this whole area of conversation.

"So you're a person who rarely feels down," I offered.

"I just don't have time for it, to tell you the truth."

"You just won't allow it," I said.

"I like doing most of what I do," he said. "Most of the ways I have of spending my time in a structured way, I like a lot. I like my work. I like being a big fish in my firm. There's just not time, you know?"

"There's just not time," I repeated.

"Well, yeah. Maybe it's escapism or something, but I don't know what I could change if I sat around wringing my hands and complaining that the light isn't just exactly the way I want it. I mean, bad stuff has happened to me, I've broken bones and had relationships end, and had business problems, and I've just learned to keep busy, to keep moving forward. To endure, you know?"

"I think so."

"I'm a successful, mature person with credible opinions," he then said. "It's taken a long time to evolve to this place, but I'm comfortable here."

"And here's where you'll stay," I teased him.

He chuckled, but then his smile faded. I think he realized the implication of what he'd said. "Oh, no, not here. Not alone, I mean. I told you, didn't I? I really do want a family of my own."

As he nodded in agreement with his own statement, I recalled something Miriam had said about him only ten days before. She'd been sitting at her desk, a tiny person with an impressively strong presence, and had stated flatly, "If there is any man in the entire world who is meant to have a family, it's my brother David. He's a wonderful man. I've introduced him to a bunch of people, but I don't think my friends are the right people for him. I don't think I know the right people. I will keep trying, but my friends, well, they're more intellectual and methodical, more like me. His life is more exciting, less organized. I think everyone would agree that he hasn't met the right person yet. It's just a matter of time until he finds the right woman."

She looked up from where she'd been carefully shifting her three piles of paper again. "Back two years ago, David was still going out with Caroline. At some point I thought he might seriously be considering marrying her, and I thought about it for a long time, whether I should tell him I wondered if it would be a mistake. I didn't want to burn any bridges if he did decide to marry her."

"What didn't you like about her?"

"She cared more for appearances than substance. She would go into a restaurant and make a big commotion about what table had been reserved for us, or that the waiter had put the water glass on the wrong side. I mean a public commotion, so that the whole place would know she was unhappy."

"That must not have been pleasant."

"Oh, it wasn't, and whatever you did, Caroline was dissatisfied and everyone knew it."

"How did David deal with her, trying to please her, or—"

"He let her do whatever she felt like," Miriam interrupted. "He didn't disagree with her complaints. I'm not sure that I would have disagreed with her complaints either. I just would have handled them differently. David lets other people be whoever they are."

"As you do?"

"Yes," she said. "I do. And so does Rebecca. We got that from our mother, who was just a great person. She always spoke her mind, but she was always willing to be convinced of a different point of view, and even say that she was wrong. She would listen to her children, even. It wasn't that she bent with the wind, it was that she really would be thinking about what you were doing."

As I watched Miriam, I thought, what an amazingly strong person she was, how worthy of respect. She continued. "Then I realized that I'm not living his life, and he's not living mine. I've been lucky so far, I've had it really much easier than either of my siblings. But none of our lives is over yet, and one never knows what will turn out right or wrong. I mean, our father died when our mother was fairly young, and her life turned out completely differently than she might have expected. So you never, never know."

"So," I asked, "did you talk to David about Caroline? Is that why they broke up?"

Miriam sat up a little straighter, edging off the chair to signal that her time was running out, that this would have to be the last question. "No," she replied. "I did not. I knew I would love him if he married her, and love him if he didn't. I also knew he was better qualified than I to decide what is best for him. The most loyal thing I could do, in fact, was to be quiet and wait for him to make up his mind."

"Loyal?" I was curious about the choice of words.

"I haven't a clue about any other way to be than the way I am," she said. "All I really know is that if I love and respect someone, I have to respect the choices they make. I think that's the definition of loyalty."

Loyalty, respect, acceptance: These were the characteristics that marked Rebecca, David, and Miriam Shulman's relationship with one another. Without a doubt, these siblings had learned, early in life, a fundamental secret of human interaction and each of them understood how to put it into practice. No matter the difficulties they'd endured or the pleasures they'd found, alone and together, it seemed clear that the Shulmans had discovered an important key to satisfying sibling relationships.

CHAPTER TEN

Art, Hank, and Ron Mahoney

"We're Fundamental"

"Which of us has known his brother? Which of us has looked into his father's heart? Which of us has not remained forever prison-pent? Which of us is not forever a stranger and alone?"

—Thomas Wolfe, *Look Homeward, Angel!*, 1929, foreword

The Mahoney brothers were, at the time when I began to meet with them, embarked upon what was, most likely, the final active phase of their lives: Children were launched, careers were slowing, marriages were happy, health was basically good. The three brothers—Arthur, Henry, and Ronald—had each produced three children. The eldest brother, Art, was in his early seventies and still maintaining a part-time practice in general medicine in the same town in which he and his brothers had been born and raised.

Art Mahoney was a round hobbit of a man, with a youthful voice and cheerful manner, and a set of big brown eyes magnified by Coke-bottle glasses. When I pulled into the driveway of his white ranch house, I was surprised to see him hovering by the front door, as if he'd been eagerly awaiting my arrival. He'd sounded less than enthusiastic on the phone the previous evening, when I had called to confirm our appointment; perhaps his phone manner was the wary

result of nearly fifty years of postponed evening meals and interrupted sleep. Any evening telephone call might be from a frightened
or hysterical patient.

His house sat high on a grassy slope: I had to climb up a steep
flight of cement steps to reach the front door, an oddly disorienting
experience, for as I hiked up the steps to Art, he seemed to grow
smaller. I had the impression that he had too much skin for his size,
almost as if the slight drooping of his jowls and the bags beneath his
eyes were the result of borrowing someone else's epidermis. I smiled
up at him, amused at the image of him as Alice in Wonderland, with
me as an observer watching him shrink.

As we shook hands, I was recalling what the youngest Mahoney
brother, Ron, had told me about Arthur. I already knew that he'd
been married extremely unhappily for nearly thirty years, and that
his marriage had ended when he embarked upon an affair with a
nurse. That six-year affair had also ended, and then, just four years
ago, Arthur had made a peaceful marriage with a widow named Ellen,
the mother of one of his patients. Ron had given me this sketchy
outline of his brother's romantic history, and then he warned me that
Art had had a very difficult life. Ron hadn't been sure what exactly
his brother would be willing to confide in me himself, but he seemed
extremely eager for me to understand where Arthur was coming
from.

I had probed sixty-one-year-old Ron a little bit, trying to discover
why it was so important to him that I approach Arthur from a sympathetic perspective. Ron's response was that Hank, their middle
brother, resented what *he* perceived as Art's life on Easy Street: a
doctor with a beautiful house, a nice wife, three successful kids, and
many civic involvements and awards. "Hank always complains about
Art," Ron told me in my first meeting with him. "We own some
real estate together, and Hank feels like Art never gets his hands
dirty, he just collects the checks we send him. See, Hank develops the
properties, and I handle the business side of things, so Hank thinks
Art gets a free ride."

"Is that true?" I'd asked.

"First of all, I'm an accountant, I manage businesses for a living.
Hank's a developer, so he's not doing anything he doesn't know how
to do. What does he want Arthur to do, take the building's blood

pressure, put it on medication? Look, I'll tell you what I should just say to Hank," Ron said, his tone more than a little peevish, "I'll tell you what I guess I want to say to Hank sometimes. What the hell's the difference? I want to say to him, look, what that man's been through you'll never understand, so leave him alone."

I nodded, but Ron barely noticed. "We're brothers. We're family. We all bring something to the relationship. It doesn't have to be even. You know how they always used to give each child exactly the same portion on his plate? It's ludicrous, that's what it is. Crazy."

I nodded again, and this time Ronald Mahoney nodded along with me. "It's so ludicrous," he repeated. "Bizarre."

"So, your two brothers, Art and Hank, they don't get along so well with one another?"

"They get along. No, we all get along fine. There's no real problem." Ron's annoyed expression seemed to wipe itself clean. He sat up straighter and opened his blue eyes a little wider. He grinned cheerfully. It was as if he'd ridden out too far along an unfamiliar road; now he backpedaled as quickly as he could.

"This is just minor—" I started to say.

"Yes, it's minor," he interrupted, clearly relieved. "It's a minor thing, I think. It's just Hank gets a little greedy sometimes. He's not as willing to share. Art and I, we're just more giving, more alike."

"I see," I said, making a note to hit upon this same area with the other two brothers, to explore where exactly in their business dealings this element of hostility was festering.

"Don't get me wrong," Ron continued. "Hank would lend me money if I needed it. He has in the past. He's just, I don't know, it's just that Art and I, we're more alike. That's all."

"Has Hank done less well in his life than you and Arthur?" I asked.

Ron shook his head, no. "To be honest, he's done better financially, and he's put more away. He's been married to the same woman for forty years, and she's just a lovely person. His kids are great, his business is good. Still, he's cheap about things, and he worries too much. It's just one of those things. He's never satisfied."

"Was he born that way?" I asked. I was trying to get a sense of where Ron thought the roots of this fraternal conflict lay, to assess how long there had been a perceived problem with Hank.

"I haven't the faintest idea. He just has tunnel vision. When you meet him, I'll be curious to know what you think. I don't know if he'll open up to you."

That was the second time I'd had a warning from Ron that one of his brothers might not be as honest with me as he himself had been. Now, as I stood in Arthur's kitchen watching him heat up the kettle to make tea for both of us, I gave myself a little mental shake to clear away the worry that I might not get the full, honest life stories I sought from the other two Mahoney brothers. As it turned out, I need not have worried, at least as far as Arthur was concerned.

From the moment we sat down in Arthur Mahoney's magazine- and book-strewn den, I could tell that he was completely willing to reveal the full story of his life as he understood it. Part of this stemmed from his natural gregariousness, but another important impetus to talk about himself grew, I suspect, from the nature of his current phase of life. Coming to terms with his actions, his impulses, and his history were important and compelling tasks for him.

The first thing Art Mahoney told me about himself was this: His birth had been so incredibly painful for his mother that she'd never again been able to approach the sexual act without an overwhelming terror of becoming pregnant. "She used to describe my birth to me, in intimate—no, more than that—in gross detail. I won't go into specifics," he said, shaking his round head back and forth in disgust, "but suffice it to say that I will never forget the things she told me." He paused to pick up his mug of hot tea and carefully take a sip.

"I was such a conehead from three horrible days of labor that my father used to call me Zip," he added. "Do you know who Zip was?"

I shook my head, no.

"He was one of the freaks in the sideshows at Coney Island. That's who I looked like." He gave me a gap-toothed smile and raised his eyebrows comically, as if to justify his father's comment.

"When did your mother tell you all this, about your birth? How old were you?"

Arthur made himself a little more comfortable, scuttling his small frame back against the cushions of the white leather couch upon which we sat. His legs nearly left the floor, and I reflected that he had probably not been the person to select this furniture. He was wearing golf shoes and blue checked pants; I had been put on notice that he needed to leave by noon to meet his regular golf partners. He stretched one arm out along the top of the couch, and began to tell me about the long, draining hours his father had devoted to running a men's clothing store. "My dad would be in the store from nine in the morning until eleven o'clock at night, except that he might walk home for dinner. And we lived in a neighborhood where Catholics weren't too well thought of, and so the only person my mother had to talk to for the first five years of my life was, more or less, me."

"Ah . . . you must have heard an earful."

"Whatever her feelings were, she expressed them to me. Whether it was love or rage, or whatever."

"She was angry at the hours your father worked?" I hazarded a guess.

"No, I don't think so," he answered, shaking his head from side to side slowly, as if to assure himself of the truth of his answer. "I think she was angry at the social isolation. The best way to describe my mother is that she was an injustice collector. She would get offended by the way someone crossed his eyes, and that was it—" He drew his right hand sharply across his neck. I noticed that it trembled slightly, that his papery skin was marked here and there by age spots. He returned both hands to his lap, where they lay gently clasped together. "They were dead as far as Mother was concerned."

"She would cut people out."

"Oh, yes," he agreed. "That was my mother."

I nodded sympathetically, then waited for him to continue. I had the curious impression that Arthur Mahoney's perceptions of his life —and his siblings' lives—would emerge only if he felt free to guide the discussion. This was a man who needed, albeit subtly and gently, to stay in charge. All the same, a faint air of grief clung to him, not only because of his trembling hands, but also because of a certain distracted sadness that seemed to underpin even his most cheerful expressions.

When he began to speak again, he was still considering the complexities of his mother's personality. "We lived on Lincoln Street, only a few blocks from here. I remember there were lots of other kids around, Mary-Jean Irvine, Tim Garfield, Maxine Hopper; we played together all the time. Once, when I was maybe five years old, we were in Maxine's backyard and I had to urinate. I proceeded

proudly to stand in the corner of the yard and relieve myself. Someone saw it, I suppose it was Maxine's mother. Well, I was a dirty
child to have done that."

I chuckled. He smiled at me gratefully, as if more than sixty-five
years later, he could still recall the humiliation of that moment.

"All of a sudden, I wasn't supposed to walk on the sidewalk of
Lincoln Street. Mrs. Hopper made a huge to-do. My mother proceeded to take a broom out and sweep the whole goddamn street. I
remember her saying, this is a public street, and anyone who doesn't
understand that can come out and discuss it with me."

"So your mother would defend you . . ."

"To the hilt," he agreed. He paused, looking down at his mug of
tea, and then he shook his head from side to side once again, this time
as if he were deliberating with himself about whether to go on. He
took off his thick glasses and began to clean them against his shirt.
He looked up at me. Without the glasses, his nearsighted eyes were
far smaller than I'd expected and deeply recessed under folds of aging
skin. "She would also," he said simply, "beat the hell out of me when
she was angry."

"She beat you? Physically?"

"Oh, yes."

He put his glasses back on, checked them for cleanliness, then
removed them again. "If she was angry, she would pick up anything
that was around, whether it be a coat hanger, or an ironing cord, and
she would beat the hell out of me. And her eyes would literally roll
in her head. She would go off the deep end. She either loved me to
death or wanted to kill me."

"A woman of great emotional extremes," I commented.

"Oh, my God, yes. Oh, yeah, she was," he said. "But nobody else
was going to touch her children."

"That was her right and nobody else's."

He laughed. "Yeah. She could beat the hell out of me, sure, but no
one else could."

"How about your dad?"

"My dad was a pussycat. He would never have laid a hand on me.
But also, you have to remember, he was an absent father, he was
rarely at home." A silence fell, and then he added, "As I was, with
my kids. That's how things were in those days."

"Did you love your mother?"

His eyes began to water, and he looked away toward the portal that opened out to the white-tiled kitchen, as if trying to will himself to stop. Eventually he said, very softly, "I loved her and I hated her. In the end, I dearly loved her."

I leaned forward and put one hand on his knee, patting him without speaking. After what must have been a full minute of struggle, he shook his head and looked up as if in wry apology. "She did what she felt was best for her kids and I know, in retrospect, that all parents do the best they can at the time. She was doing what she thought was right."

"Did your brothers have the same experience with her that you did?"

"Overall, yes, I think. Although maybe she was hardest on me because I was the oldest. You'll have to ask them."

"But what do *you* think?" I persevered. "Do *you* think the family was the same for each of you?"

"I May As Well Have Grown Up Under Another Surname"

He looked at me, surprised. In the silence that followed, I suddenly recalled Mikal Gilmore's book about growing up as the brother of the murderer Gary Gilmore, a haunting and beautifully written memoir called *Shot in the Heart*. There were four Gilmore brothers, but only Mikal, the youngest, managed to escape becoming a drifter or criminal in a family with a legacy of violence. This is what Mikal Gilmore wrote about himself and his brothers:

> The family I grew up in was not the same family my brothers grew up in. They grew up in a family that was on the road constantly, never in the same place longer than a couple of months at best. They grew up in a family where they watched the father beat the mother regularly, battering her face until it was a mortified, blue knot. They grew up in a family where they were slapped and pummeled and belittled for paltry affronts. They grew up in a family where they had to unite in secret misadventures just to find common pleasures.
>
> In the family I grew up in, my brothers were as much a part of its construction as my parents. They were part of what I had to experience, to learn from.

They were part of what I had to overcome and shun. They gave me something to aspire to: the chance to escape their fates. In fact, one of the ways my family best served me was by teaching me that I did not want to stay bound to its values and its debts or to its traditions.

The youngest Gilmore brother grew up in a family so distinct from his brothers' that he realized later that he did not even know them, that they "did not inhabit the same time and space." Yet, oddly enough, he wanted more than anything to be a part of their experiences. His anger toward his brothers was experienced not as relief that he escaped the violent and ruinous lives that killed two of the three of them; rather, as he writes, "I hate them because I wasn't included in their picture. I hate them for not being a part of their family, no matter how horrible its costs."

Mikal Gilmore was seven years younger than his next oldest brother, but more than simple chronological years separated him from the others. He was the elected, the special child, the one to whom his cruel father gave the greatest kindness and love. As a result, their fraternity was somehow closed to him. Nevertheless, even decades after his brother Gary's death by firing squad, Mikal Gilmore's psychological scars run unknowably deep. Although he managed to become a functional member of society, he doesn't *feel* that way. He, too, feels crushed under the heavy weight of his family's violent legacy.

Gilmore's book was in my thoughts as I watched Arthur Mahoney wrestling with the idea of imagining what his brothers had felt and experienced during their childhoods. Although all of the Mahoney brothers had made successes of themselves professionally—and certainly none of them had turned to criminal violence—I had the sense that their mother's violent legacy had to have made itself felt in their lives. I wondered in what different ways her mixture of cruelty and love had transmuted into addictive potions that were now needed to satisfy inner yearnings for each of the brothers.

After a long period of quiet, during which the air conditioner suddenly clicked on with a low hum, Art abruptly protested, "I was much older than my brothers. I really didn't think about them, or know them. I was so focused on the world outside." His tone was offended; it was almost as if he felt he had been accused of something.

Oddly enough, however, the comment rang with familiarity. I'd heard siblings remark frequently that, in childhood, they'd been focused on friends and school. They tended to have childhood memories of separate family experiences. Most often this statement seemed to come from eldest children and middle children with much younger brothers or sisters. Nevertheless, there seemed to be absolutely no connection to the kind of bonds these same siblings had in adulthood. Some were closer, some not; some had been through very intimate phases and were more distant at the time they were interviewed. Many were reconnecting after years of distance. Some thought of themselves as estranged and yet had a great deal of contact. Others thought of themselves as intimate, yet spoke rarely. The temptation to "discover" underlying rules of human behavior was always present; but, as always, the wisest conclusion seemed that sibling experience is incredibly variable in every family, and during every phase of life.

"There's one thing both Ron and I did that I guess sort of relates to my mother," Art said suddenly. "I mean, we both married awful women the first time, simply awful. Women who just made no sense for us. Women who didn't like us. Cruel, crazy women."

"Tell me about your first marriage."

"I can tell you this," he asserted. "I went to her mother the month before the wedding, and I told her I didn't love her daughter and didn't want to marry her. And she said the invitations were out, the whole thing was arranged, what was I trying to do to her? And I thought to myself, maybe love comes later. I just went ahead."

"Why?"

"It's hard to know, now. Millie wasn't very attractive, and she wasn't very bright, and she was just a horrible woman. I remember once she told me a story about how her father had accidentally hit her on the ear, and she went around for a week with her hand on her ear, moaning, every time she saw him. Just to bug him. She wasn't hurt in the slightest."

"When did she tell you that story?"

"Before we were married, and I never forgot it. Never."

"How did you decide to get married?"

He laughed, his lids lowering over his brown eyes as his head tilted up. "You guessed it," he said. "It wasn't my idea. I'd been dating her for a few months, and one day she said, let's get married, and I kind of said, I don't know, I guess so." He shrugged. "I let her bully me into marriage, and the bullying never ended."

"I don't understand," I said. "Why did you put up with her? Why did you stay with someone you didn't love?"

"Our father did. God knows, he couldn't have had it easy with my mother. I just assumed that when you married, it was a commitment, it was for life. And my wife always used to tell me I was crazy, I should be locked up I was so crazy, and somehow I started to believe her." His eyes were far away, looking over my head and out the window, toward the quiet street below us.

It took more than twenty years for Art Mahoney to decide to see a psychiatrist, even though his wife had been screaming at him to do so ever since he moved out of her bedroom in their sixth year of marriage. Just after his sixtieth birthday, unaccountably, he began to wonder what he might do to make his life more bearable. He went to the psychiatrist twice weekly for about half a year, and then one day, during a session, the doctor asked him, "Art, I'm curious, you've been coming here every week for months now. Do *you* think anything is wrong with you?"

Arthur said, "There must be, because people keep telling me I'm crazy. My wife, I mean. I don't feel crazy, but I'm sure that's just because I'm in such bad shape."

The doctor laughed. He said, "I have to tell you a story. Yesterday, I went downstairs to pick up your personality tests from the specialist. I asked for the Mahoney tests. He said, 'That crazy lady? Here they are.' "

Arthur just stared at the doctor, not understanding. He knew that his wife had undergone the same battery of tests that he had, but for a moment he couldn't figure out which lady they were talking about.

"What I'm trying to tell you," said the doctor, "is that if anyone is crazy around your house, it isn't you."

When Arthur Mahoney recounted this story to me, he proudly added, "You know in the cartoon when the light bulb appears above the guy's head? Suddenly everything made sense. I moved out within a week."

According to Art, his ex-wife, Millie, worked overtime to turn his grown children away from him. His eldest daughter still refuses to speak to him, while the two younger children allow him only limited access to their lives. "It's bad to say, but my oldest girl, she's so like her mother, hard and unforgiving, that I don't think I even want her friendship at this point."

His voice slowed. "I can't say I've gotten what I wanted all the time. It's been an interesting life, but it's been hard."

I nodded.

"You know," he said, his diction even more precise, his eyes sad behind those thick glasses, "a long time ago, I had a friend who was in the midst of a divorce, and once I asked him, 'What do you define as pleasure?' And he said, 'Freedom from pain.' I never forgot that. When he said it to me, I thought he was nuts. Now, I think, maybe I understand what he meant."

"Can you explain?"

"Well," he said, and he shifted forward, "I was Edna Mahoney's kid and that was hair-raising. I served in the medical corps during World War Two and I saw things I never should have seen, people inflicted with horrible, indescribable injuries. I was Millie Mahoney's husband and that was a hell all its own. But the thing is, I survived all of it. I'm stronger than I look, a little guy like me."

"Do you think you were simply born strong, or did you become that way?"

"You know, I look at Ron, who left a bad marriage after a dozen years and *told* me that life could be better. I didn't really believe him. I stuck it out for twenty-seven years. I endure." He nodded at me, almost defiantly.

"My family," he said, "we're all that way. I'm proud of my brothers, and me. We're fundamental, we don't make our lives together, but when I think of what we've done for one another, it makes life worth it. Love hasn't been so kind to me, but my brothers have never let me down."

I smiled encouragingly as he continued on, his eyes wide open and earnest, his small frame tense with the effort to say what he had to say. I could see that he was growing tired, and I wondered if he would actually make it to his golf game that afternoon. "I see my brothers for who they are," Arthur Mahoney said, "with all their weaknesses. Still, I trust them completely, wait, no, mostly Ron, I guess, I trust him to be there, to play fair, and to care about what happens to me no matter how I screw up."

His grin was weak but unabashedly proud. This man loved his little brother without reserve.

Accepting One's Life

This series of investigations into the significance of relationships among brothers and sisters began with two adolescent women, closely connected and teetering on the brink of adulthood. In musing about Justine and Edith, one was left with a sense of hope and possibility, of the potential for life's gifts to be doled out with abundance by generous hands. The best of siblingdom was theirs, ripe with sisterly confidences, loving support, and dreams of the future that seemed to halo even the most mundane moments in the present.

How do such sisterly lives—vibrant in their expectations of adventure, of romance, of future glory—contrast with the life stories of three men now rounding the corner into late adulthood, still fully possessed of their strengths and faculties and yet wistfully aware that in large measure their journeys are slowing down?

In his account of the male life cycle, *The Seasons of a Man's Life*, the late psychologist Daniel J. Levinson wrote of this period that "in late adulthood, a man can no longer occupy the center stage of his world. . . . His generation is no longer the dominant one." A primary task for a man in this phase is the reorientation of the self from an outer, worldly focus to a more contemplative self, one that is attuned to "the inner voices." This process is often described as becoming more in touch with one's feminine side, or moving from a central focus on "doing," to a central focus on "being." The richness that can result from this turning inward has been the source of tremendous intellectual and artistic inspiration: For example, some of the greatest works of the painters Pablo Picasso and Michelangelo, the architect Frank Lloyd Wright, the composer Giuseppe Verdi, even Sigmund Freud himself, were created during this latter-life phase.

In my mother Maggie Scarf's book on women and depression, *Unfinished Business,* she writes about the manner in which a person's unresolved stumbling blocks not only resurface within the family from generation to generation, but also within that person's life. Thus, an elderly woman whom Scarf interviewed continued to struggle with separation and individuation from her mother, unfinished issues of her own adolescence. For this deeply depressed elderly woman, feelings of obligation and resentment toward her own mother were being played out not only in the arena of the emotional past but also in the present, for the woman's daughter was being pressured into the same role in regard to *her* that *she* had played long ago with her now-dead mother. Significantly, her mother's obvious preference for her son over this daughter remained a major aspect of this elderly woman's distress. Although she herself had not produced a son, a similar dynamic had resurfaced in the next generation, and her daughter now felt inadequate, unable to please her mother. A sibling dynamic reverberating back an unknowable number of generations was making itself felt in this elderly woman's treatment of her daughter. The interplay of parental and sibling interaction, combined with life circumstance and genetic predilection, can produce a staggering variety of influences from life's very beginning down through the later years.

In order to come to terms with one's individual life path, the most important task is to *accept* the choices that one has made. Coming to terms with oneself in the face of the imminent likelihood of death is the primary job in later life. This means that when, for example, a man like Ronald Mahoney, Art's youngest brother, contemplated life in his sixty-first year, he had to consider not only the happy twenty years of his second marriage, but also the disastrous first marriage that had lasted a dozen years. What Ron said to me, when recalling this unhappy period of his life, was that the marriage to his first wife, Kim, had produced three wonderful children and that he couldn't discount the importance of that. In other words, even the worst experience had brought its own rewards.

The late Erik Erikson considered the last crisis of the human life cycle to be the struggle between the search for integrity (or a sense of the entire life as an experience of growth) and the sense of despair (at the ultimate meaninglessness of having lived). This is the turning point that leads to the ultimate wisdom. Having made sense of one's own life, one can accept the inevitability of death. Avoiding the despair is pointless; without an active struggle to come to terms with fear and anxiety, a person may simply sink into bitterness or depression. Without full engagement in even the most painful parts of one's life, an individual may never develop his or her full wisdom.

What is wisdom?

According to Erikson, it is "detached and yet active concern with life itself in the face of death itself." Furthermore, when one attains such wisdom, a person can maintain a sense of the integrity of one's experience, while at the same time feeling disdain for one's failings and one's fear of death.

"It Was a Long Time Ago"

Ronald Mahoney was born in an Albany hospital in 1932, his mother's third son. His two elder brothers, Arthur and Henry, were already ten and five years old, big boys out in the world, involved in childhood pursuits of their own. The family lived for several years in one half of a two-family home in an urban neighborhood; then, when Ron was three, they moved to the suburbs. Ron's father, Arthur Senior, ran a very successful clothing store in partnership with his own brother, Ron's uncle Pete. Three other uncles were in business together as well, in another men's haberdashery several towns away. The brothers in this previous generation all shared their resources, vacationed together, raised their children as the citizenry of the extended grouping. Family was family, the main focus of social and professional life. "Not that there weren't squabbles," Ron assured me. "Oh, God, no, these guys did not always get along, but they were in it for the long haul." Ron chuckled, leaning back in his big black-and-white striped armchair and twisting a water glass back and forth between his flattened palms.

Ron Mahoney was a robust and attractive man, with a neatly combed white crewcut, deep brown eyes, and well-weathered skin. When he smiled, I could see the same gap between his two front teeth that made his brother Arthur's grin so appealing. Ron, however, was clearly a more athletic man, taller and stronger through the shoulders and thighs. He had played football in high school and had continued to enjoy a succession of sports throughout his life. Now he concentrated mostly on golf and tennis, he said, playing frequently enough to maintain his physical condition, but also for the sheer pleasure of exertion and competition.

He was dressed in khaki Bermuda shorts and a cream-colored polo shirt on this first evening of interviewing; his legs were tanned to a pale oak color, and his feet were shod in boat shoes. While he did not appear nervous, exactly, he seemed to have trouble focusing in the beginning of our conversation, as if my questions were difficult or confusing. I asked about his early childhood. "I'm terrible at dates," he said, "and, uh, I'm bad at names. I just don't remember that much. You'll have to ask my brothers. They were so much older than me, they'll know more about our parents, and everything."

"What I'm interested in," I said, "is not what the absolute truth is. I want to know what you remember and what you don't. I'm not looking for right or wrong, I'm trying to understand how you viewed your family as a child."

He shifted in his seat uncomfortably. "It was a long time ago," he said.

I waited, pretending to fiddle with the volume control on the tape recorder.

Eventually, he said, "My mother was a very bright, intelligent woman. Very aggressive, much more aggressive than my father. By far the stronger personality. The women in her family were all like that, not the easiest-going kind of people." He put his glass down on the table and leaned forward, his large hands capping his knees.

"They were tough, these women," I said, encouraging him.

"They were. I mean, if they didn't like somebody, they would just shut you out. My mother had seven sisters, there were eight of them, and one of the sisters married a man nobody liked, and that was just it, blam. They never spoke to her again."

"Why didn't they like the husband?"

"I don't know," Ron said slowly. "I guess I've always thought he was a criminal, a member of organized crime, but I don't know why. Maybe someone told me that when I was little. I never met him."

"What kind of mother was she, your mother?"

"Putting it politely, she was fairly strict. I got along fairly well with her, and I would guess I got away with a lot more because I had two brothers before me. So by that time she was worn out a little bit. Still, she was tough."

"That word again," I said, smiling at him.

He grinned and nodded. "Very tough. Not loving, not . . . nice. She was strict and wanted us to perform and do well. They had never graduated high school, she and my dad, and it was important for her children to be educated. She was very involved with the business as well."

"Your father's business?"

"Yes. She was, as I said, she was a much stronger personality. She got my father to invest in real estate and so forth, and she was the one who was the pusher." He paused, looking down at his hands, which were clutching at his knees as if he were about to propel himself to a standing position. "My mother was a bright gal. I mean, she was very knowledgeable about real estate."

"Would you say she was a warm person?"

He laughed, a sort of angry snort of amusement. "She was not a warm individual. She was cold. I mean, she could cook and she did the laundry and she checked our homework, she did what was expected. I don't think she was . . . you wouldn't have selected my mother to be the ideal all-American mother."

"Did you know that when you were growing up?"

"Oh, no," he said, shaking his head back and forth ruefully. "Not until much later, when I got into my thirties. Not until my first marriage was breaking up."

"How about your father?"

Ron leaned back in his chair, his entire expression relaxing as if at the thought of his dad. "My father was a very good, warm man," he said. "He and my mom had totally different personalities, and the fact that they even stayed together was amazing."

"Did they love each other?"

"Maybe in the beginning," he said. "I never saw much love there. I know that my father was really unhappy."

"As long as you can remember, or did it begin at a certain time?"

"I would guess over the last ten years of his life, probably. He was getting to the point of being very unhappy." Ron paused and then he said, very deliberately, as if he were about to give me shocking news, "He was getting ready to divorce her."

"He told you that?"

According to Ron, his father had confided in Hank, who was working in the store with him at the time. (Oddly enough, when I later asked Hank about this, he denied it vehemently, despite the fact that both of his brothers remembered Hank reporting to them their father's intention to divorce their mother.)

"It didn't matter, though, what he intended to do," Ron said, his strong features momentarily seeming to crumple and then, just as suddenly, becoming composed again. "My dad died, of a heart attack, in the store. And he was only fifty-seven years old."

"Oh, that's terrible. Had he been ill?"

The Mahoneys hadn't known that their father had in fact suffered an earlier heart attack; even their mother hadn't been told. It wasn't until after his death when the children discovered the different vials of pills in a medicine cabinet that they realized that Arthur Senior must have been aware for several years that his health was deteriorating.

At the time of his father's death that April 1957, Ron was attending college in the Midwest, under the G.I. Bill of Rights. He had returned from a tour of duty in Germany, after the end of the Korean conflict, and was enjoying the first period of wealth he had ever known. His school expenses totaled some $150 a year, and under the G.I. bill he received $110 a month; he was living like a king and having the time of his life. "I remember I was asleep in my room; it was a Friday morning," he recalled. "The phone rang and my roommate answered it. He stood there, holding out the phone to me, and even though I was half-asleep, from his face I could see something terrible had happened. It was Hank to tell me Dad had dropped dead of a heart attack." He paused for a long moment, remembering, and then he added simply, "My roommate drove me to the airport."

Ron had been dating Kim, who was to become his first wife, for about two months. She was an only child from Ohio, the daughter of a shoe salesman father and a homemaker mother whose major pastime, according to her former son-in-law, was hypochondria. "Kim's mother was dying the day I met her, thirty-seven years ago, and I bet she's dying now, too."

"From what?"

"Nobody ever knew," he said, a smile rising from that gap-toothed grin to his eyes. "Including her, but she was very good at being ill, that was what she did. And she had Kim hooked in so tight, worrying about her, that our marriage probably never had a chance."

"When did you get married?"

"In November of that year, how does that song go, 'So in Love'? That's what I was. I couldn't wait to get married, even though lots of signs were there that it wouldn't work."

"Like what?"

"Well, people hated her. My friends kept saying to me, why? Why are you marrying her? She's a nasty person. But I just wanted her so badly."

"Then when did things start to go wrong?"

Ron looked at me directly as he answered; I had the distinct impression that he'd been waiting for this moment. Here was a memory that he had in perfect working order: names, dates, everything. "About two years after we were married, she had an affair. With the builder who was putting an addition on our house. And she came and told me, and I was just devastated, and all the love really just died."

"How long did the affair continue?"

"Not long. It was over by the time she told me. I don't think she had any other affairs that I know of, but at this point"—he shrugged his shoulders—"I really don't care."

"Did you think of divorce?"

"I thought I would take a mature view. I was going to hold this thing together, and it would be okay. I mean, you get married and you don't just destroy your marriage because someone does something wrong. I wasn't happy, and I don't think I loved her anymore, but I was brought up to believe that when you marry, you make a commitment, and therefore you go through with it. I was foolish enough to believe all that garbage. And of course what happened is it cost me a dozen years of my life."

He looked down at his hands again, watching himself knead his knees as if a stranger was in charge of the movement. "But I got the kids, you know, my daughter and my sons," he added softly. "It was worth it, in the end."

I asked Ron why he thought Kim had told him about the affair. Had she been angry or trying to get back at him for some misbehavior of his own?

He honestly didn't know, he admitted, whether he'd been working too hard or becoming too involved with his own family again. For they had both dropped out of college to get married; returning to work in the family business seemed the only logical thing to do. Ron and Hank were sharing responsibility for the store, but it was difficult for the younger brother to make a place for himself. Hank, after all, had been working in the store full time for several years, side-by-side with their father. In a sense, he was the rightful son and heir. And yet Ron desperately wanted to be an equal partner in the store as well. He'd thrown himself full tilt into the business, and perhaps he'd been neglecting Kim.

"The truth is, it wasn't even the affair so much as the fact that she never listened to me. She did not respect me. She would scream and yell at me, but she was never going to listen or change or try to work together to solve our differences. And so, when I met Beanie, she's my wife now, you know, well, I was ready to leave."

"Was the affair with Beanie your first?"

Ron sat up straight. He shook his head from side to side vehemently. "It was not an affair. I had told Kim I was on my way out, that I was going to do my own thing. I never did anything illicit. I don't count that as an affair."

"Did you ever have an affair?"

"I wanted to, but I never did."

"Why?"

"I guess I was frightened of doing it and I didn't . . . It wasn't me. It wasn't the kind of thing I did. It just went against the grain. I've been married twice, and I've never had an affair since I was married, either time."

"That's just not a thing you do."

"No." He grinned. "I'm not saying I don't think about it. All men do. But I don't do it. There's a difference, between thinking about it and actually carrying it out."

I wanted to get back to his relationship with his siblings, to get a sense of how intimate it was. "Did you talk to anybody about this? About Kim's affair?"

"Not for years. No one. I was so vulnerable, just twenty-seven years old. I think life experience makes you a little more cynical, a little stronger. Later, when I was getting my divorce and I had found Beanie and she was so warm and loving and I was so happy, I told my brother Arthur he should get a divorce, too. I said, why don't you get out of this marriage, you're so unhappy?"

"What did he say?"

"He said, 'Millie cooks my meals, she does my laundry, we don't sleep in the same room.' That was enough for him at the time. And I said, 'Arthur, there's a life out there.' "

"So you knew all the details of his life, how bad things were for him?"

"To tell you the truth, I never liked his first wife, and she never liked me. And she and Kim hated each other. There was a whole decade where Arthur and I didn't speak except on holidays, because our wives really drove a wedge between us. When I got divorced, that was one thing I said to him: 'If either of these women really loved us, they wouldn't want to see us driven apart. I don't think this is love, I think it's control.' And we agreed we would never let anyone split us up again."

I nodded sympathetically.

"That was twenty-two years ago," Ron said proudly. "And I don't think three days go by when I don't touch base with my brother Art."

"What about Hank?"

"His marriage, you mean? Hank's wife is a lovely woman," Ron said. "I remember thinking, when he married Laura, how could such a nice woman be in *my* family?"

"You mean, because none of the women in your family were nice?"

Ron shrugged. I waited.

After a long pause, I said, "Trace your relationship with Hank for me. Were you friends as children?"

He laughed, looking up above my head at nothing in particular, and smiling affectionately as if he were seeing a vision of Hank at ten years old. "Art was so much older than me, ten years old when I was born, I never saw him much when I was growing up. But Hank, I used to follow him everywhere. He was a good big brother, let me play with his friends. He was really nice to me."

Ron shifted far back in his chair uncomfortably, as if his legs were suddenly too long for the seat. He shrugged, wrinkling his neat shirt under the arms and across the chest. One large hand began to pat, pat, pat against the armrest. Then Ron Mahoney shrugged again, jumping forward some fifty years or so without further notice. "Hank can rationalize this and rationalize that," he said. "He always wants to look the best in any picture. It's not honest, what he does, because he can't bear to be wrong, to appear in a bad light. And all of us make errors."

"Like what?"

"Oh, I don't know. Nothing, I guess." Ron's expression was careful now, and I could tell I wouldn't be getting much more information out of him tonight. "I love my brothers," he said. "Both of them. We'd do anything for each other."

The Odd Man Out

Not surprisingly, I had become quite curious about Hank, the "mystery" brother. When Art and Ron talked about each other, they spoke of loved and respected equals, brothers who, despite a decade of age difference, had a great deal in common. No one denied that Hank was a loved and appreciated family member as well; and yet it was clear that Hank was different in some unarticulated way. Ron had called it "middle child syndrome," implying that because Hank was squeezed in between achieving Arthur and athletic Ron there was no other valuable role for him to fill. What about intellectual, or kind, or musical, or handsome, or one of thousands of other descriptions of positive traits? Obviously, there were many possible labels for Hank to wear. What, then, set him just that tiny distance apart from his siblings? Was it deidentification? Genetic difference? Repetition of family birth-order roles? Some combination thereof? I knew I might not find the answer, but I was eager to form my own impressions of Hank Mahoney in relation to his siblings.

I drove to Hank's home on one of the hottest July afternoons I can ever recall. It was the kind of day when air-conditioning at full blast cannot compensate for even a few minutes of exposure to the still and sultry air. The temperature had been in the mid-nineties, with the humid threat of thunderstorms, for more than a week.

After hours of driving, I found myself outside Albany in a suburban shopping district with wide, comfortable roads, a carefully designed series of solid-looking storefronts. Sprawling oak trees edged the sidewalks. This was clearly an economically stable community whose well-dressed citizens had devoted a great deal of consideration to creating a downtown area in which their needs could be met immediately and well.

Just outside the commercial district, the main street forked. I went to the right, up over a hill and past a series of stucco and brick townhouses. I found myself on a tree-lined thoroughfare, with elegant Colonial homes on either side. Each house was fenced in, either by sturdy bushes and trees or by a post-and-beam arrangement. Hank obviously had chosen to live in a far more extravagant fashion than either of his brothers, I thought, noting this first discernible difference.

I was right that he lived differently, but I was wrong about how.

The next right turn took me down into a nineteen fifties–style development, all tiny ranch homes on postage-stamp lots. This area was deserted and silent, with not a child on the streets even though it was late on a Thursday morning in the middle of summer. The house was on the shabby side of nondescript, its lawn small and recently cut, the few evergreen bushes casually shaped into soft, round forms. The weaving cement pathway ran about fifteen feet up to a gray door with a battered brass knocker. As I got out of my car, I remembered how Ron had said that his brother was stingy about spending money, that he worried more than he needed to about finances. At the same time, I was uncomfortably aware of the silence around me. Suddenly I realized one reason why the whole scene seemed so strange: There was no car in Hank Mahoney's driveway.

I rang the bell several times, used the lion's-head knocker, held my hand up to peer into the front window. Clearly, Hank was not at home.

I got back into my car, berating myself for having failed to call when I realized I was running ten minutes late. Perhaps Hank had thought I'd stood him up. I sat with the air-conditioning running, reading over my notes and trying to find the page upon which I'd scrawled his office number. It was now nearly eleven-thirty, almost half an hour after our scheduled meeting time. I decided to give him another fifteen minutes before backtracking into town to find a phone. As I waited, I kept expecting the police to circle by and question me for sitting on a deserted street in a parked car. In fact, though, Hank Mahoney's block was so empty that nobody was around to become suspicious of me.

At a quarter to twelve, I turned the car around and dispiritedly headed toward town. At the first corner, a gray Cadillac passed me, heading slowly in the other direction. Impulsively, I veered back and followed.

It was Hank.

The first words out of his mouth were accusatory, as if he'd already anticipated what I might say. "You should have waited. I had to drop some papers off with a client. I'm taking time in the middle of work, you know."

As I bit back a heat- and exhaustion-based retort, I noticed that Hank Mahoney—unlike his sweet older brother or his friendly younger brother—was an incredibly handsome man. He looked a little bit like Clint Eastwood, from his craggily etched face, to his strong jaw, to his penetrating blue eyes. I was surprised that neither of his brothers had thought to mention this.

Despite his shabby box of a home, Hank Mahoney was a real estate developer who had amassed an impressive fortune building and managing large shopping malls. At age sixty-five, he still worked four days a week, playing golf on the other three days. He had three adult daughters, one of whom was a lawyer, one a doctor, and one a social worker. The social worker was married and had several children of her own. Hank's marriage to Laura had been peaceful for forty years. This, in a word, was a man who had risen above a difficult childhood and mastered his environment very early on. I was curious to know why he, of all the brothers, had managed to free himself so completely from the curse of the yoke of Edna Mahoney.

After we'd spoken for a while about his early memories of his grandparents, aunts, and uncles, we turned to the Mahoney family proper. "Tell me about your mother," I said.

I noticed that his expression failed to change, even as he said, "My mother was beastly at times. She was the disciplinarian. She would actually use belts and ironing cords and that kind of thing."

"Why? What kinds of things had you done?"

"I think she felt that we needed discipline. I think she felt overwhelmed because we were three boys. I mean, she was only five feet four inches tall, or whatever she was."

"So that was the only power she had."

"Yeah," he said. "I remember once when I was around twelve years old, she smacked me, and I raised my hand, and I said if you do that again, I'll smack you back." He shook his head from side to side

slowly, just as his brothers had done when recalling their mother.
"She was surprised, she said, 'You'd slap me?' And I said, 'Yeah,
because you're wrong, you don't slap someone just to slap them. I'll
slap you back.' She never slapped me again."

"So that was it?"

"Yeah, that ended it." He looked at me, his face as carefully blank
as if he'd just woken up. Then he said, "She honestly believed she
was doing the right thing, that she could control us. She wanted the
best for us, even though Art never saw that. She molded him more
than us, I mean, he became a doctor, he lived the life she would have
wanted. I remember even at ten years old deciding to just put up with
her because I realized, I understood. I just decided to live my own
life.

"She was just overly protective, you know," he added, as if trying
to assure himself that I understood. "She ruled the roost. And I guess
she was sort of an angry person."

"Do you think so?"

"Well, I guess she thought . . ." He stood up, opened the one tiny
window in the dark family room, and came back to his seat on the
modular sofa. "There was a bee," he explained, and then he paused.
Eventually, he said, "I think she loved my father when she married
him. I think she thought he should have been more than he was. She
was always wanting him to be more."

"She was disappointed by your father?"

"I think."

"Was he disappointing?"

"Not in my mind he wasn't. She had certain standards, would
push us, play us against each other to be the best in school, stuff like
that. Dad was more laid back."

"Are you more like him or her?"

He laughed for the first time, and I had the feeling that laughter
didn't bring him much pleasure. "I guess of the three boys, I'm
probably the most tense, the most intense. Art is certainly much more
relaxed and Ron is by far more relaxed than I am. That's the way I
am. I guess I got more of Mother than I did of Father."

"In what ways?"

"She was more concerned with achievement, more compulsive.
Like me."

"Do you have to control your temper?"

He looked down at his hands. They were strong and well manicured, the nails buffed to a dull shine. His wrists rested upon his knees, and his palms curved like a pianist's just before beginning to play. As he leaned forward, I also observed that the blue summer suit he was wearing was a little shiny at the elbows, as if he were unwilling to spring for a new one. "I don't lose it very often," he said. "If I do, I don't show it. That's for sure. One guy, once, I almost destroyed him. So I know that I just can't . . ." His voice trailed off.

Outside, a lawn mower began to drone loudly. Aside from our voices, it was the first noise I'd heard. I looked around the family room, noting how odd the scale of everything was. The dark vinyl couch curved around two full sides of the room, the brown rug was wall to wall, the coffee table so huge it could be reached from any spot on the couch. All the furniture was well worn, even shabby, as if the room was meant to be used only by family. The ceiling was low and the room was very dark; even the white walls had hardly any brightening effect, for there was only one tiny window on the front wall from which light could be reflected. A large television set dominated a third wall, and on the last side of the room, there was a passageway leading out to the back door and another door that led to a tiny bathroom.

"The other thing is, I was lucky," Hank said. "I didn't marry a mean machine; my brothers both married these grasping, pushy women the first time. You know, my mother was controlling because she wanted the best for us. These women were controlling because they wanted control. They wanted things their way. Both Millie and Kim, they were out for themselves."

He fell silent. Of course, you didn't marry a woman like that, I thought to myself, because *you* are the one like your mother, the one who pushes, who can't rest contentedly, who needs to be in charge. Of the brothers, you are the only one who married a woman as tolerant and easygoing as your dad. History repeated itself for all of you, but *your* version worked. I wondered if Laura was as happy in her marriage to Hank as he appeared to be with her.

Oddly enough, we seemed to have been thinking along similar lines, for the next thing Hank offered was, "I'm like my mother, she had vision, she could smell a good deal. I'm a risk-taker, like her. My

brothers are more hesitant than I am about investments. They don't
understand what I do for them, how much money I've made for them
over the years.

"That's why I take a commission now, when I work for the family.
I used to do it for free, but nobody appreciated how much work I
did, how much money I made for them."

"That bothers you, doesn't it?" I asked.

"Yeah. I made them comfortable and it doesn't show in anything
they do or say. Look how nice their houses are, how well they live.
They live like kings. They're nice people, my brothers, and I like
.them, but they pooh-pooh the fact that I've made them financially
comfortable."

"Do you want to get out of the properties you share with them?
To free yourself?"

"God, yes," he said, "but the tax situation makes that impossible.
I just feel like they take advantage. I would never do anything to hurt
them, but—" He paused, still staring down at his hands. In nearly
two hours of conversation, he had barely looked up at me twice.

"It sounds like it's a lot of work for you, having brothers," I
offered.

"It's very hard for me to know how to answer that," he said
immediately. "I like them, they're nice people. If I'd never had them,
though, I'd never have missed them. They just came along with the
baggage. It's not like friends, they're brothers, but they're not friends.
We don't think in the same way, we're not in the same community.
We're family, not friends. You see?"

I nodded.

"My friends, they're the people I have to relate to, the ones I can
choose," he continued. "I wouldn't choose friends like my brothers.
I don't have to pick up the slack for my friends, they accept me for
who I am, whatever I do. So maybe I have a resentment on that part,
about that. Well, maybe it's more Art that's the problem than Ron,"
he added suddenly. "Ron sort of understands.

"I think the bee must be gone," he said. He stood up again, and
went around behind the couch to close the little window. "I mean,
Ron is my younger brother. He trailed me around until I was about
ten or eleven and my friends made me cut him loose. It's still with
me, like I raised him, more than my mother raised him. I don't have
that kind of connection with Art. To me, he's more of a dilettante."

"His life is easier, you mean?"

"I don't think he worries as much as he should. He makes jokes all the time, he's flip. Most people think Art is funny but I think he talks a lot of nonsense. Look, I just recognize Art for who he is, more self-centered than me."

We talked for a while longer, Hank and I, that afternoon, but after revealing his feelings about his brothers, he seemed to withdraw in an odd way. He continued to answer my questions, but his responses were rambling and somewhat incoherent. Later, when I went over the tapes of our talk, I wondered if the confession of his resentment of Arthur had simply drained him so greatly that he could no longer concentrate. In any case, I left shortly thereafter to make the long drive home in the sticky heat.

"He Always Needs More"

I called Ron several days later, hoping to follow up on some of the questions raised by interviewing his middle brother. We agreed to meet the following evening, and I spent the afternoon going through all the transcripts of my various conversations with the Mahoneys, marking page after page with Post-it notes.

It turned out that I had to ask very few of my planned questions, for Ron had been musing about the same matters I had. The first thing he said to me, when we were seated once again in his cheerful living room, was this: "You're curious about Hank, aren't you?"

I nodded.

"I look at Hank sometimes, and I think to myself, can we really be brothers?"

"Now that's interesting—" I began, but he was off and running.

"We don't think the same, I'm positive about it. He's less ethical than I am. In our business dealings, I confess that he's done things that I really question. I don't think he realizes it. He can't see it in himself, and I have to be careful with him, because he can get so angry. He just needs more stroking, more credit than Art and I do."

"Tell me a story that illustrates what you're talking about," I said.

Ron told me about a time, early in his career, when he'd been forced to travel for several weeks on business. The brothers had been buying a great deal of property at the time, getting involved in what

Ron felt were too many deals. He had asked Hank to refrain from any more purchases while he was away. "I asked him if we could start saving a little money, you know? When I came back, he'd spent everything we had. He'd bought more land and I was just furious. And for two years, all I did was work for nothing, for him. I finally put together enough to dig us out of the hole."

"You must have been very angry," I said, reflecting to him what he'd just told me himself.

"Oh, no," Ron said, shaking his head. "I understand him, he was reaching for the stars. I think he's always looking, he's not happy with the money he has. He just always needs more. He's driven by this need for security."

"It sounds like he is secure financially, though," I said.

Ron nodded. "Extremely secure, but he'll never be satisfied. Let's put it this way. I would never trust my brother Hank to manage the business without me, to manage my finances for me. Never. I mean, I love him as a brother, and I'll give him anything he needs. If he was in trouble, I'd do anything to help him. And I know he would for me. But I could never trust him. He can't resist a dollar."

Ron went on. "Art, though, I'd trust him about anything. You know, even back when we were kids and I didn't really know him, I always had . . . I don't know. I was always close to Hank because he was closer to me in age, but I always felt a strong communion with Art, for some reason. I always looked up to him. He was the big brother in the family."

"It's funny," I said, "but it's as if you and Art just decided not to compete with each other, but Art and Hank, there's been rivalry over the years."

"Oh, yes, there was always a rivalry, if you can call it that. Hank objects to the fact that Art does no work for our joint business. What's the difference, is what I think. I get a commission on the work I do, and so does Hank. Art just gets his check when we get ours; he doesn't make anything extra. Hank's problem is simple."

He paused, and I watched him expectantly, hoping to hear that phrase which would make all clear. When it came, it was a surprise, for it was very like a comment that—as the mother of a three-and-a-half-year-old—I heard children make constantly. "Hank's problem is simple," Ron repeated. "The guy just never learned how to share."

The Deidentified Brothers

How, I wondered, were the Mahoney brothers different from the other sets of sisters or sisters and brothers I had interviewed? Sibling researchers have shown that, overall, families with at least one sister tend to remain more connected and supportive than sibling groupings without the benefit of a more feminine or nurturing member. On the other hand, the urge to connect more deeply with one's siblings in later life is common to both men and women. Certainly, one might argue that Art and Ron Mahoney manifested a fairly nurturant, or feminine, style with each other. They spoke about intimate issues easily, thought about each other's problems, and knew without question that they could trust each other. Also, they had reconnected after a decade of distance and had, in fact, grown even closer over the past two decades.

The relationship that Hank shared with Ron was a little less reciprocal, his connection to Art even less so: Neither Hank nor Arthur thought of *their* relationship as complete and fulfilling. What was it about Hank that had set him apart from his siblings?

I suspect that there were a great many factors at work. For one thing, Hank was born a significantly different personality type from either of his brothers, and factors along the way seem to have encouraged that differentiation. The only one of the brothers sufficiently strong to stand up and defy their mother, Hank was also the most like her. That was why he alone had the strength not to cower before her. He alone of the three didn't marry a woman like Edna: His wife, Laura, was sweet and gentle, much as their father had been. Hank, like Edna, had vision, determination, and drive; he also felt bitter and unappreciated in his sibling relationships, much as his mother had in her marriage. He was not a kind man, but he was a fair one, he felt, and his brothers had taken advantage of his generosity.

His brothers, on the other hand, simply did not see the world the way that Hank did. They'd done just fine in their professional careers, thank you very much, and the joint real estate holdings were merely icing on the cake. While they originally hadn't been as lucky in love as Hank, each had managed to turn his life around. It was almost as if Hank defied his cruel mother so early that he wasn't able to learn from her hard lessons. Art and Ron, on the surface, had paid much higher prices for being Edna Mahoney's sons. By passing through fire, however, they had also reaped the benefit of emerging on the other side, more insightful, kinder, and truly capable of love.

It was an unusual conclusion to draw, but that seemed to be the truth of it—some fundamental part of Hank Mahoney had sealed itself off in response to the trauma of his childhood. Art and Ron, as different as they were physically and intellectually, seemed to be alike in being the *real* risk-takers: men who had tried, both with each other and with the women in their lives, to know and be known. Out of sadness and difficulty, wisdom and contentment had been bred.

A Final Note

Accepting Our Siblings

What types of sibling experiences have we examined in *The Accidental Bond?* From Justine and Edith, we learned that being able to be there for someone else can be tremendously satisfying, a way in which the early sibling laboratory can produce a lifetime's worth of generosity and empathy. The young sisters' relationship was a visible demonstration of a positive way in which siblings can step in and provide support for one another when it is not available parentally; Amanda and Jack's relationship was an equally vivid demonstration of how that same support can go awry. In their case, support has not been linked with increasing autonomy and mutual acceptance of difference.

Paula and Penelope's connection—or was it Penelope and Paula's? —was overwhelmingly stronger than either twin's bond with her brother Charles; his outsider status resounded poignantly and had impacted on his life decisions as an adult. Their story illustrated profoundly that most siblings *need* to make separate lives, and that brothers and sisters try their best to do so, both within the family and outside of it.

From Maria and Catherine, it became clear that siblings' relationships can alter *completely* over a lifetime, traveling the entire distance from hostility to best friendship.

And Richard, Laura, and Sara—from their complicated relation-ship, so much difficulty and competition had arisen that I couldn't imagine a more fused and crippling connection. And yet, for them, their bond had also provided some of life's richest pleasures.

With Ginger Farr and her brother Bobby, we had the opportunity to peer into the kind of family where sibling relationships are not symbolic at all; they are absolutely and completely functional. Clearly, Bobby's dependency has been life-enhancing for Ginger; nevertheless, she has made sacrifices most siblings are not called upon to make and she has made them without questioning her obligation to do so.

The Shulmans, I believe, had uncovered a key secret of successful siblingdom, for they knew that accepting one another was the way to gain the most from their connection. The Shulman sibling system was built on a strong base of underlying affection, yet it had remained somewhat dormant until real need arose. While real closeness hadn't developed until middle age, when it actually did develop, it was truly satisfying.

The Mahoney brothers seemed, in some sense, an "Überfamily" who over the course of their long lives had been through almost every phase siblings could possibly experience or endure. Survival, support, intimacy, danger, abandonment, love, mistrust: They'd seen them all and managed to remain connected to one another's lives. They were, albeit unlike the Shulmans, another variant on successful siblingdom, a credit to the tenacity of human beings.

From these eight families, one can begin to see how tremendous the variation in sibling relationships can be, even without profiling a family where there was an absolute, hostile cutoff. I did have the opportunity to meet with several members of a family who had been squabbling for more than a year over the terms of their mother's will; the emotional cost of the battle was devastating, for brother had turned against sister and the level of emotional distress was floodgate high. There had been so much family fury, in fact, that two of the four siblings refused to meet with me; as a result, I wasn't able to provide a panoramic view of each member's perspective on the dis-agreement, and so I chose not to write about them. Nevertheless, think about the emotional intensity it takes to refuse to speak to another family member: Certainly, those brothers and sisters were as profoundly linked to one another as any other set of siblings profiled here. Such tales are legion and beyond the scope of this book. An old television show used to begin, "There are eight million stories in the naked city; this is one of them." Here we have pondered the lives of eight sets of siblings; there are many millions more.

It is important to understand that each of us has control, not over our siblings, but over how we see ourselves in relation to them, and how we conceive of them. In the chapter on the Arkady sisters, I discussed the notion of unconscious defenses that help us to organize the observable world so that action is possible. In the section on twins, I discussed the genetic aspects of personality, as well as the notion of shared and unshared environment and how it helps to create differences among siblings. This book has explored in depth the *passive* aspects of our lives, what happens to us in those inaccessible internal hot spots that motivate our actions. I've examined the idea that developmental difficulty is inevitable, or as the brilliant psychoanalyst Stephen A. Mitchell has written, "All children are bent out of shape (or, more accurately, into shape) in their early significant relationships, and this is a result neither of inherent bestiality nor of faulty parenting, but of the inevitable emotional conditions of early life."

What we haven't discussed, and must, is what Dr. Mitchell calls "will," and others might call "agency." We are not simply a combination of genetic predisposition, rationalization, and victimized experience: We have choices and make choices, constantly. The choices that appear *possible* to us are limited by our powers of reasoning, the repressed and therefore inaccessible parts of our consciousness, and our interpretations of our past experiences. Nevertheless, the actions we take represent basically free choices, and we are responsible for them. As Dr. Mitchell observes, "There is no human activity which is not constituted by *both* motives *and* the will.

"Our lives are made up of a sequence of choices, always within a particular context, always within a complex set of constraints," believes Mitchell. "They are choices, nevertheless." Seeing oneself as without the will to change, solely as the victim of others, is to deny oneself the freedom to take charge, to become a player and not a pawn.

It is a very human characteristic to think of our relationships, interests, and distresses without reference to the phases of our lives. The fact is that we are, each of us, flying through time and space in the grandest of all senses. Our current phase of being is just one moment in a life's journey. Siblings, over the course of the lifespan, travel naturally from the intense and intimate circumstances of childhood through the modeling and experimentation phase of adolescence, and on to the more distant periods of young and middle adulthood. During those years, each individual tends to concentrate on forming a new family, launching a career, establishing a rounded and complete adult self. Not until the next generation itself begins to take wing does the urge to reconnect become truly compelling. This need for a reenergized sibling connection has to do with making sense of life thus far.

Psychologists and sibling experts Stephen Bank and Michael Kahn have suggested that, at any given time, approximately one third of all siblings harbor hostile feelings, one third get along well, and one third are neutral, if not disconnected. For those whose relationship is either hostile or distant, the chance for a deeper sibling connection *does* exist.

This is where the will comes into play. The first step in improving a sibling relationship is to *decide* to do so, to be ready to give up on the fantasy that only perfect connection is acceptable. Here are some other guidelines for bridging the gulf that may prove helpful.

1. Put the past in the past. If your sister was cruel to you, or Mom preferred her, forgive it even if you can't forget it. What's done can't be changed; it is the present and the future that matter.
2. Be honest but not hurtful. Let your brother *see* who you truly are, today. Don't make the revelation into a performance: Just be yourself.
3. At the same time, accept your sibling for who she has become. If you want a sibling to put *your* childhood label away, you must do the same for her, without passing judgments on her choices.
4. Try to connect with your siblings the way you do with your friends: on common ground, no matter how small the patch of land may be.
5. Don't ask for trouble. Make the most of what is good, and don't set traps to prove that a sibling is not worthwhile. In other words, if you know your brother is a little light-fingered, don't leave your wallet around.

Keep in mind that, in fact, the situations that spur us to anger with our siblings are often related to money and differing levels of achievement. As psychologists Joel Milgram and the late Helgola Ross of the University of Cincinnati identified in the first qualitative study of sibling relationships in adulthood, the issues that drive wedges between brothers and sisters are clear reflections of what is deemed important by society at large. For the most part, Milgram and Ross found that siblings feel shortchanged or superior because of differing levels of accomplishment, intellectual competence, social skills, and physical attractiveness. Achievement, looks, and intellect were by far the leading contenders as sources of competitive feelings.

For some siblings, rivalrous feelings are like spurs to a horse, great motivators. For others, rivalry serves as an inhibiting factor. The most important feature of rivalry is the fact that such feelings are rarely expressed to the sibling in question. Is this because a confession of jealousy might make the sibling feel even more superior, or embarrass the more vulnerable brother or sister? I think that, to some extent, we do hold back our feelings, overestimating the danger of acknowledging them.

The truth is that acknowledging the strengths and weaknesses of one's own position *out loud* can sometimes be the best way of bridging the gap between differences. Being different is never bad, as long as acceptance is also present. Such acceptance of difference and similarity, more than anything else, is the key to mutually satisfying sibling relationships throughout life.

Are you trying to renew the connection with your adult siblings? Honesty can help bring about resolution of sibling difference, as long as it is honesty of the "I" kind. That means saying, *I* feel so much less attractive than you, or *I* always hold back on telling you about my accomplishments because *I* sense that you don't want to hear about them, is that feeling accurate? Honesty of the "you" variety— you always bullied me, you're never interested—will only sound like accusation, and will put a sibling on the defensive.

If the gap between you and a sibling is wide enough to be considered a chasm, try putting your feelings into letter form first. Take your time, work out what you want to say, and then even ask a trusted friend or family member to screen it for you. Is the letter an attack or a confession? How do you actually want your sibling to react? If resolution is a goal, being provocative will not be helpful.

Furthermore, if efforts to make a more complete connection with a sibling fail, you may want to consult a family therapist or other psychotherapist who specializes in work with siblings. Such an expert is trained to unravel the twisted threads of accumulated resentment in a supportive way. Going into therapy with a sibling may have surprising reverberations throughout the entire web of your relationships, for as early issues resolve themselves, the present picture will alter as well.

▬▬

The Jolly Corner

In Henry James's magnificent short story "The Jolly Corner," Spencer Bryden returns to the house of his youth after more than thirty years abroad. Bryden almost immediately becomes aware of another being—a presence—who seems to dog his footsteps; it is his other self, the one he might have been had he stayed in New York and faced his own potential. He might have invented the skyscraper, Bryden muses, or been a great billionaire; instead, he enjoyed himself tremendously and accomplished little, for he spent years wandering contentedly around Europe.

Spencer actually begins to track his other self—and to be tracked by it—through the halls of his family's ancestral home. And when eventually he comes face-to-face with the other possibility of the life he could have lived, " . . . the face was the face of a stranger . . . evil, odious, blatant, vulgar." Spencer faints at the sight.

Later, he tells his friend Alice Staverton that it wasn't himself that he had seen. "There's somebody—an awful beast; whom I brought, too horribly, to bay. But it's not me."

And Alice agrees that the man who Spencer *might* have been is no one like the man he actually is. The course he has chosen for himself has preempted any other, has made him as specifically who he is *not* as who he has become.

"The Jolly Corner" is a story of one man's arrival at self-acceptance, in this case an acceptance and embracing of the life path he had chosen. He has looked deeply at the somewhat frivolous life he led and seen that, for him, it was the only path that would not have destroyed him. In order to understand this, he has had to examine himself in a dangerously intensive way, risking the destruction of his complacency and sense of well-being in order truly to love Alice —and himself.

In order to live our lives to the utmost, such intensive examination of the self can be most useful. Of course, our perception of our own family is filtered through a particular perceptual lens, for there are no absolutes in a family grouping. It may be inconceivable to a big brother that his little sister felt intimidated by his physical strength as a child; at the same time, he may never even have felt as strong as that, for he compared himself to the bigger, stronger boys whom he knew. The alter ego that Spencer Bryden perceived in himself was the ravaged, cruel face of an ambitious businessman. He had to envision this evil self to acknowledge what he had missed. In the process, however, Bryden learned that his other self was equally frightened of him, for as they tracked each other through the house, neither apparition nor man was leading the chase. It was as if each saw the other as the more horrible possibility. Our visions of our siblings are a little bit like Spencer's vision of his other self: They represent part of our own "what if?" and we are not always sure who has made the better decisions.

In much the way that Spencer Bryden comes to terms with the "might have been," we can scrutinize and accept not only who we and our siblings have become, but also who we have refused to be. One of the reasons that the sibling connection can be so fraught with difficulty is that it is the first love relationship we experience that delimits us in an arbitrary way. The boundaries set with and by our brothers and sisters in early family life are not created for our personal safety, nor to teach us the rules of society; they are the divvying up of the pie of personality and possibility. No wonder we need to move away from our siblings as we define who we are, and can best move back together once the firm boundaries of self are in place: We can only snitch a little bit from someone else's slice if they aren't around to see it. Otherwise, questions of fairness and equity may come into play. Apart from one another, we can more freely become ourselves.

We are not our siblings, and they are not us, but we are—like Spencer Bryden's other possible self—connected to one another in a way that began as randomly as it is immutably present. If we no longer know our original siblings, we find and re-create similar relationships elsewhere. The joys they bring, the problems they create—in other words, the meaning they have in our own personal lexicons—become manifest time and time again. Our brothers and sisters are with us from the start of life to its finish, as apparitions and re-creations, or as concrete, much-felt presences; they are the chance-selected partners in the accidental bond of siblingdom. If one is observant, in fact, these figures of childhood, these beautifully archetypal manifestations of where we are going and who we have been, are everywhere around us. Through them and with them, we come to know both the beastliest and the very best that lurks within each of us.

SOURCES

Adler, Alfred, *Understanding Human Nature* (Oxford: Oneworld Publications, Ltd., 1927).

———, "Characteristics of the 1st, 2nd and 3rd Child," in *Children,* 1928, Vol. 3.

Allison, Dorothy, *Bastard Out of Carolina* (New York: Dutton, 1992).

The American Medical Association Encyclopedia of Medicine (New York: Random House, 1989).

Arlow, Jacob, "The Only Child," in *The Psychoanalytic Quarterly,* 1972, Vol. 41, pp. 507–536.

Avioli, Paula, "The Social Support Functions of Siblings in Later Life: A Theoretical Model," in *Siblings in Later Life: A Neglected Family Relationship,* eds. Victoria H. Bedford and Deborah T. Gold (Newbury Park, Calif.: Sage Publications, 1989).

Bank, Stephen P., and Michael D. Kahn, *The Sibling Bond* (New York: Basic Books, 1982).

Batshaw, Mark L., and Yvonne M. Perret, *Children with Disabilities: A Medical Primer,* 3rd ed. (Baltimore: Paul H. Brookes Publishing, 1992).

Bell, Robert, *Worlds of Friendships* (Newbury Park, Calif.: Sage Publications, 1981).

Berke, Joseph H., *The Tyranny of Malice: Exploring the Dark Side of Character and Culture* (New York/London: Summit Books, 1988).

Bossard, Eleanor, and James Boll, *The Large Family System* (Philadelphia: University of Pennsylvania Press, 1956).

Bowlby, John, *A Secure Base: Parent-Child Attachment and Healthy Human Development* (New York: Basic Books, 1988).

Brenner, Charles, M.D., *An Elementary Textbook of Psychoanalysis*, rev. and expanded ed. (NewYork/London: Anchor Press, 1974).

Brown, Fredda Herz, "The Impact of Death and Serious Illness on the Family Life Cycle," in *The Changing Family Life Cycle: A Framework for Family Therapy*, 2nd ed., eds. Betty Carter and Monica McGoldrick (Boston: Allyn and Bacon, 1989).

Burlingham, Dorothy T., "The Fantasy of Having a Twin," in *The Psychoanalytic Study of the Child*, 1945, Vol. 1, pp. 205–210.

———, "Twins: Observations of Environmental Influences on Their Development," in *The Psychoanalytic Study of the Child*, 1947, Vol. 2, pp. 61–73.

———, "The Relationship of Twins to Each Other," in *The Psychoanalytic Study of the Child*, 1949, Vol. 3, pp. 57–72.

Carter, Betty, and Monica McGoldrick, "Overview: The Changing Family Life Cycle," in *The Changing Family Life Cycle: A Framework for Family Therapy*, 2nd ed., eds. Betty Carter and Monica McGoldrick (Boston: Allyn and Bacon, 1989).

Cicirelli, Victor, "Sibling Influence Throughout the Lifespan," in *Sibling Relationships: Their Nature and Significance Across the Lifespan*, eds. Michael E. Lamb and Brian Sutton-Smith (Hillsdale, N.J.: Lawrence Erlbaum Associates, 1982).

———, "Feelings of Attachment to Siblings and Well-Being in Later Life," in *Psychology and Aging*, 1989, Vol. 4., No. 2, pp. 211–216.

———, personal communication.

Connidis, Ingrid Arnet, "Siblings as Friends in Later Life," in *Siblings in Later Life: A Neglected Family Relationship*, eds. Victoria H. Bedford and Deborah T. Gold (Newbury Park, Calif.: Sage Publications, 1989).

Delany, Sarah, and A. Elizabeth Delany with Amy Hill Hearth, *Having Our Say: The Delany Sisters' First 100 Years* (New York: Kodansha International, 1993).

Dickinson, Emily, *Final Harvest*, Thomas H. Johnson, ed. (Boston: Little, Brown, 1961), p. 47.

Dickstein, Morris, *Gates of Eden: American Culture in the Sixties* (New York: Penguin Books, 1977).

Downing, Christine, *Psyche's Sisters: ReImagining the Meaning of Sisterhood* (New York: Continuum, 1988).

Dunn, Judy, and Robert Plomin, *Separate Lives: Why Siblings Are So Different* (New York: Basic Books, 1990).

Dunn, Judy, personal communication.

Elkind, David, "Egocentrism in Adolescence," in *Child Development*, 1967, Vol. 38, pp. 1025–1034.

Emerson, Ralph Waldo, *Selections*, ed. Stephen E. Whicher (Boston: Houghton Mifflin, 1957).

Erikson, Erik H., *Identity and the Life Cycle* (New York: W. W. Norton, 1980).

Ernst, Cecile, and Jules Angst, *Birth Order: Its Influence on Personality* (New York: Springer-Verlag, 1983).

Ertel, David, personal communication.

———, "The Infants of Psychoanalysis," unpublished paper.

Falbo, Toni, "Only Children in America," in *Sibling Relationships: Their Nature and Significance Across the Lifespan*, eds. Michael E. Lamb and Brian Sutton-Smith (Hillsdale, N.J.: Lawrence Erlbaum Associates, 1982).

Falbo, Toni, and Denise F. Polit, "Quantitative Review of the Only Child Literature: Research Evidence and Theory Development," in *Psychological Bulletin*, 1986, Vol. 100, No. 2., pp. 176–189.

Fox, Hannah, personal communication.

Freud, Sigmund, *Screen Memories*, standard ed. (1899; reprint, New York: International Universities Press), 3:301–323.

———, *Three Essays on the Theory of Sexuality*, standard ed. (1905; reprint, New York: International Universities Press), 7:125–243.

———, *Analysis of a Phobia in a Five-Year-Old Boy*, standard ed. (1909; reprint, New York: International Universities Press), 10:135–152.

———, *Family Romances*, standard ed. (1909; reprint, New York: International Universities Press), 9:237–241.

———, *Totem and Taboo*, standard ed. (1913; reprint, New York: International Universities Press), 13:1–161.

Frost, Robert, "The Death of the Hired Man," in *Robert Frost's Poems*, ed. Louis Untermeyer (New York: Washington Square Press, 1971).

Furman, Wyndol, et al., "Children's, Parent's, and Observer's Perspectives on Sibling Relationships," in *Sibling Interaction Across Cultures: Theoretical and Methodological Issues*, ed. Patricia Goldring Zukow (New York: Springer-Verlag, 1989).

Gilmore, Mikal, *Shot in the Heart* (New York: Doubleday, 1994).

Gold, Deborah T., "Sibling Relationships in Old Age: A Typology," in *International Journal of Aging and Human Development*, 1989, Vol. 28, No. 1, pp. 37–51.

Grolnick, Wendy, personal communication.

Harris, Irving D., *The Promised Seed: A Comparative Study of Eminent First and Later Sons* (New York: Free Press, 1964).

Howe, Irving, *World of Our Fathers: The Journey of the East European Jews to America and the Life They Found and Made* (New York: Simon & Schuster, 1976).

Ingram, Jay, *Amazing Investigations: Twins* (New York: Simon & Schuster, 1988).

Jacobs, Theodore J., "On Having an Adopted Sibling: Some Psychoanalytic Observations," in *The International Review of Psycho-Analysis*, Vol. 15, pp. 25–35.

James, Henry, "The Jolly Corner," in *The Jolly Corner and Other Tales* (London: Penguin Classics, 1900).

Jewett, Claudia L., *Helping Children Cope with Separation and Loss* (Boston: The Harvard Common Press, 1982).

Johnson, Paul, *A History of the Jews* (New York: Perennial Library, 1987).

Juel-Neilsen, Niels, *Individual and Environment: Monozygotic Twins Reared Apart* (New York: International Universities Press, 1980; Francis Galton quote from here, p. 26).

Kahn, Michael D., personal communication.

Kaplan, Howard, "And Give My Father Here Whatever He Wants," in *The Atlantic Monthly*, July 1984, pp. 42–43.

Kernberg, Otto F., "Between Conventionality and Aggression: The Boundaries of Passion," in *Passionate Attachments: Thinking About Love*, eds. Willard Gaylin and Ethel Person (New York: Free Press, 1988).

Koch, Helen L., "The Relation of Certain Formal Attributes of Siblings to Attitudes Held Toward Each Other and Toward Their Parents," in *Monographs of the Society for Research in Child Development*, Vol. 25, No. 4.

Kris, Marianne, and Samuel Ritvo, "Parents and Siblings: Their Mutual Influences," in *The Psychoanalytic Study of the Child*, eds. Albert Solnit, Ruth S. Eissler, and Peter B. Neubauer, Vol. 38, pp. 311–324.

Kutner, Lawrence, "Strife Among Grown Siblings Can Split a Family," *The New York Times*, Parent and Child column, July 16, 1992.

Lasky, Judith F., lectures on siblings given at the Institute for Psychoanalytic Training and Research, March 1993.

————, personal communication.

Lasky, Judith F., and Susan F. Mulliken, "Sibling Relationships and Mature Love," in *Love: Psychoanalytic Perspectives,* eds. Judith F. Lasky and Helen W. Silverman (New York: New York University Press, 1988).

Levinson, Daniel J., *The Seasons of a Man's Life* (New York: Ballantine Books, 1978).

Lidz, Theodore, *The Person: His and Her Development Throughout the Life Cycle,* rev. ed. (New York: Basic Books, 1983).

Matthews, Sarah H., *Friendships Through the Life Course: Oral Biographies in Old Age* (Newbury Park, Calif.: Sage Publications, 1986).

Matthews, Sarah H., et al., "Male Kinship Ties: The Bonds Between Adult Brothers," in *Siblings in Later Life: A Neglected Family Relationship,* eds. Victoria H. Bedford and Deborah T. Gold (Newbury Park, Calif.: Sage Publications, 1989).

McGoldrick, Monica, John K. Pearce, and Joseph Giordano, eds., *Ethnicity and Family Therapy* (New York/London: The Guilford Press, 1982).

McGoldrick, Monica, et al., "Ethnicity and Women," in *Women in Families: A Framework for Family Therapy,* eds. Monica McGoldrick, Carol M. Anderson, and Froma Walsh (New York: W. W. Norton, 1989).

Meyer, Donald J., and Patricia F. Vadasy, *Sibshops: Workshops for Siblings of Children with Special Needs* (Baltimore: Paul H. Brookes Publishing, 1994).

Meyer, Donald J., personal communication.

Miller, James, *"Democracy Is in the Streets"* (New York: Simon & Schuster, 1987).

Minuchin, Salvador, *Families in Family Therapy* (Cambridge, Mass.: Harvard University Press, 1974).

Mitchell, Stephen A., *Relational Concepts in Psychoanalysis: An Integration* (Cambridge, Mass.: Harvard University Press, 1988).

Moorman, Margaret, *My Sister's Keeper: Learning to Cope with a Sibling's Mental Illness* (New York: W. W. Norton, 1992).

Muscular Dystrophy Association pamphlets, "What Everyone Should Know About Muscular Dystrophy," "Facts About Muscular Dystrophy," and "MDA Services for the Individual, Family and Community," Booklets #11965, P-187, and P-105 (MDA National Headquarters, 3561 East Sunrise Drive, Tucson, AZ 85718).

The National Association of Sibling Programs Newsletter, Winter 1993, ed. Donald Meyer (The Sibling Support Project, PO Box 5371, CL-09, Seattle, WA 98105–0371).

Noble, Elizabeth, *Having Twins* (Boston: Houghton Mifflin, 1980).

Olds, Sharon, "The Couple," in *The Dead and the Living* (New York: Alfred A. Knopf, 1993).

Plath, Sylvia, "The Rivals," in *Ariel* (New York: Harper & Row, 1961).

Plomin, Robert, personal communication.

Plomin, Robert, and Denise Daniels, "Why Are Children in the Same Family So Different from One Another?" in *Behavioral and Brain Sciences*, 1987, Vol. 10, pp. 1–16.

Plomin, Robert, et al., "Behavioral Genetic Evidence for the Importance of Nonshared Environment," in *Separate Social Worlds of Siblings: The Impact of Nonshared Environment on Development*, eds. E. Mavis Hetherington, David Reiss, and Robert Plomin (Hillsdale, N.J.: Lawrence Erlbaum Associates, 1994).

———, "Nature and Nurture: Genetic Contributions to Measures of the Family Environment," in *Developmental Psychology*, 1994, Vol. 30, No. 1, pp. 32–43.

Polit, Denise F., and Toni Falbo, "Only Children and Personality Development: A Quantitative Review," in *Journal of Marriage and the Family*, May 1987, Vol. 49, pp. 309–325.

Powell, Thomas H., and Peggy Ahrenhold Gallagher, *Brothers and Sisters: A Special Part of Exceptional Families*, 2nd ed. (Baltimore: Paul H. Brookes Publishing, 1993).

Ratcliffe, T.A., *The Development of Personality* (London: George Allen & Unwin, 1967).

Reiss, David, personal communication.

Rochlin, Gregory, "The Dread of Abandonment: A Contribution to the Etiology of the Loss Complex and to Depression," in *The Psychoanalytic Study of the Child*, 1961, Vol. 16, pp. 451–470.

Rosen, Elliot J., *Families Facing Death: Family Dynamics of Terminal Illness* (New York: Lexington Books, 1990).

Rosen, Elliot J., personal communication.

Rosner, Stanley, "On the Place of Siblings in Psychoanalysis," in *The Psychoanalytic Review*, Fall 1985, Vol. 72, No. 3, pp. 457–477.

Ross, Helgola G., and Joel I. Milgram, "Important Variables in Adult Relationships: A Qualitative Study," in *Sibling Relationships: Their Nature and Significance Across the Lifespan*, eds. Michael E. Lamb and Brian Sutton-Smith (Hillsdale/London: Lawrence Erlbaum Associates, 1982).

Rutter, Michael, and Jane Redshaw, "Annotation: Growing Up as a Twin: Twin-Singleton Differences in Psychological Development," in *Journal of Child Psychology and Psychiatry*, 1991, Vol. 32, No. 6, pp. 885–895.

Sachar, Howard M., *A History of the Jews in America* (New York: Vintage Books, 1993).

Scarf, Maggie, *Unfinished Business* (New York: Doubleday, 1980).

———, personal communication.

Scarr, Sandra, and Susan Grajek, "Similarities and Differences Among Siblings," in *Sibling Relationships: Their Nature and Significance Across the Lifespan*, eds. Michael E. Lamb and Brian Sutton-Smith (Hillsdale, N.J.: Lawrence Erlbaum Associates, 1982).

Scarr, Sandra, and Kathleen McCartney, "How People Make Their Own Environments: A Theory of Genotype-Environment Effects," in *Child Development*, 1983, Vol. 54, pp. 424–435.

Schachter, Frances Fuchs, et al., "Sibling Deidentification," in *Developmental Psychology*, 1976, Vol. 12, pp. 418–427.

Schachter, Frances Fuchs, "Sibling Deidentification and Split-Parent Identification: A Family Tetrad," in *Sibling Relationships: Their Nature and Significance Across the Lifespan*, eds. Michael E. Lamb and Brian Sutton-Smith (Hillsdale, N.J.: Lawrence Erlbaum Associates, 1982).

Schachter, Frances Fuchs, and Richard K. Stone, "Comparing and Contrasting Siblings: Defining the Self," in *Practical Concerns About Siblings: Bridging the Research-Practice Gap* (New York: Haworth Press, 1987).

Schooler, Carmi, "Birth Order Effects: Not Here, Not Now!" in *Psychological Bulletin*, 1972, Vol. 78, No. 3, pp. 161–175.

Seligman, Milton, "Psychotherapy with Siblings of Disabled Children," in *Siblings in Therapy: Life Span and Clinical Issues*, eds. Michael D. Kahn and Karen Gail Lewis (New York: W. W. Norton, 1988).

Seltzer, Marsha Mailick, and Marty Wyngaarden Krauss, "Adult Sibling Relationships of Persons with Mental Retardation," in *The Effects of Mental Retardation, Disability and Illness on Sibling Relationships: Research Issues and Challenges*, eds. Zolinda Stoneman and Phyllis Waldman Berman (Baltimore: Paul H. Brookes Publishing, 1993).

Seltzer, Mildred M., "Rivalries, Reconstructions, and Relationships," in *Siblings in Later Life: A Neglected Family Relationship*, eds. Victoria H. Bedford and Deborah T. Gold (Newbury Park, Calif.: Sage Publications, 1989).

Shakespeare, William, *The Tragedy of MacBeth*, in *Shakespeare: The Complete Works*, ed. G. B. Harrison (New York: Harcourt, Brace, 1948).

Sheehan, Susan, *Is There No Place on Earth for Me?* (Boston: Houghton Mifflin, 1982).

Shengold, Leonard, "Freud and Joseph," in *The Unconscious Today: Essays in Honor of Max Schur*, ed. Mark Kanzer (New York: International Universities Press, 1971).

Slade, Margot, "Siblings: Growing Up and Closer," in *The New York Times*, July 25, 1991.

Smith, Janna Malamud, "Mothers: Tired of Taking the Rap," in *The New York Times Magazine*, June 10, 1990.

Stern, Daniel N., *The Interpersonal World of the Infant* (New York: Basic Books, 1985).

Stipp, David, "Family Matters: Blame the Birth Order for History's Revolts, This MIT Scholar Says," in *The Wall Street Journal*, August 23, 1994, pp. A-1, A-5.

Stone, Elizabeth, personal communication.

Stoneman, Zolinda, and Gene H. Brody, "Sibling Relations in the Family Context," in *The Effects of Mental Retardation, Disability and Illness on Sibling Relationships: Research Issues and Challenges*, eds. Zolinda Stoneman and Phyllis Waldman Berman (Baltimore: Paul H. Brookes Publishing, 1993).

Sutton-Smith, Brian, and B. G. Rosenberg, *The Sibling* (New York: Holt, Rinehart, 1970).

Sutton-Smith, Brian, personal communication.

Townsend, Michael, "It's a Family Affair: Ties That Bind," interview with Deborah T. Gold in *Duke University Magazine*, January/February 1993, pp. 37–39.

Trollope, Anthony, *Can You Forgive Her?* (London: Penguin Books, 1972).

Tryon, Thomas, *The Other* (New York: Fawcett Crest, 1971).

Vandell, Deborah Lowe, "Baby Sister/Baby Brother: Reactions to the Birth of a Sibling and Patterns of Early Sibling Relations," in *Practical Concerns About Siblings: Bridging the Research-Practice Gap* (New York: Haworth Press, 1987).

Van Hasslet, Vincent B., John R. Lutzker, Michel Hersen, "Overview," in *Psychological Aspects of Developmental and Physical Disabilities: A Casebook*, eds. Michel Hersen and Vincent B. Van Hasselt (Newbury Park, Calif.: Sage Publications, 1990).

Ventura, Stephanie, National Center for Health Statistics, personal communication.

Volz, Bettina, personal communication.

Wallerstein, Judith S., and Sandra Blakeslee, *Second Chances: Men, Women, and Children a Decade After Divorce* (New York: Ticknor & Fields, 1989).

Waskow, Howard, and Arthur Waskow, "Becoming Brothers," in *The Family Therapy Networker*, January/February 1994.

Watanabe-Hammond, Sandra, "Blueprints from the Past: A Character Work Perspective on Siblings and Personality Formation," in *Siblings in Therapy: Life Span and Clinical Issues*, eds. Michael D. Kahn and Karen Gail Lewis (New York: W. W. Norton, 1988).

Weisner, Thomas S., "Sibling Interdependence and Child Caretaking: A Cross-Cultural View," in *Sibling Relationships: Their Nature and Significance Across the Lifespan*, eds. Michael E. Lamb and Brian Sutton-Smith (Hillsdale, N.J.: Lawrence Erlbaum Associates, 1982).

Weisner, Thomas S., Mary Bausano, and Madeleine Kornfein, "Putting Family Ideals into Practice," in *Ethos*, Winter 1983, pp. 279–303.

Weisner, Thomas S., "Implementing New Relationship Styles in American Families," in *Relationships and Development*, eds. Willard W. Hartup and Zick Rubin (Hillsdale, N.J.: Lawrence Erlbaum Associates, 1986).

———, "Comparing Sibling Relationships Across Cultures," in *Sibling Interactions Across Cultures: Theoretical and Methodological Issues*, ed. Patricia Goldring Zukow (New York: Springer-Verlag, 1989).

————, "Ethographic and Ecocultural Perspectives on Sibling Relationships," in *The Effects of Mental Retardation, Disability and Illness on Sibling Relationships: Research Issues and Challenges,* eds. Zolinda Stoneman and Phyllis Waldman Berman (Baltimore: Paul H. Brookes Publishing, 1993).

————, personal communication.

Wilder, Thornton, *The Bridge of San Luis Rey* (New York: Perennial Library, 1927).

Winnicott, D. W., *The Child, the Family and the Outside World* (Reading, Mass.: Addison-Wesley, 1964).

Wolfe, Thomas, *Look Homeward, Angel!* (New York: Scribner's, 1929).

INDEX

D

R

T

U

ABOUT THE AUTHOR

SUSAN SCARF MERRELL has written for *Self*, *New Woman*, and *Parenting*. She lives in New York with her husband, Jim, and her children, Maggie and Jake. This is her first book.